A Tale of Two Lives

Or

A Funny Thing Happened on the Way to the Palace

Second Edition

An Autobiography by

Helen Dale

© 2015 & 2021 Helen Dale

All rights reserved. No part of this publication may be reproduced or transmitted in any form or by any means, electronic, mechanical, including photocopying, recording or by any information storage retrieval system without permission for the author.

The right of Helen Dale to be identified as the author of this work has been asserted by her in accordance with the Copyright, Designs and Patents Act 1988

Acknowledgements

Cover photograph top right of author with Princess Anne is copyright John Prater Photography

ISBN

paperback 978-1-9996329-7-7

hardback 978-1-9996329-9-1

Contents

- Part 1. RAF Brat 1
  - Chapter 1. A Funny Thing Happened on the Way to the Palace 1
  - Chapter 2. RAF Habbaniya, Iraq 1951-2 3
  - Chapter 3. Back to Gloucester 4
  - Chapter 4. Plymouth 7
  - Chapter 5. SHAPE June 60 – Mar 62 8
  - Chapter 6. RAF Stradishall March 62 – Sep 65 15
  - Chapter 7. The Cold War and Other Influences During Childhood 21
- Part 2. Hidden Issues 24
  - Chapter 8. Below the Surface 24
  - Chapter 9. Understanding Transsexualism/ Transgenderism 25
- Part 3. RAF 27
  - Chapter 10. RAF Selection 27
  - Chapter 11. OCTU 28
- Part 4. London 34
  - Chapter 12. Job Centre & Scout Shop 34
  - Chapter 13. Return to Church 38
  - Chapter 14. NDC June 67 – Spring 72 38
- Part 5. St Neots 45
  - Chapter 15. Dollings 72/3 & Foster Cambridge 73/4 45
  - Chapter 16. Wainco 74- 79 47
  - Chapter 17. Little Paxton Days 50
  - Chapter 18. Ad Agency in Luton 53
  - Chapter 19. Sanyo 1980-84 53
  - Chapter 20. The Radio Show 57
  - Chapter 21. Going For Gold and Other Perks 59
  - Chapter 22. The Benefits of Being Away 61
  - Chapter 23. Fired 61
  - Chapter 24. Bruyneel Advertising/ CAM 1985-6 62
- Part 6. On My Own 64
  - Chapter 25. JMD 1986-95 64
  - Chapter 26. Lords of the Manor 67
- Part 7. Contracting 69
  - Chapter 27. Lt Barford Power Station 69
  - Chapter 28. Connah's Quay Feb 95-June 96 69
  - Chapter 29. Fight with First National 74
  - Chapter 30. Didcot B Jul 1996 – Jan 97 74
- Part 8. Manchester 77
  - Chapter 31. CEGELEC Feb – Dec 97 77
  - Chapter 32. Helen's Haven 78
  - Chapter 33. 24/7 83
- Part 9. Coming Out 88
  - Chapter 34. Mission Improbable 88

   Chapter 35. Rocky Horror/ Coming Out to Family 94
   Chapter 36. On the Dole/ Wang End 98 – Mid 99 98
   Chapter 37. Decision Time 100

Part 10. Probation 106
   Chapter 38. GMPS interview 106
   Chapter 39. Starting on the Service Desk 108
   Chapter 40. LAGIP 109
   Chapter 41. Surgery 110
   Chapter 43. The 'Gerbil' 114
   Chapter 44. From Customer Services to IT Project Manager 115
   Chapter 45. LAGIP 2 / National Diversity Involvement 119
   Chapter 46. Work with Trans Offenders 124
   Chapter 47. Diversity Awards 127
   Chapter 48. Butler Trust Award, ... 128
   Chapter 49. Oldham Pride 131
   Chapter 50. Back to Highpoint 131
   Chapter 51. Inner Enigma 132
   Chapter 52. Counselling 134

Part 11. Moving on 137
   Chapter 53. New Start 137
   Chapter 54. Eliminating the Male 141
   Chapter 55. Flotilla in Greece 142

Part 12. Riding the Roller Coaster 149
   Chapter 56. Relationships: to Tell or Not to Tell? 149
   Chapter 57. Transphobia & Ignorance 152
   Chapter 58. Affirmations 154

Part 13. New Adventures 156
   Chapter 59. SPICE 156
   Chapter 60. Losing Mum Dec 2009 177
   Chapter 61. South Africa 178
   Chapter 62. Heart Attack 2011 187

Part 14. Retirement 189
   Chapter 63. Into Retirement 189
   Chapter 64. What next? 190
   Chapter 65. Long Haul Holidays 191
   Chapter 66. Writing 195
   Chapter 67. Covid 199
   Chapter 68. Conclusion 199

Part 1. RAF Brat

Chapter 1. A Funny Thing Happened on the Way to the Palace

In the late 60s/ early 70s, I worked at the National Dairy Council. One of the Executives, Arthur Grubb, had a letter conspicuously on his desk from Buckingham Palace and occasionally remarked "as I said to Princess Anne, if there's one thing I hate, it's a name dropper!" When I later met John Major, I made a point of repeating Arthur Grubb's remark so I could use the same line, slightly modified! Little did I know that in 2009 I would be invited to Buckingham Palace to receive an award from Princess Anne – and that the story could go full circle.

So, how did it happen?

Well, it's quite a long story that started in a galaxy far far away; actually, the start was in Werrington a village just outside Stoke on Trent in Staffordshire. The house I was born in was on the A52, the main road through the village, at that point known as Ash Bank. At the time, Werrington was little more than this main road – with Salter's Lane leading down to the school and a coal mine where my Uncle Jack worked; and Washerwall leading in the opposite direction to Wetley Moor Common – where my mother had been born. About that time (I believe) Stonehouse Road and Stonehouse Crescent were being built. At the top of Ash Bank was a borstal, now HM YOI Werrington – which reappears later in the story.

left St Philips Church where I was christened 25/5/47
right: 346 Ash Bank, Werrington, where I was born

My childhood seemed unremarkable to me – though others seem to think it was very unusual. My father was in the Royal Air Force having first served in India and Burma during World War II. He was based at RAF Records Office, Barnwood on the outskirts of Gloucester when I was born. I am, therefore, a 'RAF BRAT' – or 'Scaley BRAT' and proud of it.

My parents had married in 1945 (on 24th November, 11 days after he returned from the far east). I was born at the end of one of the worst winters ever, the youngest of three cousins: Diane, Ian and myself who had arrived at 3 monthly intervals. I was born at 3.30pm on 17th April 1947 weighing just 5lbs — possibly the only time I was below average weight! I must have been reluctant to come into the world as my mother told me that labour had started the previous evening. Perhaps I was aware of the freezing weather outside! I was christened Jeffrey Michael at St Philip's church in Werrington (next door but one to our house).

Part 1. RAF Brat

I never knew any of my father's family but there was quite a tribe on my mother's side which we'd meet up with from time to time – though with 3 of the families in the forces and 2 emigrating to Canada and Australia, we were often spread around the world.

Dad was discharged from the RAF in May 1948 and we moved back to Werrington. He tried Civvie Street eventually working at the gas works. He and my mother got tired of the smell from his work clothes and dad applied to rejoin the RAF retaining his old rank of sergeant. We moved back to Gloucester – initially into rooms while waiting for married quarters that were being built. The married quarters were on Sandyleaze and everything in them was brand new. Apparently, the furniture had been a gift from the Swedish government.

Sandyleaze — our first married quarters in Gloucester

I had repeated bouts of tonsillitis – and, in spite of being only 2½ years old I was sent to Uxbridge Hospital where they were removed. I'm told I was a right terror while there – running up and down the ward! Nothing changes! Coincidentally, or not, my daughter Joanna also suffered from tonsillitis when very young and had to have hers removed too!

Although my sister Linda and I were born in Werrington and, at times, it seemed like most of the village, certainly on Stonehouse Road, was part of the extended family, aunts, uncles cousins & second cousins, we didn't spend very much time living there – probably less than a year or so in total.

In September 1950, dad was posted[1] to Iraq. Mum was pregnant with my sister Linda at this time. Rather than stay in the married quarters in Gloucester we returned to Werrington, initially with Aunt Etty but her house was too crowded with her sons John and Roy and Diane, so we moved in with Aunty Mabel. Aunty Mabel then got pregnant – so we headed for a preliminary transit camp at Cranage

Mum Dad and me. Linda was also there — as mum was pregnant at the time

We arrived quite late, dropped off our luggage then went to the mess for a meal. When we were returning to the hut, my mother realised she had not taken a note of our barrack number. Fortunately, I was, apparently, able to take her and my sister to our rooms in spite of all the blocks looking identical. Not bad navigational skills for a 4-year-old.

---

[1] Posting: a move from one station to another; sometimes between different roles at the same station.

Part 1. RAF Brat

My memories of Gloucester prior to going out to Iraq are limited. I do remember being given a tricycle as a birthday or Christmas present and, because it was raining, being allowed to ride it around the house in a circle through the lounge, dining room and kitchen.

Chapter 2. RAF Habbaniya, Iraq 1951-2

In November 1951, we set off for Iraq. As normal, my father had gone out to Iraq ahead of us and we had to wait for a married quarter to become available.

The flight out to Habbaniya was in a ubiquitous DC3 Dakota. It's strange to think that, at the time, these were quite modern! The flight involved 24 hours flying time with a number of refuelling stops en route in France, Malta, El Adam in Libya and Cyprus. The overall trip took three days. The return flight was in a Handley Page Hastings – and took 'only' 20 hours.

Our house at RAF Habbaniya had an irrigation ditch running next to the road, fed from the nearby River Euphrates, and a sunken section of garden that could be flooded, I recall we grew melons in part of this area and splashed around in the water in other parts – but let's face it this was more than 60 years ago and I have no doubt that not all of my memories will be accurate.

rear: DC3 Dakota the type of aircraft in which we flew to Iraq; foreground Handley Page Hastings in which we returned (photographed at RAF Museum Cosford)

What I am certain about is that Iraq was where I first sailed.

Dad was a keen sailor and use to race Snipes. He would take me out with him sometimes on Lake Habbaniya. To get there we'd travel in a lorry or gharry as they were known. In Mum's memoires 'A Mellor View of Yesteryear' she says we went there most afternoons until the water mosquito season.

There was a hill on the way from the camp to the lake and I'm sure I remember occasions when the men would have to get out and push the old over-laden gharries! There was a hotel/ rest centre at the lake where (I think) we stayed sometimes –though probably not often on a sergeant's pay. I remember a veranda with large urns of cool drinking water. Lake Habbaniya had been and might still, at that time, have been a stopping place for the Empire flying boats on the Far East/ Australia run. This was, of course, still several years before the introduction of passenger jets.

I know I spent many happy days at Lake Habbaniya swimming and jumping off a pier as well as being taken sailing.

I also started my schooling in Iraq – and can remember going to and from school by RAF transport – singing 'She'll be coming round the mountain' and other songs on the way.

Part 1. RAF Brat

A less happy memory I have is when our kitchen caught fire and I gather I was torn between dad getting hurt and losing my teddy which was still in the house! Habbaniya was to be one of only two RAF stations we were posted to that actually had any aircraft while I lived at home! As the song 'Get Some In' went – 'though you're in the RAF you'll never see a plane!'

In common with many service families, we had a gardener and a bearer – or maid called Virginia. If I remember correctly, the gardener was quite old (or so he appeared to a five-year-old) – Virginia was probably mid- late teens, maybe 20s. I remember a trip to visit Virginia's parents' home. There was a hut with an open cooking fire over which they prepared flat bread (but maybe I'm transposing images from other sources).

Habbaniya is located to the west of Baghdad across flat open desert. While driving to Baghdad one day we stopped to take photographs of a local on a camel. To our horror, he started to ride towards us very quickly. Concerned that he was about to attack us we prepared to get back into the car. In fact, all he wanted was to have his photograph taken!

One of our other trips while in Iraq was to neighbouring Iran – at that time known as Persia.

Chapter 3. Back to Gloucester

We arrived back in the UK in 1952 – and, after a few months in Werrington with my Aunt Etty, Uncle Jack and cousin Diane, we were allocated married quarters at 44 Meadowleaze, Gloucester. The house is still there. As we stayed here for 5 years and I did almost my entire primary schooling here, if anywhere can be described as 'home' Gloucester comes closest.

44 Meadowleaze — home for about 5 years

The houses on one side of Meadowleaze and Sandyleaze backed onto each other with a space in the middle. As well as being able to get into this field from our own back gardens, there was an entry at the corner of the block to the right of our group of houses. This field was converted to a street party for the Coronation in 1953. From what I can see, it looks like the back gardens have now been extended into this field.

At the bottom of the garden, we had a large oil drum – with a big shop sweet bottle on top in which I had some sticklebacks at one time. I fed them with worms – but, sadly, they all died. Dad had a workshop at the side of the house where he did his carpentry – I 'helped' him build a doll's house for Linda.

Part 1. RAF Brat

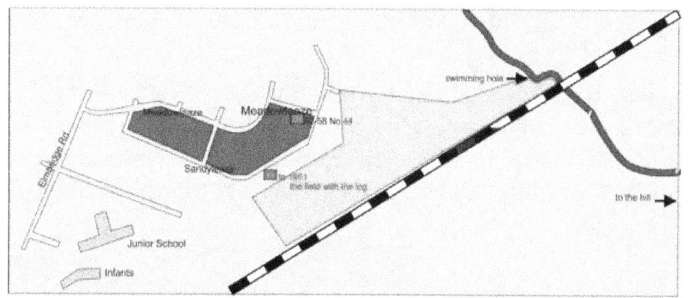

Our main playing area was the other side of Sandyleaze – in a meadow between the houses and the railway line from Gloucester to Cheltenham.

There was a regular little train that ran between the two cities (and, for all I know, beyond). It was made up from an 0-6-0 steam tank engine and one or two carriages. In the meadow was an old tree trunk/log which we played on – or watched the trains puffing by. We would also get through the fencing by the railway and put pennies (the big old, pre-decimalisation ones) or ha'pennies – maybe even farthings on the track for the trains to flatten to 2-3 times the original size. Sometimes we'd use pieces of the ballast laid around the sleepers.

The meadow is now playing fields for the old Richian's Sports and Social Club – which adjoins those of Sir Thomas Rich's School itself. If we hadn't moved from Gloucester, I think Sir Thomas Rich's would have been the school I would have attended.

Our swimming hole

We would often wander along the railway embankment to a brook that passed underneath the tracks. Just downstream of the culvert, there was a swimming hole that was deep enough for us to use to cool off during hot weather. Crossing the stream and continuing alongside the railway brought us to a tunnel for the farmer to move his cattle from one side to the other.

Once through the tunnel we could follow a path up Churchdown (?) Hill to a false summit near the top. There was a spring – presumably the one that fed the stream – near this mound and we would play or lie on the hill when the weather was fine.

While in Gloucester I attended Elmbridge Road Infants (March 53 – Jul 54) and Juniors (Sep 54 — May 58)– about half a mile walk each way (no 4x4s for kids in those days – in fact we didn't have a car at all). At the infants, we could take in a toy or pastime on Friday afternoons – one of my favourites was my Meccano set! I can remember towing it to school on a sledge one day.

The Coronation (plus the conquest of Everest) were huge events for us in 1953 and, in common with many others, we bought our first television – a Bush with a nine-inch screen (yes – nine inches). It only had one channel, of course. I was brought up on a diet of Watch with Mother: Andy Pandy, Muffin the Mule and Bill & Ben. Programmes finished well before

Part 1. RAF Brat

midnight and concluded with the national anthem (or so I heard – obviously I wasn't allowed to stay up that late).

Once in Junior school, I joined the 49th Gloucester Wolf Cubs – our Akela was Miss G Jones. She was our form teacher and one of the nicest teachers I ever had. I eventually gained my 'Leaping Wolf' and was Sixer of, I think, brown six. This was the start of a long career in the Scout movement. While I was in the Cubs, we had a trip to the 1957 jamboree at Sutton Coldfield to celebrate the 50th anniversary of the Scout movement

Holidays or excursions from Gloucester were by train. Sometimes to Barry Island, sometimes to Torbay – sometimes back to Werrington or the North Wales coast.

Other memories from Gloucester are buying yesterday's buns at much reduced prices from the bakers; visiting Bath and Bristol Zoo (where I had a ride on an elephant) – and my best friend, Alastair Webb.

A cub outing

We also used to have a number of suppliers delivering goods round the estate. As well as the milkman, who I used to help, there was the baker, the Corona lorry, the Walls ice-cream vendor on his trike with the ice box on the front and a greengrocer with his horse and cart. We would be out after the grocer had gone to collect the horse droppings for the garden. Each year the young eels, or elvers, would migrate up the River Severn and the greengrocer would have a tin bath full of them on the back of his cart. Our laundry was also changed each week with a lorry coming round to exchange sheets, pillowcases etc. Mum used to tell us that one of the national servicemen who was on the lorry had been the future world motorcycle champion Mike Hailwood.

During one holiday in London visiting my Gran and two aunts who lived in the same house, dad told me he was taking me to see a new film 'Reach for the Sky'. I was disappointed to find that it wasn't a cowboy film. I later came to appreciate the story it told of legless fighter ace Douglas Bader.

Alastair Webb

Part 1. RAF Brat

Chapter 4. Plymouth

In May 1958 dad was posted to RAF Mount Batten near Plymouth. The idea of being posted to the seaside was, of course, brilliant. Our quarters were 10 Bedford Road, Plymstock. This was on the corner at the bottom of a short hill – ideal for soapbox-karting.

Facing our house was a green with other houses on the far side. Beyond them were open fields.

Plymstock was not far from Plymouth city centre. Having been badly damaged during the war (which was still only 13 years earlier), the centre had been rebuilt with wide avenues and large modern department stores. Other parts of the city – including Mutley Pain where Gran moved to – still had 'bombed sites' which were our playgrounds.

We were also within easy reach of beaches at Jellysand (closest – but stony) where Gran kept a caravan she called 'Turestin[2]' and Bovisands (sandy but much further to walk). The beach at Bovisands was sometimes used by Royal Marines to practice assaults – and we'd watch as they stormed out of landing craft and across the sand.

RAF Mount Batten was across the Cattewater from Plymouth and was the based for the RAF Air Sea Rescue launches while we were there. It had been a flying boat base – with Short Sunderlands stationed there during the war. One of its most famous servicemen who served there was Aircraftman Shaw – better known as Lawrence of Arabia.

The breakwater at Mount Batten was a popular fishing spot. Not that I ever caught much! There was a story, however, of someone catching a conger eel that then chased him – causing him to climb on top of the pill box that stood on the end!

Mount Batten also had a sailing club using airborne lifeboats that had been dropped to the crews of downed aircraft some way from shore. They could then rig the mast and sail home. I had my second taste of sailing at Mount Batten.

I also joined the 3rd Plymstock Scouts – where I worked to gain my 'second class' badge. Summer camp was somewhere in Somerset – we travelled there in the back of a furniture lorry sitting on top of all of the camping equipment. Goodness knows what Health and Safety would have made of the arrangements!

Loading the van for camp, preparing for camp and the camp itself

---

[2] "To rest in" – because it was only for holidays!

Part 1. RAF Brat

Having arrived in Plymouth in the May, I had a couple of months at Hooe Junior School before graduating to Plympton Grammar in September 1958. The famous artist Joshua Reynolds had been a pupil at Plympton and I was in Reynolds' House.

The school was excellent – most of it was reasonably modern though there were some 'temporary' prefab classrooms erected just after the war –but still in use!

During the summer we would head into Plymouth and the lido on the Hoe for swimming.

I've always thought that Plymouth offers a great combination of facilities – a decent sized shopping centre, the nearby beaches and Dartmoor on our doorstep. It was in Plymstock that we acquired our first car – a Morris 8 or 10 from about 1947 (might even have been 1937).

This enabled us to have expeditions into Cornwall to Looe and Polperro and other exotic locations – as well as up onto Dartmoor and such forbidding sights as Princetown – location of Dartmoor prison. The scenery was, and still is, fabulous with the impressive tors, Beca falls and Widecombe in the Moor (where, according to the song. the group involving Bill Brewer, Jan Stewer, Peter Gurney, Peter Davy, Dan'l Whiddon, Harry Hawke, Old Uncle Tom Cobley and all went on the horse borrowed from Tam Pearce).

We also had regular trips to Bigbury on Sea and Modbury – home of Mrs Hubbard of the bare cupboard! The trips into Cornwall always involved long queues for the Torpoint Ferry – the nearest bridge at that time being many miles inland. It was said that it was only the chains of the ferry kept Cornwall attached to Devon. Mum would always pack a flask of coffee or tea for the wait for the ferry!

Touring in the car, we'd rarely exceed 30-35 mph – the car just wouldn't go any faster! Dad commented that he couldn't understand why anyone would want to go any faster with such glorious scenery to pass through.

Mother Hubbard's cottage

While we were living in Plymouth my gran decided to move down there from London – as did my Aunt Mary, Uncle Frank and cousin Sue; then the army decided to post my Uncle Harold down there too with his family Aunt Margaret & cousins Tim, Jackie and Christine.

While in Gloucester and Plymouth dad had been on 'Clerk Secretarial' courses for special duties. These led to him being cleared for 'Cosmic Top Secret' work.

Chapter 5. SHAPE June 60 – Mar 62

Our next move seemed very exotic – we were heading for Paris – or to be more accurate Versailles and St Germaine-en-Laye. Quite a few of my classmates were quite jealous – envying me the opportunity to practice my French.

Dad was to be based at SHAPE: Supreme Headquarters Allied Powers Europe where he was PA to SACEUR – the Supreme Allied Commander Europe.

SHAPE is about 25 km out of Paris just off L'Autoroute de l'Ouest at Roquencourt – roughly halfway between Versailles and St

Part 1. RAF Brat

Germain-en-Laye. It had representatives from all of the armed forces of 14 NATO countries (Iceland was not represented because it had no armed forces).

As well as the main HQ, there was a satellite camp, Volouceau, the other side of the motorway which housed many of the support services such as MT[3] section & stores as well as facilities for the families: a supermarket (to all intents and purposes a NAAFI[4] – except that a treaty with the French did not allow NAAFI to operate in France); there was a swimming pool, church, and a cinema, run by the Americans – so we got films well before they were released in the UK. It was at this cinema that we had our first taste of salted popcorn.

There were a number of other US bases near SHAPE – each with its own cinema so we had quite a selection to choose from – just as well as we had no English language television of course. The US bases also had a PX (their equivalent of the NAAFI) – but we were not allowed to use it. The forces ran frequent buses between the various sites – and into Paris and Versailles as well as to the main married quarters estate at SHAPE Village surrounding the Chateau D'Hennemont just outside St Germain en Laye.

Travelling to Versailles was an expedition in itself. We took the night sleeper from Plymouth to Paddington – then across London to Victoria for the train to Dover. Then after a roughish crossing, we were in Calais where we took the train to Paris Gare du Nord. The most famous of the boat trains at this time was the 'Golden Arrow' hauled by streamlined Britannia class steam engines. At one time, whole carriages were transported across the channel on the ferries to be taken on their way by French locomotives. We were not on the Golden Arrow which was 'Pullman Class'– and had to transfer from British Rail train to the ferry then onto the French train by foot.

Our first flat in France was in a house near the central post office.

In the countryside it would probably have been regarded as a chateau – in fact it was originally part of the Palace of Versailles. Built by Louis XIV for his favourite son, it had a walled courtyard in front with former servants' quarters on one side and the main house opposite. There was a turret containing a staircase going up the outside of the house. The house was divided in 2 like a semi-detached. We had the first-floor apartment on the left while the owners, the de Lavanes had the 2nd floor. Another service family occupied a flat on the right – with other relations of the owners above them.

The rooms in our flat were huge. There was a sideboard in one room that was 9 yards long. Linda and I shared a room – split in two with a partition but this was no hardship as each half was much larger than we were used to.

The house itself backed onto the Versailles Chateau Railway station (then known as Versailles Rive Gauche). Behind the house was an old coaching house/ garage with some vintage cars in which we played. They must have been worth a fortune!

We did hear that the de Lavanes were part of the family that had founded Peugeot cars, hence the vintage cars, and that they had been active members of the Resistance during the war and had helped allied airmen to evade capture. The outside staircase led into our flat –

---

[3] MT: Motor Transport

[4] NAAFI: Navy Army Air Forces Institute. In this case a supermarket. NAAFI also provided snack bars/ tea rooms at camps.

Part 1. RAF Brat

and had been used by aircrew as a safe house. Mum tells in her memoires of Mme D telling her of the times when Queen Mary visited them – and how mum was sitting on a seat that Queen Mary had sat in to do petit point. Involvement in the resistance had, of course, been dangerous and Mme D's daughter and her husband had been caught and sent to Germany.

By the time we arrived in France there was so little of the summer term left that we didn't start school again until the autumn.

English School of Paris badge

British primary school children, like my sister, attended the International School at SHAPE Village. Senior pupils attended the English (now British) School of Paris at Andrésy. Academically, ESP left something to be desired (I understand it's much better these days) – but it was certainly an experience.

It was a combination boarding and 'day boarding' school ranging from kindergarten to sixth form. Classes were very small – rarely more than 8-12 pupils and often a lot less. There was only one class per year. The forces paid the fees for us to attend and provided transport: 2 RAF Morris mini-buses driven by army national servicemen – who would race each other while we were in the bus. There was very nearly a serious accident one day with one of the minibuses mounting a pavement. If there had been an accident, I suspect we'd have been seriously hurt – even killed — as there were no safety features at all. While we arrived at school in these two minibuses, other pupils would glide up to the front of the former Manor House that served as the school buildings in their chauffeur driven Rolls Royces.

The dining room was converted stables and, if you were a 'day boarder', you had to have the school meal. One of our group tried bringing sandwiches because most of the meals were not very appetising, to put it mildly, and were much more expensive than in the UK. They were told in no uncertain terms that this was against school rules and if they wanted to remain a student, they had to comply with the rules.

I do recall one regular meal which I really did love – potato omelette served, I think, with fries. I don't know how they produced the result that they did but it was delicious! Sadly, most of the other meals were far from delicious and a protest was organised. As the meal was served one day, the dishes were pushed into the centre of the table and the sandwiches brought in by the service Brats shared with the other students. Unfortunately, this happened while I was off with glandular fever!

While living in Versailles, my sister and I would go out to buy bread and milk. Although I had studied French at Plympton this hadn't prepared me for the fact that whilst 'pain' was, indeed, bread, you had to be more specific about the type of loaf you wanted. Eventually we learned to ask for 'deux baguettes s'il vous plais'. Milk was easier. Not only because there was only one type – but because the shopkeeper had lived in New York and spoke English!

As we were returning home from shopping one morning, a car pulled up just ahead. I could see a GBJ identification plate on the back. As we walked past, the driver leant out of his window and asked in perfect French if we could direct him to the Palace of Versailles.

"Yes – you go straight ahead, turn left and it's right in front of you"

Part 1. RAF Brat

"You speak very good English" he complimented me.

Well, I couldn't let him think that French children spoke better English than we spoke French, even if this was generally true, so I explained that we were English.

Another time, Linda and I were sent out for the weekend joint of meat which we bought from a butcher near the market. Everyone agreed that it had been excellent. However, when we showed our parents the shop we'd bought it from and they noticed the horse's head above the door we didn't shop there again!

We did, however, find a delicacy that we really didn't expect in France. If you are from North Staffordshire, you will certainly know of oatcakes. I'm not talking about the hard biscuits produced in Scotland – but thin pancakes made from oatmeal. Eaten as a savoury – usually with bacon and eggs or cheese which is rolled up inside the oatcake – they are manna from heaven. The problem was that they are almost exclusive to the potteries (Derbyshire has a version but not as good!). In fact, in Stoke there used to be specialist oatcake shops. Normal village shops, such as Hills in Werrington, might stock them at weekends.

For years, if I was passing Stoke on business, I would be in serious trouble if I didn't pick up a supply. I can't remember how often I've been into Hanley market, gone to an oatcake stall and ask for twelve dozen. A request that almost always resulted in an incredulous response of "how many?" and a need to explain how I knew of this delicacy. The oatcakes froze and kept well.

As we were walking through Versailles market one day, we saw a familiar shape and colour in a shop window. "They look like oatcakes", "they can't be" but they were. We assumed that a British serviceman had married a French woman after one of the wars and had brought the family recipe with him.

These days, some Sainsbury's supermarkets stock oatcakes. For some strange reason they keep them in the bakery section – whereas they had traditionally been kept on the bacon counter.

Living in Versailles, we often explored the gardens at the back of the palace and the area around a lake at the side of the palace – where there were thousands of huge dragonflies. In the grounds of the palace was the Grand Canal where we could hire rowing boats or, during the autumn, stand under the Horse Chestnut trees while the wind blew and the conkers fell to the ground or hit our heads en route. 'We' and 'our' was usually Reg Roberts and myself. We had become best friends and were rarely out of each other's company.

It was about this time that Pete Ward, a Dutchman called Jan (?) and an American serviceman, whose name I can't remember, started the 1st SHAPE (BSWE)[5] scout troop. It was open to any son (well anyone presenting at that time as male) of service personnel at SHAPE – other than French boys. They, obviously, had their own national scout movement and we were not allowed to poach members.

---

[5] 1st Supreme Headquarters Allied Powers Europe – British Scouts Western Europe.

Part 1. RAF Brat

As I had already been a scout and had my Second-Class badge – I was the first member to be enrolled in the troop. Reg was the second. I was appointed Patrol Leader of the Eagle patrol and Reg P.L. of Ravens. The Eagles were originally all British but the Ravens were multinational.

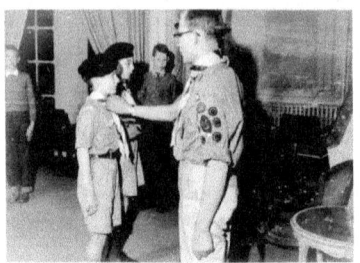
Reg being enrolled with me just beyond him

Following the first weekend camp in Marly woods, Jan's wife handmade some souvenir badges for us that we promised never to exchange. Having kept mine for 50+ years, I donated it to the Commissioner now responsible for the area that includes SHAPE. The badge has a background of vertical red white and blue stripes to reflect the fact that the camp had been in France. There was a representation of a rope bridge we had built across a chasm and the initials CUKFIBAND – to represent the countries involved: Canada, UK, France, Italy, Belgium, American, Netherlands and Denmark.

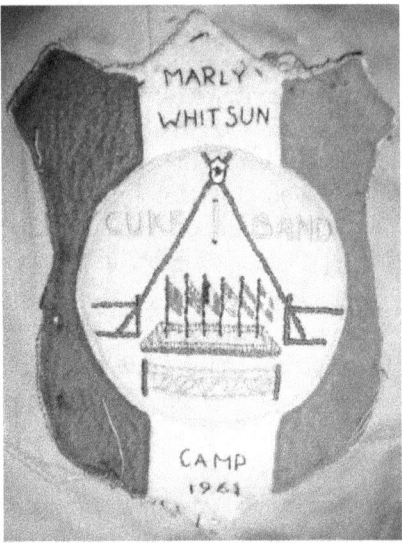

We also had a summer camp in a pine forest near Utrecht in Holland. En route we had passed through Brussels and had glimpsed the Atomium – built for the 1958 World Fair. We visited the cheese market at Alkmaar and fishing village of Volendam and hiked in the area near Arnhem where Operation Market Garden, the 'Bridge Too Far', had taken place. One ceremony at scout camps was the daily hoisting of flags. As an international troop we had more people pulling the flags up and down each day that were left to watch & salute!

The ground at the camp was beautifully soft and springy from the pine needles that had fallen – and the skies were completely dark at night except for the stars. While there we were able to watch one of the Sputniks crossing the sky.

From piston-engined aircraft taking us to Iraq to satellites in space within my childhood! Quite a thought.

Returning from Utrecht we arrived at Gare du Nord station at night passing the Sacré Coeur with its white stonework beautifully lit by searchlights – an abiding memory from my time in France.

Another holiday we had while in France was to Normandy – and the invasion beaches at Arromanches. We took two tents and all the camping kit we needed (borrowed from stores) in an 850cc Morris Mini-minor. Serving overseas we were entitled to buy the vehicle without purchase tax – so it cost under £500 new!

On the holiday there were my mother and father, my sister and Reg and me. Don't ask me how we got everything into (and on top of) the Mini – but we did. I know that the Mini was actually launched with a photograph of 4 adults and a load of luggage that could not possibly have fitted into the car – but had. I think we managed even more!

The sandy beach at Arromanches was protected by the Mulberries[6] that had been produced to provide an artificial harbour for the Normandy invasion and the supply of material following D-Day. They were only expected to last a few weeks – by which time the allies expected to have captured a permanent port. Here they were, however, 16/17 years later! There was also one section of the series of jetties that were used to offload the ships on the beach – which provided an excellent diving platform when the tide was in. They were still there when we revisited Arromanches in 1980 and, as far as I know 70 years on some of them are still there. For two 'lads' it was an ideal place for a holiday – where we could re-enact the invasion.

We visited Caen, scene of some horrific fighting and an almost total destruction of the town, and the cemetery where so many of those killed during the invasion and the weeks of fighting that followed are buried.

As well as the scouts, I was involved in the church choir as was Linda. I think dad was starting to get involved more as well – steps on his road to becoming a lay preacher and an unsuccessful application to join the church full time.

While we were in France, we heard that my cousin Roy, one of Aunty Etty's sons, had been killed serving with the Army in Cyprus. This was during the EOKA uprisings. Etty had previously lost a daughter to illness at an early age.

Cyprus was not the only place where there were terrorist activities. Paris, too, was subjected to OAS activities with bombs on the metro and attempts on the life of Charles de Gaulle. The OAS[7] was resisting plans to give Algeria independence – a portrayal of the OAS's attempts on de Gaulle was featured in 'The Day of the Jackal' featuring Edward Fox. As a result, parts of central Paris, including the Eiffel Tower, were out of bounds to SHAPE personnel. Students would also arrive at school with stories of bombs in the next compartment of the metro.

There was nearly an explosion at school too. Mr Buchannan, the deputy head and our chemistry teacher, had to investigate some vandalism that had occurred. He left us in the chemistry lab with an instruction to try some experiments of our own.

Reg had a notebook that, when opened at one end, listed poisons and how to make them and when opened at the other end listed explosives and how to make THEM!

One of our classmates was an American. I think his father was a famous musician. Reg persuaded him to try mixing concentrated nitric acid, concentrated sulphuric acid and glycerine together. I held my breath and stood by the door – ready to run for my life. Fortunately, they were unable to find any glycerine! (Nitro-glycerine needs to be mixed under VERY carefully controlled conditions – not just chucked together in a beaker!)

As service brats, we had access to British sweets from the shops at SHAPE, though they were rationed. Other students would ask us, quite forcibly at times, for some of them. One day, Reg and I came across some trick sugared almonds in a joke shop in Versailles – so we

---

[6] Concrete caissons floated across the channel to act as a breakwater.
[7] Organisation de l'Armée Secrète

Part 1. RAF Brat

bought these and some genuine ones from the NAAFI. At school, we made a show of eating some genuine ones and, inevitably, were approached with demands that we share them. We assured our tormentor that he really would not like them – but to no avail. He absolutely insisted. A quick sleight of hand and he was offered the joke – very bitter – version. He didn't trouble us again!

Having had the benefit of grammar school, I was quite advanced in maths and won a prize: the book 'Mr Midshipman Easy'. Prize-giving was quite an occasion. The guests of honour were the British Ambassador to France and the Bluebell Girls. I don't know of any other school that has ever that combination.

My test results had posed the teacher with a bit of a dilemma. When he had added up the total points there were 107 but the school used percentages for the scores. Instead of tediously converting marks out of 107 into percentages, he gave us the score out of 107 as the percentage. Then he got to my results and found that I had scored 105! Not many people can claim to have got 105% in a maths test.

The school used a flooded quarry at a camp site, Plàge de la Forêt, for a swimming pool – we went there a few times. Similarly, the school used a local municipal football pitch about half mile from the school itself – a walk that took us alongside the river Seine. We were returning one day when two Royal Navy Motor torpedo boats cruised past with their White Ensigns streaming behind – we all cheered – but I doubt if the crews ever realised that it was mainly British kids waving to them!

SHAPE village was on the edge of Marly Forest. While we lived there, most weekends and holidays, when the weather was fair, would find Reg and myself heading down the lane that led into the forest exploring – practising scouting skills or planning how we would react if and when the communists invaded western Europe (our dads were both servicemen whose roles were to prepare for just that possibility – no matter whether that seems, these days, to have been overstated).

On the main road from SHAPE to SHAPE village was a village called Noisy le Roi. Americans tended to call it noisy Leroy!

One of the less happy memories from France was mum being ill and having to return to UK for surgery – which unfortunately left her with problems for the rest of her life. She describes the military hospital where she was treated as having been built during the Crimea War – with practises from the same era.

She was in UK over Christmas so dad had permission to phone her. Dad, Linda and I went into one of the more secure areas of SHAPE, where dad actually worked, and used a phone on his boss' desk.

We were put through the various connections (no direct dialling back then) very, very promptly and were soon talking to mum. We subsequently learned that we'd been using the Hot line from the Supreme Commander Allied Forces Europe! Just as well the USSR was quiet that Christmas!

In 1962, dad was promoted to Warrant Officer – and, as his current role was a Flight Sergeant establishment, he was posted once again. At first, we thought we were going to Ternhill – but we eventually ended up in Suffolk.

Part 1. RAF Brat

Chapter 6. RAF Stradishall March 62 – Sep 65

At last. A posting where there were aircraft! Our first since Habbaniya. Strad, as we referred to it, was no 1 Air Navigation School.

Left: Vickers Varsity Crew Trainer showing bomb aiming compartment underneath fuselage photographed at Newark Air Museum. Right Meteor NF14 — similar to the type used for fast navigation training at Stradishall

The aircraft were Vickers Varsities and Gloster Meteor NF14s which were being replaced about the time I left with HS125 Dominies. The Varsities and Meteors were not exactly leading edge!

The Meteor had first seen service during WW2, the Varsity could trace its ancestry back to the wartime Wellington bomber. In fact, the Varsity first flew in 1949 and was a development of the Vickers Viking / Valetta transports. The earlier designs were 'tail draggers', the Varsity had tricycle undercarriage. It also had a pannier under the fuselage for bomb aimer training. The aircraft had been developed as a complete crew trainer – with two positions for the various main crew roles of pilot, radio operator, bomb aimer and, for its job at Strad: Navigator. The extra crew positions and the bomb aiming compartment in the Varsity gave opportunities for air experience flights for members of the cadet forces.

The Meteors were the two-seat night fighter variant used to provide high speed training for the Navigator students.

Situated between Bury St Edmunds and Haverhill (pronounced 'hayvrill' – not 'have r hill') in Suffolk, Stradishall was on the highest part of East Anglia with nothing to stop the biting winds from the Russian steppes and the North Sea. It was pretty isolated. There was a bus to Bury – and I do mean ONE bus. It would trundle through various villages en route arriving about an hour later – then wait fifteen minutes or so before the return trip. There was also a bus on Wednesdays and Saturdays only to Newmarket. If you wanted to get to Haverhill, you cycled or walked the 6 miles if you didn't have a car.

Although there was a grammar school in Bury St Edmunds, senior pupils from Strad were sent to Clare Secondary Modern or Sudbury Grammar (boys) or Sudbury High School (girls). The coaches from Burtons in Haverhill would pick us up from the entrance to the camp near the sergeants' mess and call in at various villages before meeting up with coaches covering other routes in Clare. Some of us would then switch coaches depending which school we attended.

Part 1. RAF Brat

The journey took about an hour each way – and I would have done my paper round before catching the bus so it was quite a long day.

Sudbury Grammar was NOT my favourite school. I arrived towards the end of the 4th year by which time alliances had generally been established. I had also lost progress compared with many of the students. I didn't seem to fit in and was constantly subjected to bullying – so spent most of the breaks hiding in the toilets.

SGS School photo — can you spot me? (Far right middle row)

Just as the famous painter Joshua Reynolds had attended Plympton Grammar and I had been in Reynolds House when I was there, Thomas Gainsborough, a contemporary of Reynolds, had attended Sudbury Grammar and I was in Gainsborough House! Ironically, I got the worst possible grade when I sat my Art 'O' Level; even more ironically, my career has included designing publicity material. My daughter, Joanna, however, is an excellent artist – perhaps something managed to get into her genes through osmosis – or more likely transmitted from her mum!

One aspect of SGS that I did enjoy was the Army Cadets. Whilst I would, obviously, have preferred the Air Cadets or even Combined Cadets, the ACF was OK. I'd joined a year later than most of the members – but eventually made corporal and was in the signals section. In fact, I effectively ran the signals section rather than the sergeant who was nominally in charge.

We did a number of summer camps which included battle exercises. The signals section would take our radios and try to establish a web. We also had weapons training – mainly on Lee Enfield rifles from WW1 and Bren Guns (which we learned to dismantle and reassemble – but never had the opportunity to fire). For most of the year shooting was on an indoor 25 metre range using .22 rifles; at summer camp we had a day at the external ranges with .303 rifles – which kicked like a mule and deafened you (no ear defenders in those days).

We were at a camp in Sherwood Forest one day – housed in 'Spiders'. These are number of barrack rooms off a single corridor – like legs of a spider. As we entered our block, one of our group knocked over a fire extinguisher which went off. He was sent to get a bucket and mop to clear up the mess. As he re-entered the room, he knocked over a second extinguisher with the mop!

I was also goal keeper in the school hockey team. Each year, the school played the local hockey club's second eleven. As several of the school team also played for the club, including the goalie, I was asked to play for the club. I stopped a couple of shots on goal much to the dismay of the school team members who might have expected me to just let them through and the club won the match two nil. From then on, I was promoted to the school team.

Part 1. RAF Brat

During one match, all of the action was at the other end of the field when there was a sudden breakaway and one of the opposition came running towards me. I knew that if I stayed on my line, I had no chance of preventing him from scoring – so I charged at him as he entered the scoring D. I took an almighty kick at the ball – then immediately ran backwards onto my goal line as other members of the team arrived. I wondered why the opposing player was just standing there and why the ball was just a few feet away from him. Surely, I had hit it harder than that!

Then I realised that his hockey stick was only held together by the rubber strips through the handle. It had got caught between my legs as I'd kicked and I had snapped it in half.

At SGS I gained 5 'O' levels – rather less than the average and stayed on to study Physics and Maths at A level.

By then, I'd decided I wanted to be a pilot in the RAF. I only needed the 'O' levels I already had for a 16-year Direct Entry commission. When I discussed my ambitions with the school careers officer, he suggested I should set my heights a bit lower and look at an RAF technical apprenticeship – or the Forestry Commission! I didn't take any notice of this advice and duly applied for aircrew selection with the RAF.

I also resumed my scouting at Strad – joining the 1st Cowlinge troop. Although we were in Suffolk, we were part of Newmarket District which came within Cambridgeshire County. I completed my first-class badge and went on to Senior Scouts where I eventually got the Queen's Scout award and, eventually, Rovers.

Our entire family was involved at this point with the Scouts and Guides as well as the Church and Sunday School. Linda was in the Guides, mum was a guide leader, I was in the scouts and helped with the cubs and dad was Assistant Scout Leader using his old scout name of Dixie as well as running the Rover Crew.

The Scout Leader was a local businessman, Trevor Foreman. His family had a shop in Cowlinge village and ran a mobile shop. His dark blue van was a very familiar sight around the camp and some local villages. The shop and van stocked just about anything from paraffin to bicycle tyres and wellington boots – a real traditional village shop. He also ran a taxi service and had a minibus which was ideal for scout camps.

The scouts' summer camps were usually Buckland Park in Kent or Gilwell Park just north of London.

We also took part in an annual county first aid competition. Trevor had been a medic in the services and we used the RAF sick quarters for our training – run by Sergeant Doherty. We trained every week and would be sitting listening to a lecture when there would be a blood curdling scream from elsewhere in sick quarters – we'd drop everything and follow the sounds of pain. We might find anything – in one case a casualty wrapped round a boiler that had blown back and burned him. Injuries were professionally recreated – bits of bone sticking out of plasticine with realistic 'blood' as appropriate.

I was appointed team leader the first year I was there and we duly entered the District heats. We won the Newmarket District heat and went on to the Cambridgeshire County finals. As the results were being announced in reverse order, they reached 3rd place and I thought – that's not bad for a first attempt, but it wasn't our name that was announced. Wow, maybe we've made second place then! But 2nd place wasn't us either – so where had we come? Had I missed the announcement of our place somehow? Finally, they announced First Place: 1st Cowlinge – we had won. How had that happened?

It was, of course, through many hours of very thorough training.

above: Winners of the First Aid competition: back left: Peter Butterworth; right – me; front left DavidMcGregor, right Barry Brackenborough

Right: 1st Cowlinge Scouts back row: Dad aka Dixie; me; Trevor, the Scout Leader.

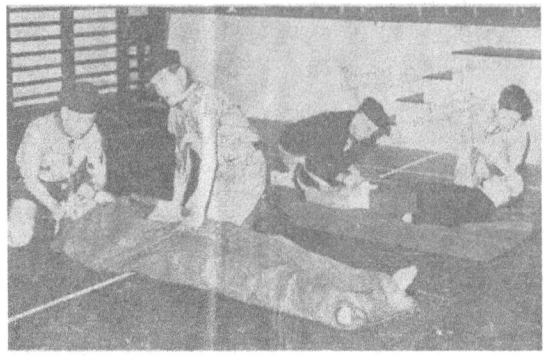

above: the winning team in action

As all the team members were from RAF families, RAF News sent a photographer and published a report that went world-wide.

The following year we came first again in the District heats and second in the finals. The next year I was too old to be part of the team but helped with the training. The troop won both District (3rd time in succession) and the County.

As Stradishall had been a bomber station during the war, the Senior Scouts patrol was named after Wing Commander Guy Gibson VC – most famous as leader of 617 Squadron, the Dambusters.

We also had a youth club at Stradishall – which used a Nissan hut. We had a record player and table tennis table. We were waiting for the club to be opened one evening when we heard that Kennedy had been shot and killed in Dallas.

Flying at Strad was limited to weekdays. At weekends, we could go over to the far side of the airfield where there was an old Hawker Hunter fighter that was used for firefighting practice. We often sat in the cockpit imagining ourselves to be top aces. Or we'd sit around

Part 1. RAF Brat

the dispersal huts that were spread around the perimeter track – or peri-track as we referred to it. The dispersal points also had huge concrete barriers designed to reduce the sounds of the engines of the Gloster Javelins that used to be based at Strad.

One Easter weekend we had my Aunty Mabel and her family to stay – including a cousin Stephen. I decided to take him over to see the Hunter.

We were on my bike; I was standing up pedalling and Stephen was sitting on the saddle. As we turned at the intersection of two of the runways, the front forks collapsed under the strain, gripped the front wheel and we were thrown over the handlebars. I landed on my face and left half of it on the runway and was stunned. Somehow, we got back to the house where I collapsed complaining about my back. My parents sent for Sergeant Doherty from sick quarters, who lived at the other end of the road. He patched me up and because I was concussed, they sent for an ambulance to take me to Bury St Edmunds hospital rather than the RAF hospital at Ely which was further away. I came round as the ambulance arrived at the hospital. After checking me out, they kept me in overnight due to the concussion but released me the next morning.

The end of the story is that the CO came across my bike while he was out walking his dog at the weekend. He was far from happy finding bits of scrap metal where they could have caused serious damage to aircraft! However, when my father explained the circumstances, all was forgiven!

On Sundays, we had a go-karting club – which was great fun. The club had a few karts for members to use but many of the adults had their own which were usually much quicker that the club ones. I could often be found leading the race for all but the last lap, with the other members toying with me before they came past me on the final straight.

I mentioned earlier that the spare crew positions in the Varsity provided the opportunity for members of the cadet forces to have 'air experience' flights. I had several such flights. These usually entailed flying up the country to about Newcastle upon Tyne – then out over the North Sea before coming back into Stradishall via a corridor between a couple of the large American Air force bases at Alconbury and Lakenheath/ Mildenhall. My favourite position on the flight overland was in the bomb aiming compartment following our progress on a chart.

On one flight, the pilot allowed me to sit in his place and take the controls for a few minutes. I managed to lose quite a bit of height and get well off course in that time – but, then, it's not normal to start your flying training on a twin-engine aircraft!

Our first winter at Strad was one of the coldest on record: 62/3. Being located at the highest point in East Anglia, we were cut off by the snow for quite a few days. No supplies could get through – but nor could the school bus! The RAF had huge snow clearing vehicles at the camp for the runways but could not use them on public roads without the Council asking for help and being prepared to pay for it. The married quarters started to run out of coal and preparations were being put in place for us to receive a supply from camp stocks when the roads were finally opened once more.

I had a number of weekend and holiday jobs while at Stradishall. These included a paper round covering the other ranks married quarters (ie excluding the officers' houses at the other end of the camp). The Sunday papers were a lot heavier than those for the rest of the week – so I decided to subcontract the deliveries of these to Peter Butterworth who had also

Part 1. RAF Brat

been in the Scout first aid team. My delivery route took me past Station Headquarters (SHQ). Outside SHQ was the flagpole. One morning I noticed that the RAF Ensign was upside down – not easy to do if you are even half awake. I went over to the guardhouse and pointed out the problem and that the CO[8] would not be at all impressed! They refused to believe me at first but when they checked they realised I was right.

I also delivered the programme for the Astra cinema on the camp. The films changed almost nightly and my 'payment' for the deliveries was to be allowed in free of charge any time I wanted.

During the winter a group of us would go beating for the local shoots – forming a line to drive the game – birds and rabbits towards the shooters. Times were quite different back then – and it was far from unusual to have rabbit stew. During the summer we often went fruit picking starting with strawberries. That really is backbreaking work. You start by thinking it's a great opportunity to eat the best fruit but soon realise that doing so affects your earnings so the biggest ones always ended up in the punnets. We would then move on to other fruit including plums and apples. As winter approached, we would be out on cold, wet autumn afternoons as it got dark picking potatoes.

I also got more regular jobs during the summer holidays. My first was in the Sainsbury's abattoir near Haverhill where they slaughtered pigs. The atmosphere was really steamy from the hot water used to clean the carcases and quite unpleasant. I had planned to be there for a week then go to scout camp for a week then back to the abattoirs. I decided at the end of the first week not to return so handed in my one week's notice which ran out while I was away.

After returning from scout camp, I heard of a job at a farm a couple of miles from the house. I worked there 6 days a week from about 9.30 in the morning to 9.30 at night –earning nearly £2 per day! My first job was to load a trailer with sacks and bring them up to the farmyard. I pointed out that I couldn't drive – well apart from karts! The farmer pointed out the gears; clutch and hand throttle and left me to it. The next job was to tidy out a barn which had a 3-ton lorry in my way – "well shift it" said the farmer. So, well before I got a licence to drive a car, I had driven a lorry and a tractor.

The farmer had devised a method of filling a tip-up trailer from his combine harvester; he would then elevate the trailer and grain would flow out of a slot in the back of the trailer and we'd fill sacks from that slot then stack them on another trailer to take back to the farm. At the end of the day, I would drive one of the tractors with a trailer through the fields while the others took equipment back on the roads.

We couldn't start harvesting until the sun had dried the dew off the wheat – so I would cycle over to the farm getting there about 9 and we would then continue working through until the sun was setting finishing off driving back to the farmyard as it became dark. The farmer would then throw my bike in the back of the Landrover and drive me home. They were tiring twelve-hour days but I was earning just under £2 per day – and becoming fitter through manhandling sacks of corn around!

When we first moved to Stradishall, our house was on Ash Walk. Later, we moved into one of two Warrant Officers' quarters on Sycamore Path. As usual, I had one main friend

---

[8] Commanding Officer

while at Stradishall – Barry Brackenborough. We had an argument about which pop group would last the longest. I favoured the Dave Clark Five – while he preferred the Beatles. We bet each other 5/- (25p) that OUR group would outlast the other. I don't claim that the DC5 outsold or outperformed the Beatles – but they did outlast them; so, Barry, if you ever read this, you still owe me 25p!

This was, of course, the era of Pirate Radio and I was an early member of the Radio Caroline Club. I tried to display a poster in my bedroom window but dad felt it was inappropriate in view of his position!

One of the sadder incidents at Strad involved two members of the Rover Crew. Rovers were the section of scouts for older members up to 23 years old (I think). We sometimes had trainee navigators from the school as members. Two of them had completed their navigator training and had some weeks to fill before joining a regular squadron so they opted to do parachute training. Unfortunately, the Hastings aircraft they were in crashed just after take-off and they were both killed.

Chapter 7. The Cold War and Other Influences During Childhood

Apart from the day Kennedy was shot, many of us who grew up in the 60s will remember the Cuban Missile Crisis. As the Russian ships approached the American blockade many on our school bus were convinced that World War 3 was about to start and it was by no means certain that we'd be going home again. If the 'balloon did go up' RAF stations would inevitably be prime targets for the Soviets.

It wasn't possible to ignore the Cold War regardless of who you were during the 60s. Being in the forces, we may have grown up with a somewhat different perspective than our civvy street school friends.

For me, there was no question that there was an important difference between the free west and the Warsaw Pact kept in line by Russia. We simply had to defend ourselves against communism – the alternative was too horrible to contemplate! As well as the attempts to put missiles in Cuba, we'd seen the Reds blockade Berlin, invade Korea and try to overrun Malaysia. Russia had invaded Hungary to smash their uprising against Soviet rule and would do so again in Czechoslovakia before the decade was out. The Berlin Wall had been built to prevent their own citizens from choosing the west rather than totalitarian life behind the iron curtain. Now the North Vietnamese were trying to conquer the 'free' south! 'Better Dead than Red' as the slogan went.

In view of all of that evidence and the overwhelming strength of the Soviet armed forces as demonstrated every year by the Red Square parades, I had no doubt that we had to maintain our own armed forces and that CND supporters were well meaning – but naive. Records released after the collapse of the USSR now indicate that the threat may not have been as real as we had assumed – but back then it seemed VERY real.

During my lifetime (even if I wasn't aware of some of the events), we had also seen the birth of the state of Israel, the Suez invasion by Britain and France, Mao Mao uprising in Kenya and EOKA in Cyprus and UDI – the Unilateral Declaration of Independence by Rhodesia (now Zimbabwe). When the latter happened there were a number of Rhodesian Air Force trainee navigators at Stradishall who, I believe, had to leave the course immediately.

They were turbulent times.

Part 1. RAF Brat

But they were also exciting times.

The jet age had started really taken off after the war, new types of aircraft were becoming obsolete almost as soon as they came into service. Pushing the boundaries proved expensive with the early Comet airliners suffering structural failures which cost the British aircraft industry most of its lead in this field. Others lost their lives trying to break through the sound barrier. By the 60s, aviation technology seemed well advanced and Britain had some of the finest civil and military aircraft in the world – what a pity we didn't exploit them as we might have done.

These included not only the Comet 4, the first jet liner to provide transatlantic services, but the VC 10 and the Trident – the first airliner to be able to land automatically. Concorde was also under development and would enter service before the end of the decade. The RAF had the Canberra and the three 'V' bombers: Valiant, Vulcan and Victor and the superb English Electric/ BAC Lightning interceptor. Anyone who ever saw the latter take off – then sit on its tail for a 60° climb will never forget that sight or sound. Also under development was the VTOL[9] P1127/ Kestrel – which entered service as the Harrier and the maritime reconnaissance Nimrod. The Royal Navy also had its share of winners such as the Blackburn Buccaneer renowned as a low-level strike aircraft. Other aircraft with incredible potential including the TSR2 had been cancelled due to spiralling costs.

Aircraft of the Cold War:
Top: Avro Vulcan
Middle: Handley Page Victor
Bottom: Harrier

The reputation of the RAF was, of course, enhanced by the formation in 1964 of the Red Arrows aerobatic display team — although it's fair to say that there had been other earlier teams such as the Yellowjacks, Red Pelicans, Blue Diamonds and the Tigers and Firebirds in their Lightnings and the 111 squadron, 'the Tremblers', flying Hawker Hunters as the Black Arrows. 'Treble-one' squadron still holds the record for the

---

[9] Vertical Take Off and Landing

Part 1. RAF Brat

largest formation flying a loop and barrel roll with 22 aircraft. I doubt if the RAF — or any other air force – could assemble a team of 22 aerobatic aircraft any longer.

The jet age had now been superseded by the Space Race – with the launch of Sputnik in 1957; the first manned space flight in 1961 and was now focussed on the race to the moon. It had also given us direct transatlantic television transmissions with Telstar and Early Bird satellites.

Transistor radios gave teenagers access to music wherever they wanted – though, until pirate radio started, this was only really of use for Radio Luxembourg in the evenings or recording the Top Ten onto tape recorders – using the new compact cassettes.

Teenagers may have been experiencing greater freedom and rebelling against the establishment, London may have been swinging – and Liverpool may have had the Cavern – but these hardly touched me in the depths of Suffolk. I was expected to set a good example in view of dad's position – and my own position in the scout group as Patrol later Troop Leader.

Dad was a very private person. Whether this was due to his own personal history or the typical male attitude of the times that you didn't show emotions – possibly partially a consequence of wartime experiences I don't know. It may also have reflected his security training in the RAF. Whatever the reasons, I don't ever recall having a 'heart to heart' talk with him. It wasn't that he was cold – but I felt there was a barrier there that I didn't try to penetrate. My childhood was comfortable. Home was a happy place as far as I was concerned. We certainly were not rich by any means but we were far from on the breadline and I didn't have to rely on cast offs from other families which some of my friends did.

On the surface I did as was expected of me most of the time and didn't resent doing so – below the surface there were other pressures that had been simmering for a while.

Part 2. Hidden Issues

Chapter 8. Below the Surface

Some transsexual individuals identified as the opposite[10] sex/ gender from a very early age and never felt comfortable in their 'assigned' role. I didn't feel this way. Most of the time I was quite happy being a boy – though I really didn't like football.

Until I was about 18, I was totally unaware of the words 'transvestite', 'transsexual', 'cross-dressing' or even the concepts that these describe. I had, however, been 'cross dressing' for some time by then.

The first incident that I can remember is wearing my sister's pink party dress. I don't know how this came about – or how old I was at the time. It was probably while we were in Plymouth – but could have been earlier. Linda did not allow me to repeat it as I was quite a bit bigger than she was and strained the stitching!

When we moved to France, there were lots of things in the attic which we could get into. I started to borrow things from there which I wore when I could. I also started to wear mum's things when left to baby-sit Linda while they were out. In Strad, there was always a collection of clothes donated for jumble sales stored in the Scout/ Guide hut – to which I had access.

In 1963, I had assembled a collection of clothes and accessories, including a pair of shoes that I had bought in Bury St Edmunds and planned a trip to London. Woolworths sold hair pieces and I thought I could apply a couple of those under a headscarf to give the impression of long hair.

I took the bus to Bury, then a train, a single diesel railcar, to Cambridge where I caught the main line train to London. The main line train had corridor coaches with toilets at the end of each coach. It was easy to slip into the toilets, get changed then re-emerge 'en femme'. I could then take my seat until we reached Liverpool Street. I left my bag of male clothes in a luggage locker and took the tube to the west end and walked around Piccadilly – buying a plastic leopard skin design mac from a 'lost luggage' shop. Then it was back on the tube and the train back home.

As I was making my way to the toilets on the return journey, the ticket inspector called out to me. Scared that he might want to challenge what I was up to, I darted into one of the toilets and quickly changed back into my male things. As I did so, there was a knock on the door and I heard "tickets please". I opened the door slightly and handed him my ticket for inspection.

I'm sure that this experience could easily have put me off – but it didn't. This was still in the days when homosexuality was illegal and I had no idea how I might be treated if I was caught.

---

[10] 'Opposite' implies that gender/ sex is binary. There is increasing evidence to suggest that gender is a spectrum. There is a brief discussion of this in the next chapter.

Part 2. Hidden Issues

A more significant issue arising from cross dressing was the cost. Whilst I could borrow clothes from the jumble sale donations, this didn't include shoes. My feet were already about a size 8 and if any shoes had been donated, they were smaller than I needed. Hair pieces, cosmetics, stockings and other lingerie also need to be bought. Funding this was a problem and I turned to theft.

Inevitably, I was caught and the police involved to my and my parents and sister's shame. There was no excuse. As I had already been accepted for the RAF and a court appearance would scupper that, I was lucky enough to be let off with a formal caution. I was also sent to see a Probation Officer in Sudbury.

Chapter 9. Understanding Transsexualism/ Transgenderism

When a baby is born, the doctors will look between the legs and declare that it is a boy or a girl. In the vast majority of cases, this is a reliable test. The individual's innate gender identity matches their physical sex.

Most people regard sex, gender and gender identity as the same. If you have a penis or XY chromosomes then you are male. If you are born with a vagina, or have XX chromosomes, you are female.

Sometimes, however, this isn't appropriate.

There has been a long debate over whether transsexualism is caused by 'nature' or 'nurture'. The nurture argument says that transsexualism is the result of experiences in childhood – and that individuals' gender identities could be influenced, even changed by the way they were brought up. In one infamous case[11], one of two twin brothers was brought up as a girl after his penis had been destroyed during circumcision. The psychiatrist persuaded the parents that the child would be happy in her assigned role. In spite of being given hormones and treated as a girl, the individual never identified as female.

There is clear and increasing evidence that there are differences between male and female brains – in the way that they are 'wired' and in some physical differences. The hypothalamus, for example, is significantly larger in males than in females.

A study in the Netherlands showed that the hypothalamus in Male to Female Transsexual individuals was more typical of a female size[12]. This included one case where the individual had not started treatment. The study was, admittedly limited, but does, nevertheless, support the 'female mind in a male body' experience reported by many transsexual individuals.

We do know that all foetuses start in a default female state and that during pregnancy, a flow of testosterone should determine whether the foetus continues to develop as female or becomes male. We also know that there are genetic influences that affect how susceptible the foetus is to the effects of the testosterone – and that the level of testosterone can be affected by the mother's physical condition. This means that the foetus may only be partially

---

[11] http://en.wikipedia.org/wiki/David_Reimer
[12] http://www.transgendercare.com/medical/hormonal/brain_sex_diff.htm

changed by the flow of testosterone – and may mean that the brain remains significantly female.

The extent to which the brain is or is not changed can clearly be infinitely variable – and produces a spectrum of results. In a male to female trans person, a low level of change causes a very powerful 'opposite gender drive'. If the change is substantially complete, the 'opposite gender drive' may be minimal – perhaps only being reflected in someone who is 'in touch with his feminine side' but happy to be a man. Between these extremes may be individuals who are driven to portray female characteristics at times but have no wish to switch permanently in the opposite role. In my view this may be manifested as what used to be termed 'dual role transvestism' (rather than fetishist transvestism).

It may also manifest itself as individuals who don't identify as male or female – or who identify as both or who switch how they feel on different days. This appears to be an increasing phenomenon in recent years and is certainly outside the scope of this chapter.

Whilst conditioning does not cause transsexualism, it certainly affects the extent to which it may be manifested – more as a 'braking force' on the 'opposite gender drive' than as an enhancing factor. From my experience of dealing with a great many trans individuals, it is clear that various factors hold them back from fully accepting their nature and doing anything about it. These factors can include responsibilities, lack of awareness of possibilities, focus on other events, religious beliefs and fear of the consequences. Testosterone levels also seem to have a part to play. All of these factors may suppress our innate drive.

As these factors diminish, as they tend to do as we get older, the innate drive can start to emerge more strongly and if they diminish sufficiently, the individual may eventually decide to transition completely.

Questionnaires that I had on the internet when I did my Diploma in Counselling course confirmed that as many as 70% of those who eventually decided to transition had previously identified as transvestite. It seems likely to me that cross dressing may well act as a 'safety valve' to a suppressed 'opposite gender drive' – preventing the pressure building up to intolerable levels. I'm quite certain that this is how it affected me.

This is a very simplistic explanation of course and much has been written and debated around the detail of how this happens and exactly why. For the purposes of my story, however, this is probably sufficient.

Part 3. RAF

Chapter 10. RAF Selection

In 1964, I applied for aircrew selection as an officer in the RAF. The pack of forms I needed to complete was huge! It included a section on medical history – with a firm warning that withholding information would be serious! As I had been treated by RAF medical staff much of my life, I included everything – including the fact that I had had hay fever while at Stradishall. I didn't want to risk the Station Medical Officer passing over information that I had not declared myself – especially as the medical centre was treating me!

I was invited to Biggin Hill Officer and Aircrew Selection Centre (OASC) just outside London just before Christmas 1964. Biggin was and probably still is iconic within the RAF. It was THE Battle of Britain station as far as much of the country is concerned. Just being invited there was so exciting!

One of the officers that dad worked with had just been transferred to Stradishall from Biggin Hill where he had been on the selection staff. Dad arranged for me to spend an evening with him so he could brief me on what the assessors were looking for and what to focus on. This proved very useful.

Eventually the day arrived for me to report to the OASC. The journey entailed the train to London Liverpool Street, across to Victoria then to Bromley South where we caught a bus to the main gates of Biggin. Guardhouses and main gates were familiar sights for me – but this was still special. 'The Few' had flown from here to defend London. This was history!

The first evening, about a hundred of us sat a series of IQ type tests. The guy sitting behind me asked how I had done with the first paper. I'd finished the questions but he had only done about half. This repeated itself as we went through the remaining papers.

The next day, we were split into two roughly equal groups. Our group remained where we were while the others were taken to another room. We had been warned that out of every 100 candidates invited to Biggin Hill only three or four would be offered aircrew training. We had just experienced the first cull.

Next (I think) was the medical examinations. This included hearing tests. The sergeant had just explained the procedure when one of our group said "Pardon". Whether he hadn't been listening or genuinely couldn't hear, this didn't seem a good response! The test included different tones of Morse code played over a background of piston engine noise through headphones. At one point the sound totally stopped in one of my headphones so I pointed this out. Fortunately, when they checked, my headphones were found to be faulty. Phew!

Another of the tests was for colour blindness using Ishihara colour charts (circles of coloured dots with numbers appearing or not). I have, I believe, anomalous trichromacy so my colour perception is different from normal in that the shortwave pigment is shifted towards the green end of the spectrum. In RAF terms this was classified as CP3, which was perfectly OK for aircrew but, as they only use even scores for ground roles, it was downgraded to CP4 for ground duties and unacceptable for air traffic control, engineering and other tasks. So, I was fine to be a pilot looking at Very signals – but not for Air Traffic Control looking at the same signals. Explain that if you can! No matter – it was flying I wanted in any case.

Another test was to use hands and feet to keep a dot in the middle of a screen – and the other hand to switch off a light that appeared randomly to test eye hand coordination.

The final stage of the assessments covered leadership. We were taken into a hangar where a number of scenarios had been set up using oil drums, planks and ropes with a general requirement to get the team across a chasm. The first of these was on our third evening. We were set the objective in groups of six but no-one was designated as 'leader'. We were told it was just a practice before we each took charge of the team for similar exercises the next day. That's not what I had been told during my briefing with the former assessor back at Strad.

He had told me that it didn't matter whether we succeeded in getting across the chasm – they were looking for someone with the initiative to come up with a viable scheme and take charge of the group. So that's what I did. I don't suppose we managed to get everyone across – but that wasn't what mattered.

Finally, we had a number of desktop exercises – "you are in charge of a patrol that has been ambushed; one of your men is injured and needs urgent hospital treatment but your original objectives remain in place. What do you do?"

The fact that I had had hay fever was an issue that had to be investigated and ultimately ruled me out for training as a pilot – though I gathered that I had otherwise passed the selection process. I was offered, instead, the opportunity of a ground commission. This couldn't be engineering or Air Traffic Control due to my colour perception rating so I settled for Secretarial — my dad's trade.

When I went back to sick quarters for my next hay fever treatment, the MO asked why I had admitted to having hay fever. When I said I thought he would have to tell them, he told me that families' records were totally confidential. I should not have mentioned the hay fever until it occurred once I was in the service – I would then be grounded for a few weeks each year.

Chapter 11. OCTU

On 5th September 1965, I made my way to the Officer Cadet Training Unit (OCTU) then at Feltwell in Norfolk. This involved a convoluted journey by train from Bury St Edmunds. The first leg was west to Cambridge – where I changed onto another train north to Ely change again and head east to Feltwell. A total of just under 70 miles – the direct journey being about 23 miles.

M4335561 Officer Cadet Dale J M

Part 3. RAF

Feltwell is in very flat countryside and the station is little more than a halt. Not the most welcoming of places. A bus waited to take us to the camp a couple of miles way. There we learned that we were part of 183 Black Squadron. There were two flights. One female, the other male. There were eleven in the female flight and six in the male flight. This was, in fact, a mistake – there should have been twelve men and six women.

We were an introductory course lasting two months before going on to the main Officer Cadet course. This had been normal practice for women entrants but the powers that be had decided that it might also benefit some of the male entrants as well. Ours was the first mixed course.

We were taken to our barracks. Ours was a two-storey block with two wings per floor. Our quarters were to the left on the ground floor as we went into the block. All of our flight shared the one barrack room. It had previously been a nursery so our first task would be to polish the floor using buffers – heavy weights with cloth underneath on long handles that you swung to and fro.

During an introductory talk we were given our programme for the training which would cover all manner of topics including 'Queen's Regulations and Air Ministry Instructions' – the RAF's own rules. I was already reasonably familiar with these as dad had had me updating his with the monthly changes. There would be drill, of course; physical training, lectures on the History, Customs and Spirit of the RAF, map reading, knots, field exercises both on the local Thetford battle Training Area which I had visited as an Army Cadet, and wider afield. We would also visit other RAF stations and stay in their Officers' Messes.

Feltwell had been a Thor ICBM – Inter Continental Ballistic Missile – site and the missile silos were still clearly visible across the airfield. It also had a number of hangars from its WW2 role as a bomber station. One of these was used as a gym; we used another for drill practice when the surfaces outside were covered with snow or ice.

The drill practice was only partly for us to learn the moves – just as important, if not more so, was for us to learn how to give the drill commands – not as easy as it may appear. On one occasion the squadron, sixteen of us, were being drilled inside by the remaining cadet when she couldn't remember on which foot she had to give the order. As one of our feet touched the ground the order to change step, turn right, left or about turn needed to be given but she couldn't remember whether it was as the right or left foot touched the floor. As we headed for the wall, she let out a shriek!

The drill sergeant yelled: "Miss *******, I don't care if you march the squadron through the wall – but you will **NOT** lose control!"

On our first PT session we were tested and told that we would be judged against that performance in future sessions. When we heard this, we didn't put 100% into the tests so we gave ourselves some wiggle room for the future. Well, officers are supposed to use their initiative!

The cadets had their own mess which was just over the road from our barracks. There we were supposed to acquire the manners and skills appropriate for officers. That meant that we were expected to behave like mature adults – in contrast to those who already had their commissions who might easily be found circumnavigating the ante-room without touching the floor; de-bagging someone or taking part in another of the traditional games. It's a funny world.

As part of this preparation, our civvy clothes were inspected for suitability. Not many of our ties passed muster anything other than stripes or plain were out – and woe betide you if you had a striped shirt! Blazers were OK in the mess – though lounge suits were far more preferable and sports jackets were most definitely not acceptable. All male officer cadets were expected to wear a hat when in civvies – so that it could be doffed to any senior officer we might meet.

In one lesson, preparing for a week in the Brecon Beacons, we were taught knots by a very large RAF Regiment sergeant. We were each given a short piece of rope and he would demonstrate each knot in turn – then expect us to do it. I'd been doing knots since I was in the Wolf Cubs and, as soon as he said which knot he was doing, I would have completed it. Seeing me just sitting there after he had done the first knot (a reef knot) he told me to get on with it – so I held mine up to show I had done it. Before he finished even saying 'sheet bend' – mine was done. Bowline (makes a non-slip loop useful for lowering someone down a mountain)? I had been able to do it one handed with my eyes closed since I was eight years old. Clove hitch? Round turn and two half hitches? All were simple for me – I might even have been able to show the instructor some knots he hadn't previously used. Another member of our flight was also a Queen's Scout and also as capable of the same knots – but I was the one who attracted the attention of the sergeant.

He then told us that he was going to demonstrate how to lower someone down a mountainside on a stretcher. He needed a volunteer he said – pointing at me! I was then tied securely onto a stretcher which was then turned upside down to demonstrate how secure I was being held in place. Having you nose two inches from the floor whilst unable to move anything defines 'helpless' as far as I am concerned! Perhaps I should have learned my lesson that being a smart Alec doesn't pay. I didn't.

Another part of our training for our trip to the Brecons was an exercise in the Thetford Battle training area. This included setting up two-man tents. "You two are Queen's Scouts aren't you" the Flight Lieutenant said to the guy I was with and me. "Yes sir" we replied. "So, you are used to setting up these tents?" "Yes sir". Good you can do mine as well as your own. We'd fallen into the trap. Oh well, they were, in fact, Scout Shop 'Rover' tents – so very easy to erect for anyone with experience and we'd finished both before some of the others had done one.

Another field exercise involved camping and canoeing in the Norfolk Broads. One of the flight was going to be a Supplies Officer – so he took control of ordering the kit that we would need and the transport. We did not go short! Once we had set up the tents – including a mess tent – we had to change into our swimming costumes and carry the canoes down to the broad. "I want you to take the canoe into the middle of the broad, capsize it and swim with it to shore".

This was October. It was beginning to get dark. It was cold.

Part 3. RAF

I took my canoe out, capsized it, held onto the bow and, lying on my back, kicked my way to shore. "That's not how you were supposed to do it" I was told, "go and do it again".

As part of our 'History, Customs and Spirit of the RAF' sessions we were shown films about famous former members and incidents. These included 'The Dambusters' about Guy Gibson VC and 617 squadron's raid on the dams and 'Reach for the Sky' – the story of Douglas Bader who, having lost both legs in a flying accident persuaded the RAF to take him back as a pilot and became a celebrated 'ace'. He was eventually shot down and after several escape attempts, in spite of having artificial legs, ended up in the infamous Colditz Castle. We were also told to get hold of a copy of the Caine Mutiny and read it as an example of poor leadership.

In common with most RAF Stations, Wednesday afternoon was for sports. At first, I volunteered for an officer cadet hockey team. We played against a group of airmen and airwomen. Whilst we were expected to act as ladies and gentlemen, the opposition seemed determined to get their revenge on their future bosses! Hockey sticks slipped up between legs, we were tripped and fouled generally. We lost the match.

I then found that gliding counted as sport.

For half a crown (12 1/2p) a flight, we could have a few minutes in the air. The other side of the deal was that we had to help with all other aspects of handling the gliders. Not that it was any hardship to deal with the tow cable, move the gliders around, hold the wing tips for the launch etc.

The club gliders were open cockpit Slingsby T21 Sedbergh with side-by-side seats. Originally designed in the 1940s and built from 1947 on, they were as old as I was! They were launched by being winched into the air using former barrage balloon winches. With luck you could reach about nine hundred to a thousand feet on the launch – enough for a few manoeuvres before returning to the circuit ready for the landing.

Some club members had their own gliders – including one V-bomber pilot who was thought to be a bit heavy on the landings with the club gliders. Well, there is a difference between a 1,000lb Slingsby T21 Sedbergh glider and a 170,000lb Avro Vulcan bomber!

You didn't wear a parachute when flying the T21 – frankly there wouldn't be enough time to bail out and deploy the parachute before hitting the ground. Flights involved signalling "take up slack" until the cable started to pull the glider along followed by "all out" at which point the winch operator would speed up and you'd soon be off the ground. At the top of the launch, you released the tow cable and were free! If you were very lucky you might find a rising column of warmer air, known as a thermal, which would take you even higher. More often, though, after a few turns or, perhaps, a practice spin you'd need to prepare for landing. If you were the last to fly on a particular day you might land near the hangar ready to put the glider away. Otherwise, it was a case of trying to land as close to the launch point as possible to minimise the ground handling and re-positioning of the glider for the next person.

Sometimes, during launch, the cable would break. If you were low enough, you could land straight ahead. If you had sufficient height, you could do a circuit and land. If, however, you were too high to land straight ahead – but not high enough to complete a circuit, you might have to lose height by side slipping first one way then the other then land.

Back in the classroom, we were taught map reading and navigation – plain sailing for those of us who were former scouts. Then we were taken out in a bus, blindfolded and driven around for a while to disorientate us. We eventually stopped and were allowed to dismount. "You are downed aircrew behind enemy lines" we were told, "you need to identify where you are then make your way back to the camp".

We had been dropped next to a large dyke that I had seen when gliding and knew to be south and west of the airfield. Sure enough I could make out the tops of the missile silos across the fields. I took a bearing, transferred this to the map and where it crossed the dyke gave our position. I showed it to the Flight Commander who asked how I'd worked it out so quickly. I explained that you could see the tops of the THOR missile silos etc. "Go and do it properly" he told me.

No satisfying some people!

One of the other RAF bases we visited was Coltishall just outside Norwich. This had been a Battle of Britain fighter station – it was where Douglas Bader had taken command of 242 Squadron. It was still a fighter station but was now equipped with the RAF's fabulous Lightnings one of the fastest interceptors ever created. As RAF Officer Cadets we were privileged to be allowed to sit in the cockpit of one of these front-line aircraft. If I had kept quiet about my hay fever, flying one of these brutes could have been MY job!

Coltishall was also an Air Sea Rescue base. We were all winched up into one of the Whirlwind or Wessex helicopters as a practice session for the crews – and an experience for us.

As part of our training, we also spent a week in South Wales and the Brecon Beacons.

The men's flight did two two-day exercises and one one-day exercise. The women's flight just did one-day exercises returning to RAF St Athan overnight! What happened to equality?

On the first of the two-day exercises in the Brecons, I think we climbed Pen-y-Fan – along a knife edge ridge if I remember correctly. It had very steep drops to one side. On the second day the cloud base was very low – making our route very treacherous. As we cut across country, I could see that we were running parallel to a road down the valley. We were due to join this road later in any case but, in view of the conditions, as Flight Leader for this exercise I suggested to the Flight Lieutenant that we should drop down to the road earlier than planned. He left the decision up to me so at the next stream running down towards the road, we followed it. As anticipated, we came to the road about a mile earlier than originally planned with everyone safe. In fact, we'd come down a stream before the one I thought we were using – but no-one else noticed.

On the second two-day exercise in place of the rain or drizzle that had soaked us, we had sunshine so ended up sweating instead. On the second day, we met up with the women's flight and were then split into three mixed sections. The overall Squadron Leader attached himself to one group, the male Flight Lieutenant to the second group and the Women's Flight

Part 3. RAF

Officer was with the third group. This section was led by Lyn Endicott (?) and I was appointed navigator.

The groups set off at 10-minute intervals – with us setting off last.

The route took us up the side of a valley – then off to the right. As the other groups reached the midway point along the side of the valley they left the track, went through a gate then down into the valley and up the other side. When we reached the gate some of the group started to follow suit. I said that we should continue up the same side then cut across the top of the valley – thereby maintaining our height.

There was a bit of a discussion which was brought to a halt by the Flight Officer saying "Dale you are not in charge, Endicott is – it's her decision". Lyn turned to me and asked if I was sure about what I was proposing. I told her that I was and she accepted my advice. The end result was that we overtook both of the other groups and got to the rendezvous ten minutes before the group that had set off twenty minutes before us. Our Flight Officer was absolutely over the moon that her group had beaten those observed by her male colleagues – and I ended up with a reputation as a top navigator!

While we were doing our own exercises in the Brecons we caught sight of other lone figures making their way across the hillside – with huge Bergans on their backs. They were SAS troopers.

While at St Athan we were shown around the maintenance hangars where they were servicing the two remaining types of V-bombers in service – the Avro Vulcan and Handley Page Victor (the Vickers Valiant not having been able to cope with the transition from high to low altitude operations). We were again, allowed the privilege of looking over the cockpits of these two aircraft that were still very much on the secret list.

Sadly, my time in the RAF was nearly at an end.

I was called into the Squadron Leaders office and told that they thought I was not yet ready to take command of a group of airmen – that I needed to get a job meeting people for a year and, if I did so, they would then accept me again for training without going through the selection process. It was a shock – but, looking back, they were right. I would have been torn apart if placed in charge of group of men!

If I had been accepted for pilot training, I would have had three years in which to mature – and even then, wouldn't necessarily have been in charge of any men. If..............

Part 4. London

Chapter 12. Job Centre & Scout Shop

Get a job meeting people! That's what I'd been told.

There was, however, something of a problem – I had entered the RAF in September; dad had been posted to RAF Khormaksar in Aden in the October and mum and Linda were due to go out to join him in a month. I could go out there with them but I really wanted to branch out on my own.

First step, then, was the Labour Exchange in Bury St Edmunds.

I told them my situation and they said they'd see what they could do for me. Next day there was a message – could I call them please. We didn't have a phone of our own so they had called my mother at the NAAFI where she worked and I had to return the call from the box by the guardroom. "The Labour Exchange in Luton had a possible job for me" I was told. "Where exactly, doing what?" I asked – "at the Labour Exchange itself"! That seemed a compliment and I duly attended for interview and was offered a post. The problem was this was the height of Luton's success as a car manufacturing location and accommodation was expensive and in short supply. All I would be able to afford on my salary would be a bed that I would use at night and someone on a night shift would use during the day.

Then I saw an advert in Scout magazine for assistants at the Scout Shop in London. I travelled down, had an interview, moved in to a hostel for scouts on Stepney Green and started work. The hostel, Roland House was back to the dormitory accommodation I'd had in the RAF so wasn't too strange!

I wanted freedom though and eventually found a bedsit between the Oval and Stockwell stations on the Northern line. It cost £3.10.6 per week rent – which was quite a bit out of my £9 per week pay – and that was before tax and there was tax to pay! Mum and dad also subbed me with £10 per month.

At work, I wore scout uniform provided as part of my job in the shop so didn't have to spend much on male clothes.

The bedsit was a single room in an extension at the back of an end of terrace 3 storey house – typical of the area. It had just enough space for a bed, built in wardrobe, a wash basin and a Baby Belling 'cooker'. Being the top floor with three of the walls external, it could get cold in the winter.

I set up my equivalent of a 'Teasmaid' with a timer plugged into the mains socket and a record player and kettle plugged into the timer. The record would start playing and wake me up – then, by the time I had struggled out of bed, the kettle would be boiled and I could make a coffee. This worked fine until I forgot to put the record arm onto the record one night and woke to find smoke filling the bedroom to within inches of my face. The record player had started – but, of course, there was no sound to wake me. The kettle had then boiled dry and continued to heat up burning into the wooden cover of the Baby Belling stand.

I spent Christmas 1965 with my friend Reg from France at his house in Chessington. On one of the days, we had a visit from one of his mother's cousins – together with her husband, daughter and a white poodle called Bobby. Her other daughter — Susan, Bobby's owner, was in the Caribbean setting up a club funded, no doubt, with proceeds from her No 1 record 'Bobby's Girl'. I was quite a fan of Susan Maughan so it was a thrill to meet her mum and dad and sister.

I joined 5th City of London Air Scout Group as a Rover – helping with the junior members when needed. One of our other regular activities was to provide crowd control and other duties at the Biggin Hill Air Fairs. These included helping to assemble a glider to be used by Derek Piggott, a renowned glider pilot who had done some of the stunt flying for 'Those Magnificent Men in their Flying Machines' (which a crowd of us had gone to see when on our gliding course at Lasham mentioned below).

left the Red Arrows at Biggin Hill C1966   *right on duty at Biggin Hill Air Fair*

I was also assigned to 'spot' for Battle of Britain Spitfire pilot and star of Tomorrows World, Raymond Baxter in the commentary tower. I had to watch out for the next display and point them out to him. While in the tower with him, a photographic supplies shop at the display sent him up some 35mm films in exchange for a mention over the Tannoy. He gave these to me.

I also went on a gliding course to the Scout Air Training Base at Lasham where they used an old Avro York as a bunkhouse

Left Slingsby T21 Sedberg 'Daisy' at Scout Air Training Base, Lasham airfield
right The Avro York bunkhouse at Lasham

Part 4. London

We flew the same Sedberg gliders that we'd had at Feltwell. Unfortunately, the weather was bad the week we had our course and we were limited in the number of launches we were able to do. I was one or two short of going solo by the end of the week. After doing the course at Lasham I volunteered to help out at the centre at weekends when I wasn't working at the Scout Shop. I bought a motor scooter to keep the travel costs to a minimum.

The scooter, a Vespa 150, cost me the princely sum of £15. Although crash helmets were not compulsory at this time – I did buy a second hand one. When I got the scooter home, I decided to check that the brakes were in good condition and removed the back wheel and brake cover. I noticed that one of the wheel studs was missing- and, when I was putting the wheel back on, a second one sheared off. Surely 2 would be enough!

Riding through South London, I felt the back wheel wobbling — when I checked it, I found that there was now only one wheel stud. It was Saturday afternoon and most places were closed – but I found a motorcycle repair shop and took the scooter to them. This was the time of the Mods and Rockers and scooter riders were the sworn enemy of bikers! In spite of this, the owner welded three new bolts on in place of the missing studs and I was back on my way before too long.

Of course, one of the principal attractions of staying in UK rather than going overseas with the rest of the family was the opportunity to cross dress. I could get in and out of my own bedsit but there was always the risk of being seen by other residents — not that there was much chance of any of them knowing who belonged to which 'flat' or caring.

Nevertheless, I developed a number of strategies to change away from the bedsit. I would tend to wear my female outfits under a thick jacket and catch a slow train from Waterloo to Vauxhall. These were the old southern region carriages with individual compartments. With luck I could commandeer a compartment that stopped close to the Ladies toilets on the platform at Vauxhall. I could remove my jacket & trousers, change my shoes and put on a wig in the four minutes it took the train to travel from Waterloo to Vauxhall. Then it was a quick dart into the ladies where I could do my make-up. I would then catch a later train to Clapham Junction and go to Victoria where I'd spend an hour or so in the cartoon cinema.

I also found a Ladies Room at Clapham Junction with a secluded entrance that I could use. Later, when I bought a motor scooter, I could use any number of toilets on the edge of parks and other secluded locations. Most weeks, if I wasn't working overtime, I would do my shopping at Tesco's at the Elephant and Castle. Sometimes I would catch the train from Liverpool Street out to Chelmsford – which gave me just enough time to change in the corridor coach toilets each way.

The toilets in the cartoon cinema at Piccadilly Circus were at the side of the screen and it was easy to slip into them – then leave by the fire exit.

For my holiday in 1966, I bought a 'Southern Rover' ticket which gave me unlimited travel throughout the south of England. I would join a train, use the toilets to get changed then spend the day dressed en femme. One trip I made was to Bournemouth where I went across to Sandbanks (before it became one of the most expensive areas in the world) and spent the

Part 4. London

afternoon on the beach in an orange bikini until I saw a guy spying on me at which point, I left. This trip became the inspiration for my first novel *'Summer Dreams'*.

Another trip was on the night sleeper from Euston to Manchester. I had booked a second-class sleeping compartment so might have had to share. Goodness knows what I would have done if that had happened. Fortunately, it didn't. Next morning, I had breakfast at Piccadilly station then caught the train back to London.

By now, I had found that I wasn't the only transvestite in the world. I had been in a bookshop in Soho when I had come across a magazine which had others who did what I did.

On 30th July 1966, I was in my bedsit, en femme as usual, when there was a knock on the door. I quickly changed before opening it to find my cousin Ian standing there. He suggested that we go 'up west'. Around the West End, we wondered why the cars were all sounding their horns. Apparently, there had been a football match at Wembley that day.

Ian was always a creative guy – making up stories that he presented as puppet shows. He had a number of novels published, including 'Cops and Other Robbers', as I.K. Watson.

Another evening, I was watching 'the FBI' on my television. The police were surrounding a house where a gangster was hiding and there was a lot of shooting when I heard a 'ping' looked at my window and saw a bullet hole! It obviously wasn't three D television – so I went out to the hall and dialled 999. "I've just been shot at" I told the police, who promised to send someone round. It was more than an hour before anyone arrived. They said there wasn't much they could do – the shooter had probably been in either the pub across the road 'The Dorset Arms' or in a block of flats behind the pub. If the police were not going to take action it was up to me – and I went out and bought an air rifle which I kept ready for a while.

Over the summer of 1966, we'd had overtime at the Scout Shop. It had been a busy time with the publication of the 'Advance Party report' which set out major reforms to the structure of the scout movement including changes to the uniform with the introduction of long trousers, new names – Cub Scouts instead of Wolf Cubs, Scouts instead of Boy Scouts, Scout Leaders instead of Scoutmasters and the elimination of Senior Scouts and Rovers and their replacement with Venture Scouts which set the upper age limit below that of Rovers.

The Chief Scout, then Sir Charles McLean, was in the Scout Shop on the day the report was published and signed copies for the hundreds of scout members who had queued to buy a copy. He was a regular visitor to the shop as we were on the ground floor of HQ when it was in Buckingham Palace Road. Another regular visitor was Ralph Reader creator of the original Gang Shows a major source of revenue for the movement.

One weekend, there was a gathering of Air Scouts at RAF Hendon – which I attended. Although I wasn't there as a member of the HQ team, I sat with them for lunch. One of the others sitting with us was the HQ Commissioner for Air Scouts – Air Vice Marshall Chacksfield. I mentioned that I had been an Officer Cadet in the RAF and planned to reapply. He told me that when I did, I should put his name down as a reference! A few weeks later he went out to Aden where he met my father who was Commissioner for Scouts for Southern Arabia as well as a Warrant Officer in the RAF. He told my father that he'd had lunch with me. It can be a small world.

Towards the end of 1966, overtime was cut with immediate effect. I had already worked the extra hours and was counting on and needed the extra money. Faced with the shortage, I started to steal again. The inevitable happened once more and I was caught. With some help from the Scout District and County Commissioners and my father paying back the money I had taken, no action was taken – but I was moved from the shop to the warehouse in Clapham.

I felt that what had happened was punishment from God for being transvestite and resolved to stop cross dressing and I dumped all of my female things into the Thames off Vauxhall Bridge.

Chapter 13. Return to Church

I joined a church near my flat and joined other young members of the congregation when they went to the Billy Graham Crusade at Earls Court in 1967. I became a Sunday School Teacher and started playing badminton at the local school that had links with the Church.

I started to go out with one of the girls from the church – but she already had a boyfriend in Southampton and didn't seem able to make her mind up. I then met Jenny at the Badminton and started going out with her. We eventually became engaged and married.

For many years there was a programme on at lunchtime on Sundays 'Two Way Family Favourites' playing requests for and from forces personnel and their families in the UK. Most weeks it was between UK and Germany but occasionally it went further afield. On one occasion it included Aden and my parents had asked for Val Doonican's 'Walk Tall' for me – a song that dealt with an individual who had gone off the rails but had recognised his mistakes and was determined to go straight in future.

I was also determined to remain on the straight and narrow from now on.

Chapter 14. NDC June 67 – Spring 72

In 1967, the warehouse was relocated from Clapham to Littlehampton. Rather than move, I looked round for another job. The Guide Association was looking for staff and I was offered the same role as I had with them at £12 a week compared with £9 that the scouts were paying. I was also told of a position with the National Dairy Council. I was told to phone, ask for Mr Henkinshaw and mention that Mr Speakman had told me to do so.

I did so, was invited to an interview at the offices in Charing Cross Road, and asked to sit a very simple test of arithmetic and to say which county three towns were in. I got one of the counties wrong – I think I had confused Skegness with Scarborough. I was, nevertheless, offered a job as 'Despatch Clerk'. I asked how much it paid. When I was asked how much I was on at the time, I said £9 but I've just been offered £12. "We'll match the £12". The week after I started at the NDC, they relocated from Charing Cross Road to John Princes Street, just off Oxford Circus. It wasn't much of a move – but it was on different north/south tube lines so there were a number of staff changes.

Part 4. London

The week after we had moved to John Princes Street, the Director came round to meet the new staff. Mrs Bradshaw, our section manager, introduced each of us in turn: "This is Miss Lawson"; "Hello Miss Lawson"; "this is Mr Whateverhisnamewas", "Hello Mr Whateverhisnamewas"; "This is Mr Dale who has just started with us", "Hello Mike, how are you settling in?"

This was the Mr Speakman, County Commissioner, on whose instructions I had applied.

Chins dropped! "So, who is the blue-eyed boy then?" asked Mrs Bradshaw once Mr Speakman had left.

At that time, it was quite amicable but it didn't stay that way.

My role was to transcribe requests from dairies and other organisations for posters and point of sale material onto forms that were sent to our despatch agents. We also had some supplies on racks in our office – which were untidy and disorganised. I set about reorganising the racks and putting the material into envelopes. I made the mistake of not asking permission first!

I also used envelopes to store the material without permission – to the annoyance of Miss Waring who was secretary to the director. She was also Mrs Bradshaw's best friend.

It may also have been that the reorganisation was sensible and that I had done something that Mrs Bradshaw should have done before. The end result was that I was now in Mrs B's bad books.

My work was simple and I could do it in no time. I started to visit other departments to collect requests rather than wait for the internal post sometimes saving a day in meeting those requests. But, every time I left the office Mrs B was into the Office Manager, Mr Henkinshaw, "Mr Dale's missing from the office again!"

I eventually instructed to report to Mr Henkinshaw one morning at 9.15. I knew I was in trouble. I fully expected to be dismissed. When I got to work the next morning, full of trepidation, I learned that Mr Henkinshaw had suffered a heart attack the previous evening and had died.

The NDC's role was to promote milk, cream, English cheeses and yogurt. It was funded by the Milk Marketing Board on behalf of the producers and a body that represented the distributors. One of the ways it did this was to hold cookery demonstrations at the centre during the day and in the evenings. I volunteered to help with the evening demonstrations by operating the film projector and helping with the washing up. For this we received the generous 'evening meal allowance' of 17/6 (87.5p). As there were plenty of ingredients for the cookery demonstrations, especially eggs and dairy products, we didn't need to spend the money on food.

The evenings involved an Executive doing an introductory talk, a film (often 'A Million Pounds A Day' staring Richard Todd himself a dairy farmer as well as film star) then the cookery demo and, finally coffee (made with milk of course).

When I found myself on duty with Valerie Boyd, one of the PR Executives, I mentioned that if there was ever an opening in her department, I would be very interested.

Part 4. London

A few weeks later I was told that there was an opening. One of the PR Assistants was not up to scratch and was being moved into the typing pool and I could take her place if I wanted. The role entailed sorting out press cuttings that came in each day and distributing them to the relevant Executives; doing more projecting and dealing with bookings for the demonstration theatre. This was extended to include dealing with film requests and involvement in other PR activities.

During my first year in the PR department, I received four pay rises taking me from £600 per year to £800.

Pints of View — the NDC staff newsletter which I edited — also described as Comic Cuts by one member of staff

I started to study Public Relations at evening classes – initially at the East London College. On the first night I found that one of the other students was a guy called Graham who had been at the Scout Shop at the same time as me. That first lesson was a nightmare. I don't think I understood a tenth of what the tutor was speaking about. He had warned us that this might be the case but that if we managed to stay for the first few weeks it would gradually fall into place. He was right. Nevertheless, as the exams approached, I was nervous about my chances. Then the tutor took me to one side and told me that he wanted to put me in for the following year's exams as well as this year's! He also wanted me to think about becoming a tutor myself. I was stunned. In the end it may just have been very good psychology on his part – boosting my confidence but I did, in fact sail through the 'Certificate in PR' and passed three out of four papers for the 'Associate Examination'.

I went on to complete the Associate Exam and to join the Institute of Public Relations as an Associate Member. The following year I did the Final Examination. This included a Viva Voce at which I was asked what I had thought of the course and the exam. My response was that I had thought both had been OK – I just wished that they had been related! When asked to explain what I meant, I explained that the course had spent many weeks on legal aspects of PR which I realised were important but the exam had been more about influencing members of parliament or local councils on behalf of our organisations or clients and the course hadn't dealt sufficiently with this. "You must have missed my talk on that topic" the examiner replied. OOPS! No, I hadn't missed it but I felt that the topic needed much more than just one session. I hoped I had removed the foot from my mouth!

I had. I not only passed but received a distinction in the Viva Voce.

I was now qualified to be a Full Member of the Institute of Public Relations but, at 23, was still too young as you had to be 25.

The NDC used all sorts of publicity activities to promote milk – often involving celebrities. As a result, we got to meet all sorts of television personalities including Bruce Forsyth, Ken Dodd, Tony Blackburn and other comedians, DJs and singers from the period. One day I was told to go out to the front of the building and watch out for Jimmy Tarbuck's car. "How will I know which it is", I asked. "You'll know" I was told. A Rolls Royce came round the corner – bearing the registration number COM 1 C!

As my career developed, I was entrusted to organise events myself. On one occasion, there was an attempt on the World Dance Marathon record at a venue in Crawley. The attempt was to be started on an edition of the Radio One Roadshow – a popular live show at lunchtimes. This edition was to be hosted by Emperor Roscoe and Anne Nightingale. My task was to organise milk for the competitors and ensure that the photographs of the event featured them drinking the white stuff. Another time, I was sent to interview the Arsenal goalkeeper Bob Wilson.

The NDC also ran a series of 'Dairy Festivals' around the country – the largest being at Weston Super Mare. The Festivals were launched on the forecourt of the Royal Exchange in London – usually by the Prime Minister of the day or, on one occasion, HRH Duke of Edinburgh. The Dairy Festival also featured a Dairy Queen competition in association with Young Farmers' Clubs – culminating in a Dairy Queen Ball at venues such as the Grosvenor House Hotel on Park Lane. As I was one of the organising team for the event one year, I was placed, with Jenny my wife and two friends of ours, on the 'workers' table which included Shaw Taylor (from Police 5) who was the compere for the evening. This was the first time that Jenny, Anne, Mike and I had been to such an event and we were all dressed to the nines in Dinner Jackets and Evening Dresses. A popular dance of this time and one that I remember doing at the ball was March of The Mods.

The NDC also produced a large number of films aimed mainly at consumers, typically, young housewives, nurses or schools to inform them about the dairy industry and the value of milk and dairy products. They also produced a film each year aimed at the Dairy Industry itself. This featured a celebrity to explain how their money would be spent. I was asked to take a briefing pack and meet the current year's presenter at Kings Cross station so that he could study the script on a train journey. It was Raymond Baxter – for whom I had spotted at the Biggin Hill Air Fair.

The NDC ran a promotion to win a new Morris Marina car one year. There were 6 cars to be won – roughly 1 per week. I realised that the first of the prizes would be announced during the Motor Show, then at Earls Court. I suggested that we should try to tie in with this and see if we could get a champion racing driver to award the prize. This was agreed and I was told to see what I could do. Jackie Stewart, that year's champion, had a contract with Ford so was unable to do it – but Graham Hill was available and we were able to arrange to organise the ceremony on the British Leyland stand. The advertising agency filmed the presentation and it went out as an advertisement the same evening. This would be quite easy to do in these days of video editing – but this was using film.

Another task I was given was to persuade each of the local BBC radio stations to allow a representative of the dairy industry to be interviewed regarding Margaret Thatcher's removal of free milk from schools — the infamous 'Maggie Thatcher — Milk Snatcher' incident.

Part 4. London

Another photo opportunity that we organised was bringing a Jersey or Guernsey cow into the west end and having the Dairy Queen standing on the rear platform of a double decker bus apparently trying to get the cow on board!

While all of this was going on, I had moved out of my bedsit, first sharing with a friend from the church – then into the YMCA between Stockwell and Brixton. I sold my motor scooter (for twice what I had paid) to a friend – Hugh and had bought a car a 1953 Austin A40 Somerset Utility. It looked like an enlarged Morris Traveller with timber frames on the exterior. With the rear seat folded down, you could fit a double bed mattress in the rear without folding it at all. (We did – when helping to move someone). With the seats up, you could fit two in the front, three on the back seat and four in the luggage area.

Shortly after I had joined the NDC, my sister and mother flew back from Aden. They had been warned that they were due to leave – then their flight was postponed so they, and other families on the same flight, headed for the beach only to be rounded and told to get to the airport immediately as their flight was leaving that day after all.

It was just after the Israeli / Arab Six Day War and there was no possibility of overflying any of the countries involved – so the flights went up the Arabian Peninsula, in through the Persian Gulf then to Istanbul (or, perhaps, Ankara). Whichever it was mum commented later about the stench! The flights then also had to avoid flying over Eastern Europe and the Warsaw Pact so had to detour through the Mediterranean. By the time they landed at Gatwick I think they'd been on their way for 24 hours.

I had arranged to meet them at Gatwick and was expecting mum and Linda to take a while to come through customs so went to get another coffee when I heard words to the effect of "go on then, ignore us!" I had just walked past the two of them.

Their travel arrangements had originally been based on arriving on Saturday so all of their further train times were wrong as it was now Sunday. They needed to get to Honington just north of Bury-St-Edmunds where they would be housed for the time being.

I think all of the families were quite shell-shocked from a combination of the travelling and the release from the tensions of being in what had effectively been a war zone. I'm sure it took them a while to stop reacting instinctively to loud noises.

I stayed with the group heading to Honington until they were on the train at Liverpool Street – helping to sort out train times and platforms.

I went up to see them the following weekend. When making some coffee for everyone, I instinctively reached into the cupboards and took out the bottle of coffee and sugar. "How did you know they were there" mum asked. "They're always there!" I replied. Well RAF quarters tend to be to a similar design and I suppose we got into habits of where things lived.

Dad had to stay out in Aden until virtually the end of the British presence – helping with the shut-down of RAF Khormaksar including the disposal of the remaining Hawker Hunter aircraft which were given to the South Yemini Air Force I believe.

Later that year, cousin Diane got married in St Philip's Church, Werrington. She and mum had been close and Diane had waited until she was back in the UK before tying the knot! I bought another motor scooter to get up to Werrington – going up the M1 to Birmingham

Part 4. London

then on the A5 as the M6 hadn't been built. It was a very long trip on something that only did about 35mph and I had taken the precaution of joining the AA the day before setting off.

Jenny and I got engaged in April 1968.

A couple of months before, Hugh and I had seen posters advertising the chance to be paid to learn to parachute. We just had to join the TA. No problem – I had done my training in the Army Cadets as well as with the RAF. How bad could it be? We went along to sign up at the beginning of February 1968. Unfortunately, Hugh was just too young to join – but I was accepted.

I'd read some of the history of the regiment and their wartime exploits so had a bit of an inkling about what would be expected of me. I started to walk/ run to and from work carrying a loaded rucksack, or Bergen as they called them, wearing Tuf boots. It was about 4 miles each way. At least it wasn't hilly – unlike the Brecons where I knew we would eventually be subjected to much harder 'tabs'.

All of my time with the TA was spent in the classroom / drill hall – we never did any seriously hard stuff at this stage. Then the week after Jenny and I got engaged, we were in the mess and saw the preceding course come back from their parachute training. Every other person had a broken arm or leg. I decided that maybe this wasn't such a good idea for someone who had just committed themselves to another person – and who was just starting out on a career. I asked to leave and, as I hadn't completed the training, this was accepted.

About a year later, I met one of the other recruits who had started the same night as me. He told me that two of the group had been killed in training accidents. One had fallen off the ridge at Pen-y-Fan, the other had been killed when a Land Rover turned over. I think I made the right decision – but I can still produce a Service Record to show that I was Trooper 24139430 Dale of 21st Rgt. SAS Reserves as well as A/C M4335561 Dale RAF.

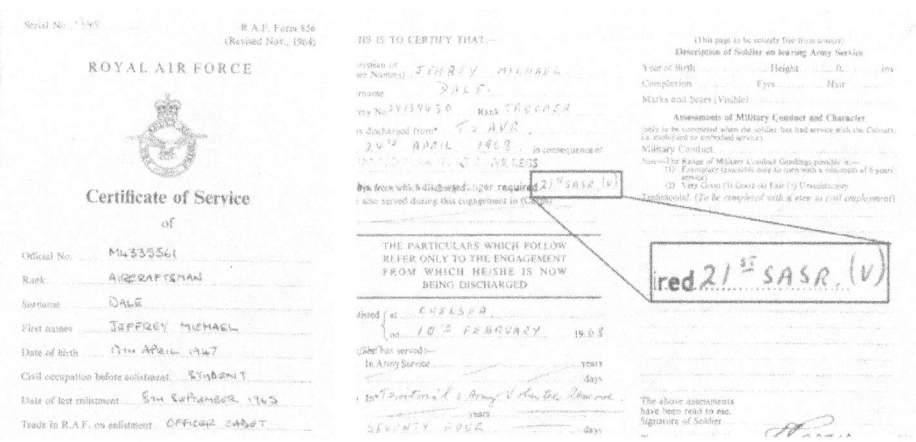

Part 4. London

Hugh and I had become very good friends – in spite of my having sold him a scooter for twice what I'd paid! Hugh eventually replaced the scooter, after riding it to Scotland a couple of times, with a Triumph 350cc motor bike – and I followed suit. This was still the time of Mods and Rockers and, although I was neither, I thought that if I was on my scooter and caught by a group of rockers I would be in trouble; if I rode a bike and encountered some Mods, I'd only have to twist the throttle and I'd leave them in my dust! I also bought a Triumph 350cc.

We often went out just for the pleasure of a ride – if we came across someone on a scooter, we would, I'm (almost) embarrassed to say come up behind and go past on opposite sides opening our throttles wide as we did. Naughty I know – but seemed like fun at the time.

Jenny and I were married on 5th September 1970 at St Edwards Church, New Addington, Surrey – her parents having moved there from South Lambeth. We honeymooned on the Isle of Wight at Pontin's Little Canada holiday camp. We had planned to go overseas but wanted to save up for a house of our own and buy a car.

The Triumph bike was replaced by a Triumph Herald car.

Hugh Johnstone was our best man. He and I had moved out of the YMCA earlier that year into a flat – the understanding being that he would leave when Jenny moved in.

Jenny and I realised that we couldn't afford a house in London – so we calculated what we were spending on rent and how much we had spare; then looked at developments out of London where the mortgage and the season tickets fell within our budget. There were two options: near Chelmsford in Essex or at St Neots in Huntingdonshire. St Neots was about 40 miles south of Stamford where my parents lived whereas we knew no one in Essex.

We had to wait for the house to be built so we moved in with Jenny's parents for a few months which also allowed us to save some more money for the deposit. At this time I was on about £1,200 pa; Jenny was Secretary in the Marine Superintendents' Department of Cable and Wireless on a little less than me. Our brand new three-bedroom house cost £4,250. Commuting from St Neots to London meant leaving the house about 7.15 am and getting home nearly twelve hours later. The route wasn't electrified so the trains were hauled by diesel electric locos. It was quite common for the train to arrive with two engines – the first having broken down before reaching St Neots – in spite of it being only the third station.

The NDC had a set hierarchy. At the top was the Director: George Speakman; below him were two heads of department: Advertising and Education and Public Relations. Below them, were a number of Executives and below them the Assistants.

I was one of the Assistants – arguably, by now, the senior Assistant in the PR department. There was, however, no prospect of promotion until one of the Executives retired – and that was several years ahead. Valerie Boyd, my line manager, recognised this and actively encouraged me to look elsewhere so that I could develop my career. She was the first to congratulate me when I was successful in this quest and we stayed in touch until she died.

She had been a personal friend of Douglas Bader and his wife, Thelma, perhaps I could have persuaded her to introduce me but I never did.

Part 5. St Neots

Chapter 15. Dolling's 72/3 & Foster Cambridge 73/4

I applied for the role of PR Account Executive with Dennis Dolling Limited in Potters Bar, Hertfordshire – on the northern outskirts of London. Their clients were mainly technical/scientific / industrial organisations making electronic components, oscilloscopes, industrial instrumentation, electronic keyboards and word processing machines. I initially missed out on the PR position but was offered an equivalent role on the advertising side. When the original successful candidate for the PR role left, I moved back onto the PR side.

The word processors at this time were complete desks with built in VDUs and stored data on cassette tapes rather than discs and cost thousands of pounds each. I don't think anyone really saw the extent to which they would become an integral part not only of business life but also just used for day-to-day correspondence etc.

By now my Triumph Herald had quite a few miles under the bonnet and as I would need a car for work, we bought an MGB GT (green, of course). Our neighbour, Brian, worked at Hatfield so we arranged to give him a lift to and from work to share the costs and Jenny then caught the train from Potters Bar station rather than St Neots.

The company organised a car 'Treasure Hunt' one weekend. There was a time penalty built in which was illegal as I pointed out but it stayed. The route took us out from Potters Bar to Welwyn Garden City then on to the A1(M). There was an error in the clues in the first section so we were behind time when we reached the motorway. I was about to put my foot down to make up a few minutes when I spotted a white MGB GT behind me. I knew there was a police MGB GT on this section so looked very carefully to check that this wasn't the one. There was no 'Police' flash on the bonnet and only one occupant. He stuck with me as I accelerated up the road. When I turned off at Stevenage, he followed me. That was when I found out that there were two MGB GTs on that stretch and one did not have any markings.

He said he was surprised that I hadn't seen him. I didn't think it would help to say that I had but that I was racing him. He reported me for doing 105mph and I eventually received an 'endorsement' and a fine. We didn't win the Treasure Hunt either!

After I had been with Dolling's for about a year, one of our clients, Foster Cambridge Ltd, asked us to quote for a brochure announcing to their staff that they were to move from sites around Muswell Hill to St Neots. I had a chat with their Publicity Manager and when they advertised for a Publicity Assistant, I applied and was offered the position. I was the first person from St Neots to join them.

My work mainly covered PR, Exhibitions and maintaining the direct mail list. The organisation produced a wide range of industrial instruments, recorders and controllers as well as a few other devices. One of the senior managers had a daughter who suffered from kidney problems and Foster Cambridge designed a dialysis machine. They supplied them at cost and didn't publicise this work as the manager didn't want it to be seen as just a publicity stunt.

The company also made 'endoscopes' an optical device for examining inside anything hollow. These days flexible versions using fibre optics are used extensively for medical

Part 5. St Neots

purposes. In the 1970s, they tended to be rigid and used more in industry. I visited a couple of customers to develop PR application stories. One made fire extinguishers and the endoscope was used to ensure that the interior of the barrel was flawless. The other was Westland Helicopters who used them to examine the inside of rotor blades.

Foster Cambridge also planned an exhibition tour at major hotels around the country. They would take over a conference room and set up a display of products and invite potential customers. One of the venues was the Golden Eagle Hotel in Middlesbrough. We were all relaxing in the bar after the exhibition had closed and everything packed away when we heard a ringing.

"That sounds like a fire alarm" remarked my boss who had recently joined the company from Reliance Systems who made such devices for hotels. "Shut up John and have a drink" he was told. The ringing continued. "I'm sure that sounds like a fire alarm". "Shut up John and have another drink". A few minutes later John again said he thought the ringing was like as fire alarm. To put his mind at rest, I went out into the lobby. There were firemen with hoses and the corridor was partially smoke filled.

"It is a fire" I reported back. We finished our drinks then left the hotel.

Sometime when I was on one of the business trips for Foster Cambridge, I was in a shopping centre somewhere around Newcastle or Gateshead when I walked past Lilley and Skinners. They used to have a 'Tall and Small' section which included larger sized women's shoes. On a sale rack outside the shop was a pair of high heels in a size 9 very much reduced in price. Just seeing them connected with the drive I had been suppressing for several years.

As an academic exercise I made a mental list of what I would need to be able to 'dress' again. The mental list became a written list. I wondered how much the various items would cost. I decided that, in theory, I would be able to afford no more than £100 total. Could it be done for that amount? The two critical items had always been shoes and a wig. The shoes were available but what about a wig?

There was a market in the shopping centre. Maybe there would be a stall selling wigs. This wasn't likely and, in any case, wigs tended to be expensive and would almost certainly breach the budget. IF, however, there was such a stall AND they had a suitable wig for less than £20 (or whatever the figure had to be) – then surely that would be a signal!

I wandered into the market. There was, indeed, a wig stall. But how much were the wigs? They had some within my budget! That settled it.

I bought a wig and the shoes and everything else I would need and went back to my hotel where I got changed then went out to a cinema. The drive had been unleashed again.

Foster Cambridge's move to St Neots was delayed. Nearly a year later, they had not even started to dig the foundations for the new factory. I had bought a new car on the strength of my new job and the planned move. I had recognised that the first year would involve as much as 20,000 miles commuting but this would then be balanced in future as I'd only be doing 25 miles a week.

I received an allowance for petrol – in exchange for which I agreed to give other St Neots residents a lift. Unfortunately, the petrol crisis had resulted in a huge increase in prices. We'd even faced the possibility of rationing at one point. All of which had started to make the position untenable and no one could give me any assurances about when the move would now take place.

When I saw a vacancy for Publicity Assistant advertised at Wainco, a local engineering company, I applied and was offered the job.

Chapter 16. Wainco 74- 79

Not long after I joined, a new Marketing Director, Mike Wilmore, was appointed. He compared my background with that of the then Publicity Manager, Peter Robinson and concluded that I was better qualified. He made me Publicity Manager and Pete was appointed Sales Coordinator. It might have helped if Mike had told Pete what was happening! I started to take decisions that Peter thought he should be making and he queried what I was doing. I had to suggest that he have a word with the director.

Wainco made 'dip and dunk' film processing machines and paper processing machines for prints. They also made a daylight operating, transportable machine for processing photoreconnaissance film up to ten inches wide. The 'dip and dunks' had a series of tanks and a lifting system. Films would be attached to metal frames and the machine would lift them from the loader and lower them into various tanks in turn before a final rinse then through a lightproof chamber into the dryer located in the light. The tank configuration was specific to the type of film being processed. Most common was Kodak Kodacolor II negative film used by most amateur photographers; there were also models for Kodak Ektachrome E6 slide film and Agfa films. Kodak also did Kodak Kodachrome – but Wainco did not make machines for this process. The machines came in three widths – allowing larger volumes per frame and higher outputs.

Wainco was part of the Woburn Studios Group headed by Peter Peck. They had three large studios in London, Leeds and Manchester. The group handled much of the photography for mail order catalogues. The studio in London had a door in one corner that looked quite small from the other end – but was big enough for a double decker bus to drive through. The studio in London was above the 'Film Exchange Club' on Quay Street – a dining club favoured by the cast of Coronation Street and other shows recorded at Granada just down the road. I was in there one day with Peter Peck and Pat Phoenix (Elsie Tanner) was at the next table. The unwritten rule was that you didn't bother the stars; they were there because they could relax.

Much of the publicity work involved major trade photographic exhibitions including Photokina in Cologne, Germany and similar shows in London, Paris and Chicago and elsewhere in the USA – which was an important market for us. We also displayed the photoreconnaissance film processor at the Farnborough Air Display.

Another machine developed by Wainco was a desktop processor for strip film up to type 120, including 35mm aimed at professional photographers. The film was transferred to a cartridge using a dark bag – the cartridge was then inserted into the machine and about 35 minutes later dry strip of negatives would emerge. The whole machine was about forty

Part 5. St Neots

inches long, fifteen high and about twelve deep. Mike Wilmore kept the case of one of these on a table in his office – and referred to it as his drink's cabinet.

We took the 'drinks cabinet' to Photokina in Cologne along with several other larger machines. We then looked at the 'drink's cabinet' and realised it would, indeed, hold several bottles of wine – about fourteen in total. Throughout the show, Mike continued to refer to it as his drinks cabinet not realising how accurate his description was.

When the equipment was brought back to UK after the show there were delays at customs because one of the larger machines had been seriously damaged on the way to Photokina and we had had to dismantle it and hide it behind the exhibition stand so the numbers of machines coming back didn't correspond with the items shown on the carnet. There were a number of very worried staff at St Neots until the lorry reached us.

We exhibited at these shows as part of the British Photographic Export Group partially funded by the DTI. One of the other exhibitors was Harkness Screens. They used to demonstrate their products by projecting images of RAF World War II aircraft including Lancaster bombers. Not the most sensitive of subjects in the city that had suffered the first of the RAF's Thousand Bomber raids. Some Belgian and Dutch visitors to the show would also spit at the feet of the German security guards. It was, after all, less than a generation since the end of the war and many of the visitors had seen their countries occupied by the Germans.

It's often said that exhibitions are only for 'flying a flag' but Wainco really made use of the opportunity and usually came back from Photokina, in particular, with a full order book for the next year or so. After each day, we would go out for a meal then gather in Mike Wilmore's room to discuss the enquiries recorded that day – taking our preferred drinks with us. I had bought a bottle of Bacardi on the ferry. As we were leaving Mike's room one evening, Pete asked if he could have a swig of my wotsit! I thought it was a strange way to refer to it – but he was welcome to some if he wanted. He took a couple of gulps. The second was on its way down before the first hit and he realised that I wasn't drinking bottled water!

There were political changes at Wainco. The original founder, Eric Wain, had retired. As well as Mike Wilmore, a new Financial Director had been appointed. Peter Peck wanted a shake up and brought in a new Managing Director, Gerard Campbell. It seemed that the other directors didn't get on with him and there were battles that started to affect the rest of us at times.

One of the instructions Campbell issued was that we should not fly to an exhibition in Paris – but should use trains instead. He was staffing the stand on one of the days. Goodness knows why he chose to do so – he knew nothing about the industry or our products – but, in accordance with his instructions, I booked him on the overnight train back from Paris. He later told me that he had had to share with a Frenchman with a supply of very smelly cheese.

I had arranged to visit some of our major customers while on the continent. One was in Munich the other in Dusseldorf. I was given special permission to fly to Paris – then on to Munich and Dusseldorf and back to London. Munich was beautiful in the snow with the mountains providing a backdrop and I had a successful meeting with the client. I then learned

Part 5. St Neots

that the Baader Meinhoff Gang had acquired some Surface to Air Missiles and were threatening to blown a number of Lufthansa aircraft out of the sky starting the day I was due to fly. The only airline operating between Munich and Dusseldorf was Lufthansa. I tried to contact the client in Dusseldorf to postpone my visit and travel by train instead but there was no reply.

I decided I had no option but to continue with the original plan. The airport was a lot less busy than normal and the Boeing 727 had very few passengers – there was sufficient room for each of us to have a set of three seats to ourselves. I'm not normally nervous when flying but that was an exception.

Press releases proved to be a sore point as far as the Managing Director was concerned. He would want it written his way – which was full of statements about how wonderful the company was – known in PR as 'puff'. It wasn't professional and against my principles because it didn't work. If left to do it correctly, I could virtually guarantee that what I wrote would be used by at least two, probably all three of the target magazines. If 'puffy' they would go straight into the waste bin.

Eventually, Mike Wilmore and the Finance Director left and the Technical Director focussed more on other interests. Without the protection that Mike had given, I was now exposed directly to Campbell's attention. He told me that he thought I was no good at my job and as long as he was there, I would never have another pay rise.

I spoke to one of the other directors, a designer who had been promoted when the original Technical Director had left. He said he couldn't say much but that I should do nothing.

We were due to exhibit at both Photokina and Farnborough that September. I had planned new display material for both shows – using a supplier that had seemed promising. When their material arrived, however, it was very poorly produced. We had no option but to use the Farnborough panels – there simply wasn't time to get them replaced. I rejected the Photokina material, however, and decided to use panels created for another show.

Having seen the lorries loaded and on their way to Cologne, we had a day before we were due to leave. I had previously been instructed by Campbell to ensure that items on notice boards didn't stay up longer than a month so I used the time to do some housekeeping.

Out in Germany, while setting up the stand, Campbell asked me if I was aware of any rumours about him leaving. I wasn't — apart from the conversation I'd had with the Technical Director a few weeks earlier. Campbell told me that it seemed that the rumours hack been sparked because a load of notices with his name on had been removed from the notice boards. I told him that I had done that –in accordance with his own instructions. "That's the only reason?" he probed. "Yes" I replied. He went off apparently satisfied.

During the show Campbell sold a machine, off the stand, for immediate delivery at a discount. There were a number of problems with this. Firstly, it would mess up the customs carnet. Secondly, it wasn't the right machine. The sign I had had to use because the new ones had been rejected said it was designed for Kodak film – but, in fact, it was for Agfa. The variations were shown on the sign and all of the other staff on the stand knew which machine it was.

Part 5. St Neots

Not long after we got back from Photokina, Campbell came storming into our building and went straight into Mike Wilmore's old office. We heard him on the phone to his solicitor asking if "they can do this to me". He had been fired. I don't think anyone shed any tears.

It did, however, leave the company in limbo. I decided to write a report to the Chairman about the state of morale in the company. I showed it to the Technical Director who had hinted that there would be changes. "I really wouldn't send that to Peter Peck" he advised. "Too late, I've sent it!" Fools rush in where angels fear to tread!

I soon received a message from Peter Peck's office. Would I come and see him in London? I thought I was either in trouble and about to be fired – or I might be thanked for the report.

With Peter Peck was the Deputy Chairman. They thanked me for having produced the report and told me that I was being given an immediate pay rise of a thousand a year – equivalent to about 25%.

Not that anything was done with my report – but another new Managing Director was appointed. He and I got on well together but he made me redundant less than a year later.

Chapter 17. Little Paxton Days

Jenny and I moved from Eynesbury to Little Paxton– a village just outside St Neots in about 1976. The front of the house faced out onto a green, making it safer for children to play – with car access and the garages at the back of the house.

The road out from St Neots to Little Paxton crosses some water meadows before dropping into a dip then rising over the bridge over the Ouse and past (then) Samuel Jones paper mill. Part of the Ouse tumbles over a weir – while the other branch passes through a lock allowing pleasure boats to cruise along the river. The village is then just to the right lying between the Ouse and the A1 — Great North Road. Just on the edge of the village are gravel pits one of which had been made into a sailing club and all of them teem with wildlife.

Our daughter Joanna was born 18th August 1977 – a year that was also famous for the Queen's Silver Jubilee and Virginia Wade winning the women's championship at Wimbledon.

My sister Linda also had a daughter, Sarah, who was a few months older than Jo. My mum had made each of them a stuffed toy – I think Sarah's was a camel called Humprey.

Our best man Hugh had got married in this time. Unfortunately, he had chosen the same day as Jenny's sister Lorraine so we were unable to attend. Anne and Mike had also got married – a ceremony we had been able to attend.

Joanna (left) and her cousin Sarah

Part 5. St Neots

After Hugh moved out of the flat, he lived in London for a while before going to horticultural college at Askham Bryan near York. When he completed the course, he rang to tell me he had joined the prison service and was being sent to a place near Stoke.

"Where?" I asked

"The borstal at Werrington"

"Give my regards to my Uncle Jack and Cousin Brian – they both work there."

He moved into a house a few hundred yards up the road from the one I had been born in.

A year or so later he rang to say that he was moving again.

"Where now?"

"Highpoint Prison, in Suffolk"

Highpoint had previously been RAF Stradishall and was named because it is the highest point in East Anglia. Hugh, Janet and Alastair moved into a house a few doors along from the first one we had lived in when we were there.

A couple of weeks later; I was over that way on business and called in to see Trevor Foreman, the scout leader. I asked how things were going and he told me that there was a new Farm Manager coming to the prison and they didn't know if they'd be allowed to keep using the Scout & Guide hut. I told him I thought I could fix that as it was my best friend.

While living in London, Hugh and I had taken the twelve-foot dinghies out on the Serpentine in Hyde Park – where we would chase the ducks. It's excellent tacking practice.

I had started sailing again at the council's residential training centre at Grafham Water next door to Grafham Water Sailing Club. Courses were quite affordable and once you'd been on one, you could use the centre's dinghies on a Thursday evening for just £1 per year. The centre also organised trips to the coast each year for sea experience. The first time I went on the coastal trip, we were leaving the little harbour at Southwold and it was becoming choppy, when one of the other crew members asked "what do we do now". "I don't know, you've got as much sea sailing experience as I have"[13]. "This is my first trip" he replied. "Same here" I told him. "I think I'm going to be sick" he said "well don't do it into wind" I instructed. Full of heart I was!

The centre also took part in a 24-hour sailing race on behalf of RNLI. The team used one of the Wayfarers – a stable but relatively slow dinghy. We couldn't expect to compete with some of the others in much lighter and faster craft. However, the race day was windy. Being cautious, we reefed our sails – potentially making us even slower. Caution paid off though. Several of the other teams were overpowered by the gusts and capsized – while we sailed majestically on. We may have been slower through the water – but those that capsized lost a lot more ground while getting their dinghies upright again and bailing out the water they'd shipped. I can't remember whether we won the race or not. To be honest that didn't matter

---

[13] I had overlooked sailing in Plymouth.

Part 5. St Neots

– but I believe that we'd raised the most money as a team as I'd asked a few of our suppliers to sponsor us.

Following my pay rise for the report I'd written at Wainco, I pointed out to Jenny that she had been against me joining the sailing club due to the cost but that the extra I was getting meant we could afford it. She agreed.

Highpoint was only about an hour's drive from Grafham Water and Hugh was keen to sail so we decided to buy a dinghy between us. I was reasonably experienced but Hugh was a beginner. So, should we buy something that was easy to sail which we might tire of quite quickly – or something with more potential but which might initially be a handful? We decided on a Fireball.

Fireball racing dinghies at Grafham — if you didn't capsize occasionally, you weren't trying hard enough (or were much better at controlling the boat than we were!)

These are racing dinghies. Light weight, with mainsail, jib and spinnaker, they can fly! To balance the force in the sails, the crew hooks a trapeze wire onto a harness at their waist and stands on the edge of the boat. Fireballs, like many high-performance dinghies, are designed to plane – skimming across the surface rather than forcing their way through the water. It's exhilarating planing on a 'three sail reach' with the main, the jib and spinnaker driving you, the crew on the trapeze and the helm leaning out as well. It's a fine balance and easy to misjudge. A stronger gust, or a drop in the wind, and you have to adjust your position – or end up swimming.

Hugh had never seen a trapeze before the first time we took our Fireball 1087 'Turn Turtle' out onto the water. We'd already had the boat a few weeks by now but the weather had stopped us going out. Even that day conditions were marginal. We were on the plane and Hugh was out on the trapeze before we'd gone fifty yards and that was with just two sails up. We just headed straight towards the other side of the reservoir. Sooner or later, we would have to turn round. Chances were, we'd end up capsizing. We didn't. We successfully turned round and headed back to the shore, got TT on the trolley and removed the sails. Then it was time for a shower and a well-deserved drink.

Although we didn't capsize that day, we often did so over many subsequent sessions. Turn Turtle was quite old and heavy and we were not competitive. We usually brought up the back of the Fireball fleet – but we didn't care. We had fun.

Many of our holidays at this time involved either Hugh and Janet or Mike and Anne and their families as well – sometimes all of us.

Part 5. St Neots

Quite a few of them were in the Southwest – Salcombe was a particular favourite of ours. Sometimes we took the Fireball dinghy 'Turn Turtle 2' with us – sailing it in the harbour. On one occasion we gave the children a ride in 'Turn Turtle 2' – Mike was supposed to come with me to handle the jib and keep an eye on James or Joanna. Instead, he shoved us off from the shore before I realised he wasn't getting on board and I had to do a circle to go back and pick him up.

We also took trips to France especially St Jean de Monts on the west coast. One year I had my Laser dinghy with us and a Dutch guy asked if I'd let him have a go on it while I played on his windsurfer. I then saw him sailing back to shore and signalling to me. "There is a girl in trouble out there on a windsurfer – can you take me out to her so she can come back on the Laser while I bring her windsurfer back". We headed back out, found her, he swopped places with her and she wrapped herself round the front of the mast out of my way while we returned to shore where she ran into the arms of her parents.

Chapter 18. Ad Agency in Luton

Following my redundancy, I applied for an Account Executive job with a small advertising agency in Luton. They took two of us on at the same time – both of us called Michael Dale. I was asked to use my first name instead, a name I had only ever been called at school.

The agency was asked to bid for two advertising accounts at the same time. One was for a range of plastic model kits – I think it may have been Revell, but I'm not sure. The other was for some new small computers being introduced. As they didn't see much of a market for computers, perhaps one or two per large business, maybe some in farms, they went for the model kits account instead. I suspect that Apple spent a lot more over the next few years than the model kit company!

I had been with the agency for about a month when I was told that I wasn't mixing sufficiently with the people in the studio. I had made the mistake of thinking that my job was to get on with some work – not spend time gossiping. I was given notice to leave.

Chapter 19. Sanyo 1980-84

I was then offered the position of Advertising and Exhibitions Manager with Sanyo Marubeni (UK) Ltd.

Having fought the Japanese during the war and in view of my Dutch-Indonesian mother-in-law having lost most of her family in Japanese concentration camps, my father wasn't happy about me working for the enemy – but I needed a job.

As I joined Sanyo, sales of video recorders were about to explode. In 1980 turnover was around £37 million. Over the next 4 years that shot up to £120 million with around £90 million from one model of video recorder.

The company was also about to appoint a new advertising agency at this time. We had presentations from some of the leading London agencies. One of them sent several staff to a meeting with us in Watford and each of them arrived in their own Porsche, Ferrari or similar expensive car. If this was intended to impress, it failed.

Part 5. St Neots

As well as day to day (rather than strategic) responsibility for advertising, I was responsible for exhibitions around the country. The first week, we were at the Cunard Hotel in Hammersmith for a Hi-Fi show. While setting this up, we were supplied with a sample of a new model – with all of the connections marked in Japanese. We did manage to sort out what plugged in where. At the end of the exhibition, we had to dismantle the displays quickly – the demonstration units were fed from power points hidden behind the panels. The mains plugs would not pass through these panels and rather than disconnect each plug in turn, we cut the leads. I checked with the contractors that the power was off to the section I was working on and was told it was.

Must be a lot of static around then I thought as I got a few tingles cutting through the leads. "No Not that section!" someone called.

The stands themselves were set up by contractors but I tried to be at each show to check all was OK before it opened. One week this entailed Edinburgh one day, Manchester the next and Truro on the third.

The travelling around the country did mean that I had plenty of opportunity to dress in the evenings. I also soon identified a number of hotels where it wasn't necessary to go past reception when leaving or returning.

Sanyo sponsored the show jumper Harvey Smith and we were often present at UK and Irish events where he competed. We created an exhibition trailer and bought a Jeep Cherokee Chief with which to tow it. The trailer had originally been bought to store exhibition materials rather than as a mobile display unit. It was the maximum length allowed for towing and about the same height and width as a shipping container. It was fitted out by our exhibition contractors who were used to displays where weight was not a problem. As a consequence, the trailer was an absolute pig to tow – aggravated by the fact that it only had two wheels not a tandem arrangement.

One of the first trips I did with the unit was over to Dublin – catching the ferry from Liverpool. Driving up the M1 and M6 was a nightmare. Anything over about 35mph and the trailer would start to fishtail. At one point having crested a hill, I found that my speed had built up to nearly 50 and the trailer was starting to swing from side to side. I had to accelerate to pull it straight – then very gradually let the speed fall of. It was a very nasty experience. When I got to Liverpool, I had to back the combination onto the ferry. The next morning, I delivered the unit to the showground where Harvey Smith was competing and was then driven to the airport for my flight home.

A while later, I was allowed to appoint an assistant who would drive the display unit and look after a large store of display stock of our products. On one occasion he was asked to help set up an exhibition in Belfast to support one of our dealers in the province. He was not at all happy about this explaining that just being around people trying to kill each other would be too much a of a mental strain and he would need time off afterwards to recover. I wasn't particularly happy with this response – but did the job myself.

In 1982, the Marketing Manager decided that it would make more sense to swop some responsibilities within the team – taking exhibitions off me and giving those to Bob who also

Part 5. St Neots

looked after in store displays. In exchange I would get Sales Promotions to go with my Advertising role. We were in the middle of preparing a promotion with trips to the World Cup in Spain as the prizes. The week before the promotion started, England lost a match which effectively meant we stood no chance of making the finals. Then just as the promotion was ending, another team lost a match which meant that England WOULD be at the finals after all. It wasn't the most successful of promotions!

The advertising agency that we used also worked for Rover Group and persuaded us to sponsor the Rover team in the BTCC[14]. Being a keen motor sports enthusiast, I attended as many events as I could with Donnington being one of my favourite circuits. The original lead driver was Jeff Allam. It became a common sight to see the two Rovers leading the races and they were originally declared Champions only to have the title taken away when (I believe) the wheel arches were found to be a few millimetres too wide.

To tie in with the Rover sponsorship and to launch a new range of In Car Entertainment, we organised the 'Alsace Ice Run' – a rally/ treasure hunt for leading motoring journalists and major clients in the Ballons Des Voges around Colmar and Mulhouse in South East France. The area was very hilly and wooded with an escarpment on the eastern edge that overlooked the Rhine; indeed, our hotel was perched on the edge of this escarpment giving fabulous views. The hills were so long that you needed to be careful with the brakes as they could fade going downhill.

The participants flew into Basle airport and allocated cars hired at the airport. We replaced the standard car radios/ cassette players with our own for the duration of the trip (without, obviously, informing Hertz and the other hire companies).

I had driven out in advance and test driven the route – created by, I believe, a former head of motor sport at Rover. I vetoed one section which had the participants driving down a steep track on the side of a hill – with nothing to stop them going off the road and rolling into the valley. The aim was for the journalists and dealers to have fun – not be scared to death.

At the end of the rally, we had lunch at a motoring museum in Mulhouse before most of those present caught their flights back to the UK and I drove back. I aimed to get to Paris for my overnight stop. It was four hundred miles but Autoroute all the way. I just kept my foot to the floor and did it in four hours driving time.

Having checked in, I went out to Pigalle where I was accosted by a couple of 'ladies of the night'. One of them told me that the other was 'transvesti' – I wanted to say "so am I" and even pay for a chance to spend an evening dressed – but I didn't. I later realised that they had picked my pocket.

The managing director at this time had been a driver with Nissan and when the UK arm asked if we would sponsor a new young driver, called David Llewellyn, in the Welsh Rally, we agreed. I thought this would provide a nice filler for the Sales Conference that year so went over to film him. I met him before the start at Aberystwyth and took some shots there of him

---

[14] British Touring Car Championship

Part 5. St Neots

starting – then headed for stage three knowing that I had no chance of getting to the earlier stages before he did. I parked at the bottom of a hill and started to trudge up the slope. The 'portable video recorder' I had available was effectively a household unit with batteries and separate camera. It weighed a ton! It was damp, very damp. The clouds were shrouding the top of the hills and it was drizzling. I finally reached a corner before the end of the stage that I thought offered potential for some good action shots. I knew I would only get one chance – I could hardly ask him to repeat the stage!

When I set up the kit, it wasn't working. In spite of everything I tried, it would not record. The damp had got into the machine and electronics don't like moisture.

Thankfully, I had my 35mm Nikon camera so could, at least, still take still shots which would have to serve.

I waited for the first cars to arrive on the stage – then for David to make an appearance. I thought he was running third or fourth on the stage but when more cars had gone through, I checked with the marshals "where's David Llewellyn running"; "oh – he went out on the first or second stage, quite a big shunt".

My trip had been wasted – fortunately, in spite of the accident, David and his co-driver were reasonably OK though they had been taken to hospital.

Part of my role was now to organise the sales conference. The first year that I was involved, we used a comedian who was about to star in his own TV show – but was still available at a reasonable price. I organised a room for him to use to change in and met him there to brief him before the dinner. I'm not sure that I should admit it, but I can, therefore, claim to have been in Michael Barrymore's bedroom!

Other celebrities that we used for sales conferences and other events included James Burke who had been one of the presenters on Tomorrows World and Peter Allis and Alex Hay for an annual golf tournament that we ran for major clients. When we were involved in launching the first sub-£one thousand IBM compatible computer, I contacted Raymond Baxter who agreed to present the launch. When I met him to discuss arrangements, I mentioned our previous meetings – he remembered having given me the films at Biggin Hill. He was a real gentleman.

The leading sponsors of Show Jumpers – such as Sanyo with Harvey Smith – tended to also sponsor one of the Shetland Ponies in their 'Grand National' at the Christmas Horse Show at Olympia. A representative of the sponsor was the official 'owner' for the evening and would go down into the arena for the race. One evening it was my turn to be the owner so I took Joanna, who was about 6 or 7 at the time, down into the arena with me. Our little pony race round the course, jumping over the fences with its rider urging it on to win!

Harvey Smith was a total professional when it came to promoting sponsors; as soon as he'd finished a round, a groom would be there with a blanket with the Sanyo logo in the corner; all of the horses were named Sanyo this or that – including Sanyo Music Centre, Sanyo SanMar[15], Sanyo Video etc etc. I confess I was responsible for a couple of the names.

---

[15] The UK company was Sanyo Marubeni (UK) Ltd

During the Radio Shows, Harvey would make himself available to chat to dealers – I'd sometimes keep him company when he wasn't otherwise occupied. He loved his red wine and when I was watching an episode of 'Through the Keyhole' and we were shown views across open moorland and boxes of red wine under the stairs, I said "That's Harvey Smith's house". It was. There were also rumours that when a horse box returning from an event in Spain overturned, its water tank had been full of red wine!

The following weekend, we were at my parents' house in Stamford and were watching the show jumping when the Shetland Pony Grand Prix was shown. I told my mother that Jo and I had been in the arena for one of the races – then said "in fact, there we are!"

Chapter 20. The Radio Show

Each year, in May, the major consumer electronics companies, such as Sanyo, held exhibitions in big hotels around London at the same time – known overall as The Radio Show. Sanyo had started to use the Royal Garden Hotel in Knightsbridge. We took over the entire Palace Suite – some thousand square feet – together with the annexe. We also took over the restaurant where we served lunches. An associate company, Fisher, had one of the other suites in the hotels. Over two to three days we set up displays of our entire product range on units around the edge of the Palace suite – and had a central display in the centre of the room. We had to work around the clock to get ready on time.

In the annexe, we set up discussion booths where the sales team could take dealers to discuss their orders for the next year. The Radio Show was a major event for the organisation – almost every member of the sales team was expected to attend.

There were well over a hundred products every year including portable radios and radio cassette players, music centres, hi-fi systems, televisions of all sizes from 2.5 inch to 45-inch projection models, video recorders and cameras – plus microwaves, cash registers, computers and calculators and other office equipment.

Almost every item changed each year – only the commercial equipment tended to have a longer model life. That meant that we started with a photographic session to shoot each item in January. On one occasion, we took had three photographers working non-stop in one studio for three weeks to photograph the range. I even had an assistant whose sole job over those three weeks was to remove the items from their boxes, clean them and check they were perfect (or quickly obtain a replacement) – and record that they had been photographed before repacking them and having them returned to the exhibition store. We had a Home Economist to prepare food for the shots involving the microwave ovens and a Stylist to obtain other props for the feature shots for the new brochures.

The copy also had to be written, and agreed, for the brochures. Some were straightforward product specifications – others were more descriptive.

By the time we got to the hotel and were setting up the exhibition, it was only adrenalin that was keeping us going. On the couple of days, we might well work through until 4am – take an hour or so break – then be back setting up at 6am. Once the show opened, our job in the marketing team was still not over. We still had to help deal with the dealers. Where

Part 5. St Neots

possible, their Sales Representative would have arranged appointments for them rather than just have them turn up on spec – but this didn't always work of course. We did, however, have a strict rule that dealers were not allowed to just wander around the display unaccompanied.

Due to the success of Sanyo's VTC5000 series of video recorders, the company was seen as one of the rising stars of the industry and another newcomer tried to take advantage of our progress by using the same hotel for their Radio Show. No doubt they hoped that our dealers would then also visit them. We were not prepared to allow this to happen and, in view of the amount of business we were doing with the hotel they turned Amstrad away. We did hear later that Alan Sugar had not been pleased!

The Radio Show was used to launch new ranges or make major announcements. In 1980 Sanyo announced that it was slashing the price of its VTC 9300 video recorder from £699 to £499. This clunky old top loader model weighted a ton and could only record one programme up to three days ahead. It was later replaced by the VTC5000 series and the price dropped eventually to £249 at which point the European manufacturers protested to the EU that they (and other Japanese videos) were being dumped in the UK at below cost price. Rather than fight the claim the Japanese companies agreed to restrict imports the following year to the number imported in the previous year. As video sales had been doubling each year Philips and Grundig hoped, no doubt, that they would pick up the unfulfilled demand. Sanyo and the other Asian manufacturers felt there was no point advertising products if they would be unable to satisfy the demand so they stopped advertising and sales collapsed.

The VTC5000 disproved the theory loved by marketing teachers that the cheapest product in a range is never the biggest seller. It was. In fact, one year the VTC 5000 outsold, I believe, all other video models combined. It was certainly the top selling video in Curry's with two Fisher models in second and third place. Sanyo was firmly committed to the Beta format although VHS was the most popular. Rather than lose face by switching, Sanyo established a hold in both camps through Fisher which was a subsidiary of Sanyo.

I was able to borrow whatever equipment I wanted from the Exhibition store (I needed to be familiar with the products in order to write copy about them well that was my excuse) – and had both Sanyo Beta and Fisher VHS recorders at home. This led to an interesting exchange at the local video library. Unable to find a film I wanted to see in the beta section, I took one from the VHS shelves.

"You usually have Beta," said the assistant.

"Yes," I replied

"That's a VHS tape."

"I know."

"You can't play VHS on a Beta machine."

"I know – but I have one of each."

This at a time when only around 5% of households had even one video!

We also launched new products at the Radio Show. Sony's success with the Walkman meant that everyone else in the industry wanted to jump on the bandwagon. Sanyo launched a range called MG1. At that time, Rover was about to resurrect the MG brand car brand with the launch of the MG Metro. Our ad agency also handled the Rover account and was working on the launch of the MG Metro. With our established links with Rover through the BTCC team, we agreed to a promotion where we would give away two MG Metros; one to consumers, one to the trade.

The trade promotion asked dealers to estimate how many MG1 personal stereo boxes we'd squeezed into an MG Metro on display at the Radio Show. The winner was from a dealership in Bedford – just a short detour from my way home from the show.

I called in at the shop and asked for the lucky winner. I asked if he remembered entering the promotion then told him that he had won the car. His face was a picture! "You're kidding!" "Err, no! What colour do you want?"

The consumer winners lived in Essex and, again, I went to see them. They too asked if I was kidding. "Yes, I've driven seventy miles to play a trick on you – what do you think?" I loved being able to give folks the news that they had won a prize like this – it made such an impact on their lives. I still look forward to someone doing the same for me – or even just an e-mail from Lottery HQ to say I've won more than £10.

Chapter 21. Going For Gold and Other Perks

In 1984, Sanyo sponsored the British Olympic Teams at both the winter and summer games.

To tie in with these, we ran sales promotions. The winter promotion was only aimed at the dealers but the summer games promotion was for consumers and dealers. The main prizes were trips to see events at the games.

The accommodation for the Winter trips proved to be a long way from the events and there had been some adverse comments from some of the winners. I convinced my boss, therefore, that I needed to check out arrangements for the summer games personally. He agreed – providing it didn't appear as a separate item on the invoice.

The prizes were to be a week in Los Angeles, three days in Las Vegas and four in San Francisco. My fact-finding tour was for just a week. I had anticipated seeing a show in Vegas and riding the Cable Cars in SF. Unfortunately, many of the shows were closed in Vegas due to a strike (though I did see one) and the Cable Cars were out of service in SF as they were being overhauled ready for the Republican Convention later that year.

On the flight back from San Francisco, some scruffy individuals wandered through the economy class section although they were from first class. When we arrived at Heathrow, there were crowds waiting at arrivals – even the customs officers were getting autographs before taking apart all of the kit Duran Duran were bringing through! If you ever intend to smuggle something – try to ensure you're on the same flight as a pop group; the rest of us were just waved through!

Part 5. St Neots

As I mentioned earlier, we produced a large number of brochures each year – a significant part of these through a design agency that the Marketing Manager had introduced to the company.

The agency did a lot of work for other large companies and Len, the owner, realised that several of his major clients were keen sailors. To keep us happy, he bought a Sadler 32 yacht which he kept on the Hamble. He was no sailor himself but hired a professional skipper to take us out with him for weekends.

There would usually be three or four clients, Len and the professional skipper. Most of the trips were around the Solent including, around 1982, entering in the Round the Island Yacht Race. This started and finished off Cowes. The start time depended on the tides but was usually between 6 and 7 am. The fastest yachts set off first and the slower classes at ten-minute intervals. The route would take you anti-clockwise round the Isle of Wight with the tide with the yachts for the first leg to the Needles.

The faster yachts would complete the course in around 4 hours, the record is just under 3 hours, while the last finishers might creep over the line after racing for 12 hours or so.

On another occasion Hugh and I joined Len on the boat. As he knew that we were experienced sailors, he didn't bother with a professional skipper for this weekend. As we emerged from the Hamble into Southampton Water, Hugh and I looked at a pole secured to the deck. It was about eight feet long and about four inches in diameter with shackles on each end.

"Is this a spinnaker pole Len?"

"Yes" he said apprehensively

"Have you got a spinnaker on board?"

"Yes – but I have no idea how to use it." Came the worried reply

"We do!"

We found the spinnaker in its blue bag and hauled it on deck; identified the spinnaker halyard and the two lines that connected to the tack and the clew. Running the lines outside of everything else on the yacht we hanked on the spinnaker. As we hoisted the spinnaker, we attached one end of the pole to the bottom corner of the sail which would be upwind – and hooked the other end of the pole onto the mast.

The secret is to gradually ease the spinnaker sheet until the leading edge begins to curl then draw it back in an inch. As the wind is never constant this has to be done all of the time.

We emerged from Southampton Water into the Solent – the Isle of Wight in the distance. "I think we need to drop the spinnaker" called Len on the helm. "Plenty of room yet!" we replied.

Eventually we took pity on Len – it was, after all, his first time as skipper and I don't think he really expected to be tested so much!

Part 5. St Neots

Chapter 22. The Benefits of Being Away

The exhibition work in particular entailed a great deal of travelling around the country – and being obliged to stay away overnight. This increased the opportunities for me to dress in the evenings. Sometimes I would go out to a cinema – hiding in the anonymity of the darkness. Other times I would just go for a drive, perhaps calling in to a Little Chef for a coffee or even a meal. On very rare occasions, I would visit a transvestite/ transsexual support group if one happened to have a meeting when I was in the area.

I got to know lots of hotels that had access that didn't go past reception desks – or were far enough from the desks to let me slide past without close attention.

This didn't always work out. Returning to a hotel one night, I headed from the front door to the stairs when the night porter called to me to ask for my room number. I mumbled a reply. "Sorry couldn't catch that"; I mumbled again; "Sorry I STILL couldn't catch it". "241" I exclaimed – practically running through the door to the stairs and up to my room. In the room, I tore off all my things and dressed in pyjamas in case the night porter decided to check out what was going on.

I don't know if I was imagining it – but there did seem to be a hidden message in the "did you have a good evening" when I checked out the next day.

On another occasion I had seen a sign outside a beauty salon in Potters Bar (just round the corner from the offices I'd worked in during my time with Dollings) offering treatments for men and women. I enquired and was told they would be happy to give me a range of treatments as a transvestite and for me to leave afterwards en femme. The salon was called 'Helen of Troy' – which is why I chose the name Helen. It's a good job it wasn't called 'Emma' – or I could have ended up as Emma Dale. (Emmerdale is a TV soap opera!)

When I visited coffee shops I was always on edge. Would I be 'read'? What would happen if I was? If someone laughed or giggled or I saw them glancing at me, I'd be paranoid that 'they knew'. Yet there were rarely any comments that I heard. One exception was in the coffee bar at a Tesco's in Coventry when I did hear someone call me disgusting. Another time, in a Little Chef – probably on the A45 somewhere near Newmarket/ Bury St Edmunds, I heard one of the chefs ask the waitress if I was a man or a woman. She said she didn't know. When she returned with my order I coughed and made some comment about having a bad throat. I then heard her tell her colleague that I was a woman but just had a bad cough.

Chapter 23. Fired

In 1984, with the decision not to advertise videos, our marketing budget was slashed. The Marketing Manager decided it made sense to use it on a poster campaign during the summer to boost sales at a relatively quiet period. I had serious reservations and pointed out that this would leave us without any budget for the pre-Christmas period and that even a 100% increase in sales in the summer would be less than a 20% increase pre-Christmas. He was convinced that a boost in sales during the summer would mean we'd get extra funds for later. It didn't work.

Part 5. St Neots

We had moved as a family from our 3-bedroom semi in Little Paxton to a four-bedroom detached house in Great Staughton. The mortgage we needed to pay had jumped significantly between deciding to buy the property and completion – rates had risen by 2% in one go!

I made the mistake of asking Len if he needed any copywriting doing to bring in some extra cash. This was reported to my boss who took it as an attempt to coerce Len into paying me backhanders for the work he got from Sanyo. Nothing was further from the truth – but it cost me my job. Perhaps I'd trodden on some toes, perhaps it was because my boss had made some pretty bad decisions that year that I'd disagreed with and he saw me as a threat. Maybe they even believed that I had been trying to put pressure on Len.

I again saw this a punishment from God for my cross dressing and got rid of my female stuff in a picnic site not far from Northampton – burning some of it in the metal waste bins.

Chapter 24. Bruyneel Advertising/ CAM 1985-6

I joined Bruyneel Advertising as an account manager/ copywriter. The agency was run by Rod Bruyneel and his Australian partner Andrew Davies – known to everyone as 'Blue'. I was soon told that Rod and Blue were gay and not just business partners. Several of their clients were also gay. Although I was in one of my denial phases, I didn't have any problem with their sexual orientation – except as far as the risk of aids was concerned.

This was at the beginning of the Aids epidemic and I confess to have been as ignorant as most people were at the time – Rod and Blue's coffee mugs were kept separate from those of the rest of the staff!

One of our major clients was the Spectrum Photographic franchise and the associated Spectrum Computer franchise – not to be confused with Sir Clive Sinclair's Spectrum computer company.

On my first day, I was given some proofs of newspaper ads for Spectrum. As I had worked in both photographic and computer industries before, I had an extensive knowledge of terminology. When I checked the first proof, I identified a large number of mistakes; after finishing checking and marking up the page, I took it into Rod. I asked if I had found them all. "What do you mean?" he asked. "I assume this was a test to see if I'm any good at proof reading". It hadn't been.

Mike Stern, Managing Director of Spectrum often attended our meetings. One day he advised us that he had to cut the price of MSX computers in order to get rid of a large backlog of stock. I pointed out that when I'd been at Sanyo I'd raised serious doubts about the prospect for these computers. I told him that I'd thought the concept of a standard design from all of the major Japanese and European companies all with the same specification and sold at the same price wasn't likely to succeed. I'd believed that, as the UK had its own manufacturers such as Acorn and Spectrum, UK buyers would prefer to have a homemade product rather than an import. The fact that the MSX range were all the same would cause confusion – with no unique selling propositions for any particular brand. "I wish someone had raised those points with me before I bought a million pounds worth of them" he ruefully admitted.

The staff was invited to Rod and Blue's housewarming – they had moved from London to just outside Biggleswade in Bedfordshire. In the corner of their lounge was a 26inch Sanyo television. I'd last seen that set in the exhibition store that I'd managed.

I said to Blue that I knew where they'd got the set. "We bought it," he claimed. "That's not possible – that's a sample produced by the factory in Spain and it was the only set brought into the UK. It was sent out to Spectrum for a photo shoot and not returned with the rest of the products. I know because it was my job to manage the items!" Red faced, he asked what I intended to do about it. "Nothing. I work for you now and don't owe Sanyo anything!"

Later that year the agency lost one of its clients – which meant that there would be redundancies. Rod couldn't stand having to fire anyone from his 'family' and had a breakdown. I arrived at the offices one day to find him sitting on the floor in his office with furniture strewn around, much of it broken.

He told me that he had thought of jumping from his office window – but as it was only on the first floor, had realised the fall wouldn't kill him but would result in serious injuries and pain. Blue took Rod home and I don't think we ever saw him again. He later died, we were told, of hepatitis.

Blue continued to run the company, now renamed 'CAM', and tried to sell it to some of the staff but, in reality, any good will with clients was held by the staff he was trying to sell to and there were very few assets apart from some typesetters.

Instead, four of us set up our own companies and moved into shared offices in St Neots.

Part 6. On My Own

Chapter 25. JMD 1986-95

The first-year trading as JMD Advertising was quite successful. I managed to retain many of the clients that I had worked with at CAM and picked up some more small accounts in the computer field and through the Cambridge Branch of the Chartered Institute of Marketing – where I was now a member of the committee – producing the newsletter and annual programmes for members.

I regularly represented the CIM at Cambridgeshire County Council 'Small Firms Workshop' – providing ad hoc advice to visitors and, occasionally, being commissioned to do further work.

CIM also organised social events as part of the monthly programme. These included a visit to the Maclaren Formula 1 factory and a Gliding Evening at the Cambridgeshire Gliding Club. As I was Branch Vice Chair, I offered to act as host for the evening and arrived well before the other members. I was asked if I'd ever done any gliding before. I mentioned that I had done some in the RAF then at the Scout Air Training Base at Lasham – both times in a T21. "We've got one of those here" said the instructor – "would you like us to get it out for you".

I helped take the T21 to the launch point and carry out at DI (Daily Inspection) ready for use.

I left my flight until last but it was eventually my turn.

As we sat at the launch point, the instructor reminded me of the procedures. We were hooked onto the launch cable – gave the signal "take up slack" then as the glider started to move forward "all out".

Up we went like a lift; stick slightly forward to ensure not too much pressure was applied to the cable or it would snap. I remembered the signals to the winch operator – waggling the wings indicated – faster please; yawing from side to side with the rudder meant slow down.

At the top of the launch, the instructor pulled the cable release setting us free, stabilised our position then turned to me and said "OK – let's see what you can remember. You have control". Whoa! It's been nearly twenty-five years!

I was a bit tentative at first but was encouraged to make firmer movements of the controls and it came back. After a few manoeuvres, we had to fly the downwind leg, then turn cross wind before another turn to line us up for the landing.

Joanna started to get much more interested in nature and spent many weekends at the nature reserve at Grafham Water while I was sailing. She became very good friends with the warden Jo Thomas and when her school took part in a 'tourism and the environment' competition, Joanna decided she would do a 'radio interview' with Jo Thomas. She won the national competition in her class and was invited to the Natural History Museum in London to receive the award.

Part 6. On My Own

Joanna and her award at the Natural History Museum, London

All of the other award winners had been part of teams – she was the only individual winner

During the 80s my brother-in-law, John, and a few others formed the Huntingdonshire Motor Club. As John and I were attending a local business meeting that the local MP was to address, we were delegated to ask him to be our President – which is how we came to be having tea with John Major in the George Hotel in Huntingdon and, incidentally, where I was able to drop the 'I hate name droppers' statement into the conversation. Shortly afterwards, John Major was promoted to Chancellor and I was able to include an article in the club magazine headed 'Major Promotion for Club President' and ask the question 'where next John?'

During this period, I continued my interest in motor sports both as a competitor/ organiser through the club and as a spectator – particularly the RAC Tour of Britain Rally (when it really did tour the country).

As I was Managing Director of an advertising agency, I was seen as a prime target market for Lotus when they launched their new Elan. I was invited to take a test drive then go to the factory in Norfolk to look around and have a go on their test track. They didn't realise that JMD Advertising was myself, a YOS trainee and a part time book keeper.

On the M11 on the way to the factory, I was overtaken by a Lotus. It reminded me of an incident I'd been told off when I was with Wainco. We used the same agency then as Lotus and the agency's chairman raced single seaters. He'd been at a meeting on the south coast and had put his car into the protective tyre barrier. Annoyed with himself, he'd collected his guest and told him they were going back to London. He didn't even change out of his racing overalls.

As they drove up the M23 in his Lotus, his guest has asked "so what will this do?" Foot to the floor he demonstrated only to be pulled over by a police patrol. "Right little boy racer" said the officer when he saw the agency chairman's overalls.

The day at the factory was very interesting and it was fun driving their sports cars around the test track – getting up to well over 100mph on the straights. I 'toe and heeled' the throttle and brake as we approached one corner prompting the professional racing driver with me to ask where I'd learned to do that.

Hugh and I also continued to get in some sailing. He'd move to Farnborough so we no longer shared the Fireball – but we'd sailed on a 'classic' yacht in a rally in Brixham and had been invited by the owners to crew for them on 'Mary Poppins' on some cross channel races. After being asked to tidy up the lines at the mast during very heavy weather, which I considered risky and unnecessary, we both left the boat in Cherbourg and returned by ferry.

Part 6. On My Own

I had just arrived at work one morning in January 1992, when I had a phone call from my mum. She said that she had some bad news. I immediately assumed it was that my gran had died – she was approaching 100 and we'd not really expected her to survive the previous couple of winters. Her next words were however "It's your dad, he's gone."

I hadn't any client appointments that day – but it wouldn't have mattered if I had. I just said "I'm on my way".

Mary Poppins; Hugh and I crewed on three cross channel races

For some reason my parents had decided they wanted a downstairs toilet at the house but instead of having it in or even attached to the house, it was a few feet outside. Mum had gone to bed the previous evening while dad stayed up to watch TV. Rather than disturb mum by flushing the upstairs toilet, he had gone outside. We don't know exactly what happened; he may have slipped or had a heart attack – but his body was found the next morning. The cause of death was recorded as heart attack – but whether that was the cause of him falling or as a result of it or the cold that night, I don't know.

His funeral was held the following week. We had just arrived home when mum rang again. Gran had just died so we were back for another funeral the following week.

Other difficulties at this time included Jenny being diagnosed with breast cancer and needing chemo and radio therapy and a mastectomy. After this, she told me that she had been reflecting about her life and had decided that she wanted a divorce. It was Joanna's last year at secondary school so I said I wasn't prepared to disrupt her at that stage.

The business was also in trouble.

I had a client who had asked for some design work to be done – including a new corporate design for his new company. He had wanted a number of changes which I did but he still wanted more. Eventually, I invoiced him for the work he'd commissioned but he refused to pay. The matter went to court but he kept making promises so the case was suspended. In the end, with interest and court and legal fees, the outstanding amount was several thousand pounds.

Being owed this money, I took some risks with other work – some of which did not work out. I had been commissioned to produce a sales folder for a double-glazing company in Peterborough. I had previously produced a range of recruitment adverts which had proved effective. Due to late changes and shortened deadlines by the client, I had to change the production method for the sales presenter from full photographic pages to photocopies. The folders were delivered on time as a result. All except three pages came out perfectly satisfactorily and I offered not to charge for the other three and to replace them at my own expense.

Instead, the client withheld all payment and the matter eventually had to go to court.

As I hadn't been paid by these two clients, I couldn't pay my own bills. So I was being sued. Other clients started to use desk top publishing for some of the work I had previously handled.

These factors combined with the result of the next chapter meant that JMD Advertising was put into liquidation. As it happens, by the time the Official Receiver took over, we had won the case against the double-glazing company and there were substantial funds in the account. Sadly, not sufficient to meet all debts.

Chapter 26. Lords of the Manor

Merv and me as Lords of the Manor

One of the annual events in Great Staughton was the Brains of Staughton quiz. Two friends, Merv and Rod, lived on a road just opposite our house called Manor Close – so we formed a team called the Lords of the Manor.

We reached the finals one year. There was a tradition that the finalists and the beaten teams from semi-finals wore fancy dress for the finals night. We obviously dressed as medieval Lords of the Manor

The following year, we were back in the finals. We obviously couldn't wear the same costume – so one of the wives suggested that we be the 'Ladies of the Manor' instead.

I made a token objection – but secretly thought this might be an opportunity for me to come out if Jenny's reaction wasn't too critical on the night. I knew from past experience that the biggest problem for me would be shoes – so I went over to Cambridge and the Saxone 'Tall and Small' department. They had some suitable items and, for once I could claim honestly that they were for a fancy-dress event and even give some background.

Unfortunately, either Rod or Merv flatly refused to go with the idea but the genie was out of the bottle once more.

The shoes were soon joined by other items.

I was my own boss and could easily cover time out of the office – finding somewhere to change and just driving around or going for a coffee at a Little Chef.

Part 6. On My Own

One of the clients I was approached by at this time was a company in Grantham who were launching a range of bridal lingerie. I was asked to design and produce new leaflets and point of sale material for them.

The client's publicity manager wanted to use a photographer and stylist she knew in Manchester and asked if that was OK with me. I had no problem with going up to Manchester – especially as it meant an overnight stop.

We all met up at the studio in Manchester and set to work. I'm sure that most guys surrounded by some attractive ladies clad only in underwear would have been turned on. I was too – but by the thought of wearing the products!

As the day went on, it became apparent that we wouldn't finish that day and the client asked if everyone was available to continue the next day. That meant staying another night in Manchester – what a disaster! The stylist then mentioned that she was OK for the morning but had another client in the afternoon. She was booked to make up a transvestite for a photo session – a regular job for her. She then revealed the individual's name and where he worked. I was appalled but not in a position to protest without outing myself.

That evening, in the village, I asked around and found someone who knew the individual concerned and asked that he be advised that his stylist was being indiscrete to say the least.

Part 7. Contracting

Chapter 27. Lt Barford Power Station

With the business in trouble, I started to do some temping work at Little Barford power station just outside St Neots. They were constructing a new combined cycle gas turbine plant. These employ a large gas turbine – similar in principle to jet engines – to drive generators; the hot exhaust is used to heat water for a steam turbine which also turns the generator. I was in the Electrical Department which was responsible for installing all of the cables from thick cables for high voltage down to those connecting telephones and computers. The department also installed the instruments and all of the electrical devices.

My initial work was mainly secretarial/ admin – dealing with correspondence. I also did some spreadsheet work and this resulted in the department manager asking how good I was with computers. I told him I was brilliant! He then told me about a spreadsheet they had had on another project that took data from the database and gave them up to date reports on the status of the work. "Could I do the same?" "Of course!" I replied. "If you can then there will be a job for you on the next project!" (If it could be done – then I was confident I could find how to do it)

That afternoon, I went to a bookshop in Bedford and bought the best manual I could find on Lotus 123.

Eventually, I produced a spreadsheet that gave up to date information about the progress. I was demonstrating it to the manager, Brian, when his boss rang him from head office in Manchester. Brian said he could give the answer to one question he'd been asked immediately but couldn't answer the second question. I had heard the question too and found the appropriate section of the spreadsheet and pointed to it. "Hang on – I've now got the answer here".

After the call, Brian gripped my shoulder and said "I want you with me on the next project!"

Chapter 28. Connah's Quay Feb 95-June 96

The next project was at Connah's Quay in North Wales. It would mean living away from home – which, in view of Jenny wanting a divorce meant she got the space she needed while not disrupting Jo's education with a divorce. Connah's Quay was not that far from Manchester which suited me down to the ground.

Brian asked me what I wanted to join him at Connah's Quay. My immediate response was a Pentium computer rather than the 486 we had at Lt Barford. "I meant salary" he said.

I'd found out that if your salary was above about £19K, you didn't get paid overtime. If you asked for just a bit less, they gave you the £19K instead – so I asked for £17,000.

I arranged to borrow a caravan off Hugh and moved onto a site just outside Chester. It wasn't a residential site so I had to be away for a few days each month which fitted in with visits home. I started at CQ in February 1995. Hugh had been good enough to lend me his caravan as a temporary measure but he would obviously need it back for holidays so I bought one of my own. The first one was just 12 feet long and I replaced it with a fourteen-foot

Part 7. Contracting

Musketeer which I fitted out with a proper mattress and other home comforts including a portable TV. It wasn't ideal but I wasn't in the caravan much. I was working very long hours – typically 15 hours per day – except Wednesday and Saturday when I finished early to go to the gay village.

Doing around 100 hours a week really boosted my salary – I was on around £50,000. However, by the time I paid out £1,800 a month for the mortgage and another loan secured on the house and other credit cards; transferred money to Jenny and supported Joanna at university, I was left with about £200 per month.

Before I left for Connah's Quay, I told colleagues on the Chartered Institute of Marketing Branch Committee of my plans and was invited to a farewell dinner where I was awarded the Presidents Medal for services to the CIM.

Evenings in the Village fell into a routine. Wednesday was Northern Concord, Saturdays I would have dinner in the Blue Café on Sackville Street then wander round to Paddy's Goose for the early part of the evening before visiting some of the other venues and, inevitably ending up in Napoleons.

Receiving CIM President's medal

Getting to the Village entailed leaving the caravan with my female outfit under a padded male jacket then driving to a lay-by or other location where I could remove my jacket and trousers, swop shoes and put on a wig then do my make-up. Coming back to the caravan was easier as it would be totally dark.

At that time, Northern Concord met upstairs in the Rembrandt on the corner of Canal Street and Sackville Street. I soon became friendly with three transsexual members Faye, Jackie and Gwen. Either Jackie or Gwen lived in Warrington and I often dropped her back home. I think, sadly that she died of cancer. I started to realise that I had far more in common with Faye, Jackie and Gwen than with most of the transvestites in the club. Yet I hadn't always felt that I'd been born in the wrong body – or hated my penis – which seemed to be the key factor that determined whether or not someone was TS rather than TV.

I always maintained that the Blue Café was the best place to eat in the village – although a friend thought that the honour should go to Metz. I knew that I could go to the Blue Café and most weekends have the 'special' and it never disappointed. On the rare occasion when I didn't want the special, their burgers were fabulous.

Paddy's Goose was directly opposite the coach station and, to all intents and purposes, looked like thousands of pubs around the country. Thirsty travellers would cross the road and order their pints if they arrived before about 7.30pm. If the next stage of their journey wasn't for some hours, they might even remain there until the regular evening crowd arrived

Part 7. Contracting

– at the back of the right-hand side of the bar was 'Tranny Corner'. As we arrived some jaws would drop; watches glanced at and pints would be speedily finished as though they had suddenly realised their coaches were due to leave. Those weary travellers who arrived after us might take one look and back out again.

There were, of course, many who were more tolerant or less afraid of what mixing with us might result in. Two couples that were frequent visitors and sat with us were Barbara and Dave and Sal and Martin. We also mixed with lesbians and gays including Gilda – who was later to become an important part of my life.

Due to my size, I had problems finding clothes to fit so had started making my own outfits using a hand sewing machine I had bought. I was wearing one of the dresses I had made one weekend when Barbara complimented me on it – "just something I ran up" I told her.

"You didn't make that."

"Yes, I did."

"No, you didn't."

"I did."

Pause

"You didn't really make it did you?"

"Yes!"

"Well, if you are that good you can make me a trouser suit!"

"What size?"

Next time I saw her, I passed a package to her.

"What's this?"

"The trouser suit you ordered!"

She took it out of the bag and examined it.

"You did NOT make this," she insisted.

"Look at the material and compare it with my dress and compare the buttons". I had deliberately used the same buttons on both outfits. Barbara finally accepted that I had, indeed, made her outfit.

Just as Paddy's Goose was the first stop on a Saturday night, Napoleons was our last. There was a dance floor upstairs surrounded by mirrors and most trannies love to see themselves in the mirror.

Winter in the caravan was cold – particularly when I was away for the weekend. I came back after one home visit to find that my two-gallon water bottle was a two-gallon ice cube.

As spring became summer, an election loomed. Due to boundary changes, we now came within John Major's constituency. For years, Screaming Lord Sutch had stood against the Prime Minister of the day. I was looking forward to voting for the Monster Raving Looney Party – but it was not to be, Screaming Lord Sutch's mother was ill and he was not standing.

Part 7. Contracting

While at CQ, I discovered that you can tell people you cross-dress and they think you are joking!

I was shopping in a supermarket one day when I saw a white handbag which was perfect to go with some 3" heel court shoes I had.

At the checkout I was packing my groceries into a carrier bag when the girl said "I'd better put this handbag in a carrier for you as well — don't want people wondering what a man is doing with a handbag."

"It goes with my white high heels," I told her.

She laughed.

I was tempted to go back there dressed and prove I hadn't been joking!

On another occasion, I had CorelDraw on my pc which was ideal for producing posters. I had done one for near the coffee making facility with a picture of a maid and the message "we haven't got a maid — so clear up after yourself."

Someone else wanted one for a golf tournament. So, I used clip art of a golfer on it.

"Brilliant programme you've got here to do these posters," my colleague said as I gave it to him.

"Yes — it will even merge images together — so you could merge the golfer and the maid and have a transvestite golfer!" I replied.

"What's wrong with that?" he demanded in a camp voice and hand on hip!

"Nothing at all, I do it all the time," I answered.

His mouth dropped to the floor as he stared at me.

"No that's not true," I said .... leaving a pregnant pause .... "I haven't played golf in years."

"Nice one!" he exclaimed laughing.

Oh well. Two hours later I was at a Northern Concord meeting dressed and relating the same story!

The main part of my job was to produce the progress reports for the electrical department. I had received my Pentium computer and, each morning, I would import the latest changes from the design team into the database and the latest progress from the cabling contractors. Both of these sets of data were correct to 5pm the previous evening. I then opened the report spreadsheet. This had a list of every one of about 150 systems in each of the four CCGT units. For each system we identified the number of each size of cable and the length used against the planned length and the status of each cable – 'pulled', 'glanded at end A', 'glanded at end B', 'terminated at end A', 'terminated at end B', 'tested'.

The spreadsheet was a mass of around 5,000 cells each containing complex calculations looking up the data in the database. Progress for each of the four units against planned was plotted on a graph. With the figures printing at just 9 point, it covered an A1 sheet. The spreadsheet had to be set to manual recalculation otherwise it was impossible to use. When set to recalculate each morning it still took about 20 minutes using my Pentium 90 (which

Part 7. Contracting

had been the fastest available when we started. Most of the team was still using 486 computers – one of them also had significant calculations to process and felt he, too, needed a Pentium. I suggested that it made more sense to provide me with a faster machine and pass mine to him – he agreed that this was sensible. We then had to go and see the overall site manager.

"Why do you need another computer? Your team has already got more than they had for the moon mission!"

I pointed out that the Apollo Mission had had ten years to achieve their goals whereas we only had eighteen months; that when he wanted information, he wanted it urgently and that the faster machine would halve the time to produce his figures. We got the new machine!

The fact that we could produce data up to 5pm the previous evening proved to be a cleft stick. Brian knew exactly where we were in relation to planned work – whereas other sections were still working with data that was up to a couple of weeks old so no one could check the accuracy of their claims that they were on time. I got the impression that this led to friction between Brian and the overall site manager.

One of Brian's deputy managers had left the project after being told that he could no longer stay on his contract and needed to take a permanent position which meant a very large cut in salary. He had gone to work for Siemens at their Didcot B project.

Brian asked me to re-type his CV which he gave to Cliff. A little later, Brian called me into his office and told me that he had been offered a job with Siemens. He told me that as soon as he got there, he would persuade Cliff that they needed me too. I then told Brian that Cliff had already been in touch and offered me a position but I'd told him I wouldn't drop Brian in the proverbial.

When Brian left, one of the section leaders took over the Electrical departments. My contract had originally been planned to end in the September but I was now told that I would be finishing in June instead.

The project was virtually complete and we had started the snagging phase. I developed another spreadsheet to monitor progress on this work. One of the other departments saw the work that I had done and asked if I could do the same for them.

They were pleased with the result and my new manager asked when my contract was due to end – I told him it was in about 3 weeks. "We'd better get that extended" then he looked at my face. "Have you got something else lined up?" "Of course I have". "Well, what are we going to do then?". "Perhaps you should have thought about that before bringing my end date forward".

As well as going to the Village on a Wednesday and Saturday, I would often do my weekly shopping 'dressed' – typically in a Sainsbury's and usually without attracting any attention whatsoever. One weekend, however, I was in a branch near Chester when I was aware of people giggling and glancing at me. What had I done wrong today? Had I messed up my make up? Was my wig on back to front? Were my clothes inappropriate? I hadn't ordered anything from the deli counter so it couldn't be my voice. Then I realised, I wasn't dressed en femme.

I was in male mode. The glances and giggles were nothing to do with me! As I said earlier, it's easy to be paranoid and assume that we've been read and that all of the laughter etc is aimed at us – when it isn't.

Chapter 29. Fight with First National

Although I was now keeping pace with loan repayments, we had an ongoing battle with First National Bank with whom we had taken out a loan for the business. When we had taken out the loan, I had deliberately queried a clause that said that if Bank of England rates went up then the loan payments would go up. My question was about what happened if the rate fell. I was told that our monthly payments would stay the same but that the difference would start to reduce the balance.

That sounded reasonable so we had signed the agreement.

It was only when we got into trouble and were arguing in court what we should owe that we discovered that the clause meant no such thing. If interest rates went up, our payments would go up. If interest rates fell there would be no change.

We had a long debate over this with the bank and, while I was at Connah's Quay, eventually had a meeting with the general manager at their head office in Harrow. He was accompanied by their head of legal services. They proposed to Jenny and me that they would reduce the interest rates by two percent – not particularly generous when the bank rate had gone down by six percent. We wanted them to abide by what we had been told and recalculate the outstanding amount using that basis. They refused. I said that in that case, we would sell the house but the value wasn't likely to cover their loan but they could whistle for the rest. They threatened to make me bankrupt – I told them to go ahead. During the meeting, they had admitted that their terms and conditions had been found to be misleading in court – but they still insisted on applying them.

In the end we sold the house and, as expected, the proceeds left a balance that First National said was due to them. They chased us for this money and I asked them to sue us for it. I hadn't been able to instigate an action against them for the misleading terms – but I would certainly be able to use that as a basis for a counter claim. The outcome was that First National 'took no further action' over the alleged outstanding balance.

Chapter 30. Didcot B Jul 1996 – Jan 97

I hired a Transit van with a towbar for 24 hours to move the caravan from Chester to a site next to the Thames at Abingdon. I transferred as much as I could out of the caravan into the Transit for the journey. Rather than use the M6, I took a scenic route down the A41 before using the M5 and M40.

Once I reached the site at Abingdon, I set up the caravan – then headed back north with the Transit. I needed to be close enough to the hire depot to return the van before my 24-hour hire ran out so I slept in the back of the van near Chester. Then it was back in the SRi back to Abingdon – rather quicker than the day before.

Part 7. Contracting

I started at Didcot B the next morning. Our offices here were some individual Portacabins set apart from the main linked complex. We also had a store about half a mile away and part of my job was to open this for an hour each morning and afternoon so that the work gangs could collect components that they needed. I also had to estimate likely demands based on work to be done and ensure that we never ran out of stock – but also that we were not tying up too much money in the stores. Trudging to and from the stores twice a day through the mud in Hi-vis jacket and overalls and protective boots certainly burned calories. As the campsite was only about 3 miles from the site, I bought a bike and cycled to and from work. On the other hand, there was a tradition of a large breakfast on Friday mornings – piles of bacon and sausages, eggs, fried bread, tomatoes, beans, mushrooms for those that wanted them (I didn't). Goodness knows how many calories were piled onto each plate but it must have been at least 2-3,000.

When we started at Didcot, we had about 5 computers in the electrical department – all standalones. I was asked if it was possible to link them as a network and connect them to the internet so that we could exchange emails with head office in Germany. It seemed that the most cost-effective way would be a simple peer to peer network and a simple modem for the internet. We could do all of this for a couple of hundred pounds. We put the proposal to the IT team in Manchester. They told us that it would cost a lot more as they would need to organise proper cabling for the network – we shouldn't do it ourselves. I then asked if they knew what our role was at Didcot. They didn't. I explained that we installed all of the cabling, including all the computer cables for the entire power station. We thought we could manage a few links between Portacabins. We heard no more from them and our network was up and running within a few days.

One of the side effects of the internet / email link was that I could get on line myself in the evenings. I came across 'Donna's Den' – a TV/TS chat line. I was on there most evenings establishing contact with trans people across the world – and much closer. I had also learned of trans groups in Oxford, Watford and Swindon – all within easy reach of Didcot. Most met monthly but I think Watford (which was, strictly speaking, Gay and Lesbians Of Watford but admitted trans people as well) may have been weekly. The Oxford Group met in the top floor of an Italian restaurant north of the city centre. Swindon met in a community centre not far from the M4 motorway.

I made a number of local contacts on line. I invited one person back to the caravan picking her up from the railway station. By then I had moved the caravan from the site near the river which closed during the winter to the car park of a pub. On another occasion, I was chatting to Lynette, a Canadian trans person in Oxford, who didn't know anyone in the UK – I'd been invited to a bonfire party at a friend's house in Hemel Hempstead so asked if she wanted to come with me. One of the other guests at the party was Janet Scott, then president of the Beaumont Society.

Siemens had been planning to develop a team that could move from one power station project to another – but the new Labour government had decided that to protect the coal industry, they would stop any further gas turbine power station projects. Instead of moving to another project when Didcot was completed, I was given my notice on Christmas Eve. As

Part 7. Contracting

we only got paid when working, this seemed to me to be a deplorable way of dealing with staff – most of our notice would be spent on our Christmas leave.

I packed up the caravan and towed it back to a bungalow Jenny had rented in Grafham after the house in Great Staughton had been sold.

When I went along to the Job Centre, I was told that I would have to wait for benefits. I then asked about training opportunities as there was a poster on the wall. "Are you ex forces" I was asked. "Yes" I replied quite honestly. "When did you leave?", "1965". Apparently 30 years was too long a gap!

I was then asked if I had been in prison. I said I hadn't but was he telling me that someone who had been in prison got better treatment than someone who hadn't? Apparently, this was the case. I did appreciate once I was working for Probation, some years later, the justification for this – but at the time it did seem totally unfair.

Part 8. Manchester
Chapter 31. CEGELEC Feb – Dec 97

When we were leaving GEC at Connah's Quay, it had been suggested that I mess up the IT system – which I could have done. I didn't follow that suggestion which is just as well.

A few days after my appointment at the Job Centre, I had a phone call from Terry who had been Brian's deputy in the electrical department. He had heard I was available – would I be interested in a job in Manchester with CEGELEC – who did the designs for power stations built by GEC Alsthom. Could I attend an interview the following week? We agreed on the Wednesday.

When I arrived, I was told that the job was split between two sections and I would be interviewed separately by both managers. After the interviews, neither of which had involved Terry, I was asked if I wanted a chat with him. I asked him how many other people were being interviewed for the roles and was told that I was the only candidate and I could expect to start the following week. I'd be phoned at home on the Thursday.

I stayed in Manchester that night and resumed my acquaintance with Northern Concord.

As Thursday afternoon dragged by, I still hadn't heard anything from CEGELEC. Perhaps Terry's confidence had been misplaced. It was on the Friday that I had the call. It had been felt that my experience on the main side of the job had been a bit weak though I was more than OK for the other part of the role. At that I thought the job had gone! Instead, I was told that they had decided to change the job and focus on my strong side. When could I start?

The following week, I visited the Bank Manager – who had asked to see me about our overdraft. He obviously wanted to hear how I planned to reduce it. Instead, I pointed out that I had been offered a job in Manchester but in order to take it, I needed to be able to pay out some expenses and I asked for the overdraft facility to be increased by £1,000. I pointed out that if this was not agreed, I would be unable to pay off what I already owed but if I could start work in Manchester, I would be able to continue reducing the overdraft. He eventually agreed.

I went back up to Manchester on the Wednesday and, after looking at some private flats/bedsits in the afternoon, went to Northern Concord in the evening. Someone there suggested that I try Salford Council for a flat. When I said I thought Councils had long waiting lists I was told that this didn't apply to Salford. I duly went along to a housing office on Churchill Way and explained that I had been offered a job in Manchester and asked if they had any accommodation. They had. They offered me a one-bedroom flat on Graythorpe Walk. This was on the first floor of a low-rise block that ran parallel to the M602 motorway. Fortunately, it was screened by some bushes so the noise wasn't too bad. I went back to the housing office where they asked what I thought. I told them that it looked as though it needed redecorating as you could see where the previous tenant had hung paintings. They then told me that they had had another tenant hand in keys that morning for another flat in the same area – this time on the ground floor.

Apart from a cracked power socket and a light fitting that was dangling from the ceiling, this one was in better condition so I decided to take it. I was given some forms to fill in –

including an application for housing benefits. I told the housing officer that I had a job. "You HAVE?" he exclaimed.

"When can I take possession", I asked as I start work on Monday.

"We need to do an electrical safety check and sort out a plug and a light fitting – so you can't move in until middle of next week but to all intents and purposes the flat is yours as of now". I didn't tell them that I had already tested that the socket was safe and that the light fitting worked.

"We'll give you a voucher that you can spend at a DIY store on decorating materials but we can't do the work for you" That was no problem.

I asked if I could borrow the keys again so that I could drop off some of my things that were in the car while I went back down to Cambridgeshire to pick up the rest of my kit. I then took the keys and had a spare set cut and moved in as soon as I came back with my other belongings.

The flat was empty so I needed to find a cooker, fridge, wardrobe, bed, table and chairs and sofa.

I bought the cooker and fridge from a second-hand shop and obtained the rest of the items from a church store near Salford precinct. They even leant me their van and a couple of volunteers to move the furniture to the flat.

The work at CEGELEC lasted until the end of 1997. I was told that there was another contract in the Philippines due to start in the spring and they would want me for it – probably initially in the UK but also on site.

As it happens, CEGELEC was absorbed back into GEC Alsthom – from where it had originally spawned. There were redundancies which meant they could take on contacted staff. It was unfortunate that they didn't say this as soon as it became clear instead of keeping me hanging on for nearly six months.

When the contract ended, I discussed the position with Jenny and we agreed it was best for me to stay in Manchester for the time being.

Chapter 32. Helen's Haven

Although I might still be Mike at work, I was Helen for almost all of the rest of the time and the flat soon became 'Helen's Haven'. Being on the ground floor, I could easily enter and leave without normally being seen – the path outside was rarely used and it was only a few yards to the road at the side of the flats where I would park the car if going out that evening.

Occasionally I'd get a bit of abuse from local youths and the area was not safe for cars. My Cavalier SRi was stolen within three months of me arriving – in spite of having put padlocked flaps over the key holes and removing the door lock studs from inside the car. It had been written off after being chased by the police in a Transit. (I don't think a Transit was ever likely to catch an SRi – no matter how well driven and the end result was inevitable).

For the rest of the time that I was at Graythorpe, I drove old cars that would be unattractive to thieves. This was such a successful strategy that I found one day that my car had been left but they'd stolen the number plates! It seems they valued the petrol they could obtain using my plates on their vehicle higher than my car!

The first of the 'low value' cars was an Astra. Jacqui gave me a lift to the seller on an estate in North Manchester. She then sat in her car while I took the Astra for a test drive. She has never let me forget that I abandoned her to the local youths for (she claims) hours. The Astra was not the pinnacle of my motoring history! It drank more oil than petrol. In fact I think we were lucky that it got us to Blackpool and back for a weekend.

In that weekend lies another story. It was a VC UK event. Most of the girls were booked to stop at Linda's B&B but there wasn't room for all of us so Jacqui and I (as the most confident of the members) were asked to use a B&B run by a friend of Linda's a few doors away. Jacqui asked the landlady if she could borrow an iron to do her outfit for the evening. "Give it to me, I'll do it" she was told. A few minutes later the item was returned. "I've done the top, does the skirt need doing as well?" The top was, in fact, Jacqui's dress. Short? You could say that – but that was Jacqui's style. I suspect some of her skirts were shorter than the width of some of my belts!

We were looking round Blackpool on one occasion (may even have been the same weekend) when Jacqui dived into a charity shop – in spite of my attempts to head her off. She found a green (I think) dress that she tried on. It wasn't quite right but when she discovered that she'd got make up all over it, we made a quick escape from the shop.

When we weren't in the village, the chances are I would be on Donna's Den. I now had a circle of friends from the village including some who lived in Albion Towers, a tower block a few hundred yards away. Chatting on Donna's Den, I'd often ask where people were from and where they went out. All too often the answer was that they had never been out dressed. "Come down to Manchester, stop at my place if you like and we'll go down the Village".

Almost every time there would be protests that they wouldn't have the nerve, they'd be too scared or too shy. They didn't believe assurances that after half and a hour in the village they would be totally relaxed and feel they'd been doing it all the time. None of them believed me – but all of them accepted that I had been right when they tried.

I'd come across Vanity Club on the internet, a group of more confident trans people. When I enquired about membership, I was referred to Lisa who was setting up Vanity Club UK. Lisa and BJ, another friend of hers, who had set up a scheme awarding trannies 'stars' depending on how confident they were and what they'd done. A one star meant they'd only ever dressed in private five star meant they had been out in public in daylight mixing with other people (or something along those lines).

When we organised a first meeting, possibly in Blackpool, Jacqui (one of those from Albion Towers) and I found that whilst we were totally confident going out dressed, the scheme organisers had hardly done anything. In Blackpool, most of the girls stayed in male mode during the day and only dressed at night to get a cab from the B&B (run by a post op transwoman) to one of the gay clubs such as the Flying Handbag. If everyone went out for lunch or a drink during the day it tended to only be Jacqui and I that would be dressed.

Part 8. Manchester

AS VCUK grew, we had some transsexuals who were already on the transition path – but it remained mainly transvestites. Eventually, Lisa decided to resign as President to concentrate on a business she had set up importing (mainly) exotic shoes and boots. She asked if I was interested in taking on the presidency and I agreed.

At this time, I was also a member of an internet message group TG UK – open to all trans people. Some transsexuals eventually decided that they wanted their own group and set up TS UK.

Inevitably someone suggested on TG UK that it would be great to organise a get together for members. Several of us lived in Manchester so we offered to accommodate some of those from wider afield and a crowd of us gathered at Metz restaurant for the first Face to Face (or F2F) gathering. Walking up Canal Street after the meal, en route to one of the other clubs, we were spotted by a group of youths crossing Sackville Street bridge over the canal. "OI! Are you lot men or women?" they jeered. "More of a man than you'll ever be; more of a woman than you'll ever have" I replied. Thankfully, the person next to me had been a major in 22 Regiment SAS – so I felt quite safe making this comment.

Amongst the friends who stopped at my flat were three who gave me cause for concern.

One was an individual who was teetering on the edge of accepting that she was TS rather than TV. She told me that if she did ever make that decision then it would cost her marriage and she would not be able to live without her partner and would commit suicide. I persuaded her to at least call me to say goodbye if she ever decided to end things – obviously my intention was to then try to persuade her to at least postpone her actions.

The second was Fran. Fran had been in a car accident and had been seriously injured. She had been led to expect a very large insurance pay-out but this fell through. She'd moved not far from Manchester and was due to attend Gilda's 50th birthday party one weekend. When I called her to check that she was coming, I was told that she wasn't; she had taken every pill in the house! It appeared that her boyfriend had dumped her on top of everything else that had been going on. I tried to persuade her to give me her landline number as all I had was a mobile. She refused, knowing that this was a ploy to be able to get an ambulance to her. I went on line and eventually found someone who had her address. I called the police.

About midnight I had a call from her. "I've just had the police at my door; you promised you wouldn't say anything". "Well, you didn't believe me did you?" "No" "That's ok then". The following Saturday evening she was at Gilda's party and gave me a hug.

The third individual, I'll call her Carol, was someone from GLOW in Watford. I'd told my friends down there that if they wanted to visit Manchester, give me a call and I'd put them up.

I had a phone call one night reminding me of my offer to put her up if she visited Manchester. But before Carol agreed to come, she needed to ask me a question.

"Did I believe in God?"

"Yes."

"So, if you die, you believe you'll go to Heaven."

Part 8. Manchester

"Yes."

"That's good because I'm being chased by some drug dealers!"

Well, what can you do when faced with such a statement? I just thought that the chances of a local drug dealer following her up to Manchester from London were remote to say the least.

When she arrived, Carol explained what had happened. She was a social worker and her team leader (who I'll call Phil) had become addicted to drugs and this was affecting his work. Carol had gone to the drug dealer and had asked him to stop supplying Phil. She was sure the dealer was really a very nice person and would understand the impact the drugs were having on Phil and his clients. The dealer didn't respond well to the suggestion – so Carol had reported him to the police. The dealer was now after her.

As she sat there, chain smoking and refusing coffee because it wasn't good for her, Carol was absolute gushing in her praise of me letting her stay. I was a cross between Princess Dianna and Mother Theresa!

Carol was constantly talking – going on and on and speaking very quickly. It was the early hours before I could make her stop talking – and only then because I had a phone call from another friend who had problems (this was at 3am).

The next morning Carol started talking twenty to the dozen as soon as I saw her, carrying on from the night before – hardly taking a breath. By now I was convinced that she was not well. I told her that I needed to do some work and she would have to leave the flat for a few hours.

While she was out, I called social services who said I needed to get a GP to certify her before they could take action. My GP was still in Great Staughton. If I could wait until 6pm I could use the out of hour's service locally they said.

When Carol returned, she told me that she had been over to Salford Precinct where she'd been preaching about God. She said she had to tell me something. Before she did so, though, she would pack her bag in case I asked her to leave.

She then me that she had had a message from God that she needed to expose the hypocrisy in Social Services over drug use. She was going to give up her job and focus full time on this mission. When I asked how she would support herself, she told me that God would provide.

There was one problem – to undertake this mission she had to give up being transsexual. "Did I think she was Transsexual?"

"Yes."

Wrong answer! I now became the devil incarnate as she ranted and raved at me.

I felt quite threatened by the anger she was expressing so I told her to leave.

She pointed out that it was raining and did I have an umbrella she could borrow. I almost threw one at her and yelled "There you are – GET OUT NOW."

Part 8. Manchester

I heard later that she had been sectioned within a day or so and I know she spent many years in and out of mental health hospitals.

Some months later a group of us were going to Northern Concord and, as we parked across the road from the venue, I saw what was clearly a trans person go into the main entrance of the Showbar on Bloom Street. At that time, NC met in the basement so I guessed that the individual was looking for the group meeting. I left Jacqui to finish parking the car while I ran across the road and into the main bar. As I approached the back of the individual, I asked if she was looking for Northern Concord. She turned round and her face lit up "HELEN, it's me. Carol!", I'd recognised her as she turned round. She was absolutely the last person I'd wanted to bump into. I walked back out of the bar and towards the entrance to the basement. Jacqui and the others could see my face which must have been like thunder. "What's up?" "It's the tranny from hell!" I whispered. They knew this was the person who had turned on me at the flat.

We opened the basement door and let Carol precede us down the stairs. "Are we going down?" asked Jacqui. "No!" I said brooking no debate. We turned on our heels and headed for Paddy's Goose instead. Perhaps it hadn't been nice of us to treat Carol like this – but I really couldn't face her again at that point.

The issues with the friend who threatened suicide and Carol convinced me that if I was going to continue supporting other individuals then I needed professional training. It simply wasn't good enough to operate by the seat of my pants which is what I had been doing.

As well as going on to Donna's Den, I set up my own website as part of the Geocities community – my address was WESTHOLLYWOOD\5604

One of the sections was on Helen's Havens – giving details of places that trannies were welcomed. It included clubs from around the country – including a lot about the Gay Village in Manchester.

I also started a diary – what we'd now call a blog I suppose. At this time, I used the name Helen Williamson – deliberately distancing myself from my real name.

There was a bit of friendly rivalry between my website and 'Pam's Palace' set up by Pam Sexton, a friend. She would boast that she got more visitors than I did – but I pointed out that if anyone searched on 'sex' her name would come up.

The two sites were amongst the first in the UK to provide serious sources of information for and by trans people.

As I was going into Napoleons one night, I was stopped and asked if I was Helen Williamson – as the other girl had seen my website. FAME!

Another of the sections on my website was an article about the difference between transvestites and transsexuals and the usual perception of hierarchy within the trans community. I said that I was concerned that if my theories were correct – then I could easily face the prospect at some stage in the future of deciding that I was TS rather than TV. I said that I hoped this wouldn't happen as I thought TVs, far from 'playing at being female' had the best of both worlds able to express their feminine side without the dreadful consequences of having to go through transition. I suggested that instead of TVs being seen as 'failed TSs', it was more appropriate to consider TSs as 'failed TVs' as they couldn't cope with switching back and forth. The comment was made with tongue in cheek – but I still think that there is a grain of truth it it.

I lost count of how many trans people visited my flat – it had to be up in three figures. Quite often after a night in the village we'd all go back there and chat over wine and cheese or ham on baguettes. Sometimes we'd go on to Donna's Den – where there would be plenty of Americans on line. One evening we logged on as Helen Jacqui Lisa Jane Lyn Debra Sue (or something similar). One of the Americans asked "What's with all the names?"

"That's the names of the girls here," we replied.

"Seven of you all together in one place?"

"Yes."

"I don't even think there are seven girls within 500 miles of me."

It really was a different world in Manchester!

Chapter 33. 24/7

When my contract at CEGELEC finished, I had been told that I would be wanted again in 2-3 months. At one time it had been my dream to live a complete 24 hours as female; once I'd achieved that, I wanted to try at least a week. This was my opportunity. I was now living 24/7 in role. I had often wondered if living like that for long periods would become boring. This was my opportunity to find out. Other than signing on or other 'official' appointments, I lived entirely as female.

This did result in a bit of embarrassment one day. I had been trying to get a transfer out of my flat on Graythorpe Walk to Albion Towers. This offered better security for my car – and those of any visitors as well as less risk of hassle from the neighbours. I was dealing with some mould in the bathroom caused by damp – my hair held back by a headband, open toed slippers exposing painted toe nails and tastefully dressed in leggings and a T-shirt. Not a good look for a 50-year-old, overweight person. I could see, through the opening section of the window, an official looking individual coming to the front door of the flats and ringing a bell. My bell.

When I opened the door (having removed the headband), he introduced himself as from the housing department – here to discuss my application for a move. I invited him in. I explained that as well as the reasons I had given in my written application, one of the other reasons I wanted to move was because I was transgendered and wanted to avoid problems with the neighbours.

I subsequently had an interview with the manager at Albion Towers and was eventually offered a flat on the twelfth floor. Two floors above Jacqui's and immediately below Garry, one of the bar staff at Napoleons. The car park at Albion Towers was secure so I would finally be able to get a decent car again – when I could afford one.

After the visit from the guy from housing, I posted a report of the incident on line and received the following reply from one of my friends:

Part 8. Manchester

Really, Helen, you could save yourself a lot of grief, not to say the confusion engendered (pun intended) in your pals, if you went whole hog and joined me in having a little [snip]

After all, how can you ever turn up at the Northern Concord again after coughing (police term for admitting) that you were seen wearing that outfit? Now anyone that knows anything knows that no self-respecting TV or TG would ever be seen dead in an outfit like that. Only TS that have had their dress sense removed at the same time as the [snip] would even consider it.

Oh hell, good on yer girl! I wished I had seen that council bloke's face — I'll bet his day was not quite as planned as well. :)

I had been increasingly suspecting that I might be transsexual rather than transvestite. As I wrote in a blog at the time:

There is a verse in 'Some Days are Diamonds (Some Days are Stone)' on a John Denver CD which reflects my current position (it's playing as I write this posting):

> ...now the face that I see in my mirror
> more and more is a stranger to me,
> more and more I can see
> there's a danger in becoming
> what I never thought I'd be.

I DO look in the mirror when male mode and see someone who I 'used to know'. And I certainly see myself becoming something I never thought I would be.

I continued to attend Northern Concord and go out in the Village. I had a number of trans people stop with me overnight and they usually paid for my drinks in exchange for the bed and being shown around the scene.

As I met more and more trans people, I developed theories about causality based on what I could observe. A very high percentage of those who now identified as transsexual had previously identified as transvestite. Were the two conditions really totally different – or was there a link? I became convinced that there was something innate in the brain that provided a feminine drive in us. This wasn't something we learned or were conditioned into. It was there effectively from birth. I didn't understand how this might occur – but all the evidence I'd seen indicated that it existed.

Against this, there were clearly 'braking forces'. These seemed to come from a number of sources and were typically conditioned into us. They included the expectation that men should be men; religious views; obligations; the fear of the reaction of family and friends; the impact on careers; ignorance about possibilities. It also seemed to be linked to hormone levels. My observations suggested that many of these 'braking forces' generally diminished as one got older. It seemed that a significant number of individuals who had previously identified as transvestite but now identified as transsexual came to that conclusion when one of these factors was completely removed – the loss of a parent or a divorce for example. It seemed that the removal of that braking force released the innate drive.

Part 8. Manchester

It was as though the driving force was the lift in a hot air balloon – that was kept on the ground by ballast that was the braking factors. As the ballast was released – either gradually or suddenly, the balloon would start to rise.

It seemed obvious that the driving force and the braking forces both varied – you could have a powerful drive held back by powerful braking forces or a much smaller drive, restrained by a much lower braking force. It seemed likely that the critical factor was the net drive, the difference between the lift and the ballast.

How far this drive would carry someone also varied. If the net drive was powerful then it was clear that only full transition was sufficient to satisfy it. At a lower level, it seemed to me that transvestism might act as a safety valve that released the pressure for a while. Certainly, the manifestations of the drive were very different – but I saw little reason to suggest that there are different drives. It seems to me that it's like the gradual blockage of arteries in the heart. At a low level it's manifested as Angina – often resolved by a spray or tablets. If the blockage is more serious, the patient suffers a heart attack and more drastic steps might be needed.

I hoped my ideas were wrong because if they were right, there was a very real risk that I would eventually identify as transsexual – with all the drastic consequences that this would entail.

Well, I'd worry about that if and when it happened! In the meantime, I was having fun in the village – just being myself. Napoleon's was really the place to be in Manchester for trans people of all types on a Saturday night. There would be TVs dressed in anything from leather and chains, the shortest of short skirts or more girl next door outfits. Drag queens in outrageous outfits and huge wigs; showgirls perhaps down for a night out in Manchester from Blackpool where they might often work at venues such as Funny Girls. These girls often had breast enhancements for their work – and were sometimes referred to as 'supertrannies'. There was a definite hierarchy of trans folks – with the post op transsexuals seen as the top of the tree!

I used to joke that you could easily tell the difference between a transvestite, a transsexual and a 'real' girl. The transvestite would be wearing the shortest of skirts; the transsexual would be showing off her newly developing boobs and the 'real' women would be in trousers. I know this is stereotyping, that it's inappropriate to use 'transsexual' as a noun (it's an adjective) and refer to 'real' women as though transwomen are imitations or imposters!

Some of the regulars upstairs in Napoleons would be there just to dance and watch themselves in the mirrors; some to chat; some because it was where they could be who they really felt themselves to be; some would be high on poppers – and some were there to pick up a punter – either one that paid or just as likely just treated them as a female. Nap's reputation for trans people meant it attracted a lot of Tranny Chasers[16]. I was in there, taking a break from dancing on one of the sofas with a couple of friends when a guy approached

---

[16] There is another, cruder, term!

me. "What does a guy have to do around here to get a fuck?" he asked smiling. "Go out the door turn right, walk up the street and ask one of the girls standing on the corner" I replied. "I'm serious!" he insisted. "So am I," I said. He then turned to the girl sitting next to me "What about you?" she shook her head so he turned to the third girl "what about you?" Not the brightest of chat up approaches!

Napoleons looked after the trans people. We got in free or charge while Ernie stopped everyone else and demanded an admittance fee. If another customer started to cause trouble they would soon be forcibly ejected. I once saw a guy bundled down the stairs so quickly that his feet didn't touch one of the treads!

We were also protected in Paddy's Goose. I was in there one evening with a small group when a gay guy started to chat up one of our younger friends and stroking her hair. She asked him to stop but he ignored her. I asked him to stop – "Or what?" he demanded; "or I'll have you thrown out." "Really?" "Really!". He looked at me and stroked her shoulder – daring me to do something. I stood up and walked over to the bar, had a word with one of the staff who came to our table. By then the individual had gone back to his boyfriend who was now giving him an earful! That developed into a scuffle and both of them were 'asked to leave'.

One of my favourite bars: Dotz with owner Foo Loo Lamar (right) and Chris (left)

One of my other favourites was Dotz – a piano bar on Sackville Street. It was owned by Frank Pearson aka the famous female impersonator Foo Foo Lamar and managed by his boyfriend Chris. I had my photograph taken in there one evening with me en femme and Foo Foo in male mode – which was a reversal of roles at the time. I'd be in there most Saturday nights – often with whoever was stopping at the flat – I was jokingly know as their membership secretary because I introduced so many people to the club. One evening two of us went in, we were asked what we wanted to drink; I asked for a white wine the other girl wanted red. A bottle of each was put on the counter with the compliments of the house!

Just across Princes Street from the village was Follies Galore which featured a drag comedienne. This became one of our regular haunts for a while. It was also popular with groups of women on a night out. A crowd of us arrived one evening to find there was a coach load of out-of-towners. They gave us some stares as we walked into the club – apparently horrified at the thought of sharing a venue with a bunch of weirdoes like us! Then Lucy, the star of the show, spotted us "Hi Helen, Hi Jacqui" she called from the stage. The frost suddenly evaporated and we were now welcome to chat with the earlier guests!

Part 8. Manchester

Julia Grant, of 'Change of Sex' (and 'Four in a Bed') fame also set up her Hollywood Showbar on Bloom Street. As well as the ground floor Showbar, there were other bars on the first floor as well as some shops including one selling stuff for TVs. At one point she came round to my flat to try to encourage me to take over the T Shop but it didn't feel right so I declined. When Dotz closed down, the piano bar was moved into the first floor of Julia's establishment.

By now, Jenny and I had mutually agreed that we wouldn't be getting back together but I wasn't actively looking for any sort of replacement relationship.

I'd known Gilda for about three years — since soon after going out regularly in the Village in fact. We had often been part of the same crowd — and we gradually became friends. We would joke together. Occasionally dance with each other. She came back to my flat one evening with a crowd. Unfortunately, she has a medical condition which is affected by drinking and smoking and results in attacks which are extremely painful for her for an hour or so. I'd previously seen the result of one such attack while she was in the Village. This particular evening, she had such an attack while at my flat and I put her in my bed while her medication took effect. Samantha remained with her and held her hand until the attack subsided. By the time Gilda had recovered, nearly everyone else had left.

Some of the girls were stopping over — which meant that the lounge was full and the only place left for me to sleep was in the same bed as Gilda. As I joined her, she turned to me and asked what we were doing in bed together. I told her that as long as she didn't try to take advantage of me — she was welcome to stay. She hit me! As it happens, I had no intention of letting anything happen between us and, in any case, she had to get back to her own house to be there for her two girls the next morning (they were sleeping over at friends). I called a taxi for her and she left.

We met up several times after this before anything actually happened between us. One evening, after a night out in the village, I offered her a lift home. I'd had no ulterior motive in making the offer. But when she invited me in, I was more than happy to accept. That was the start of an affair that lasted a couple of years.

Her two girls and most of her family accept me as Helen. The girls even sent me a 'like a mother' Mother's Day card.

It may seem difficult to understand but, although I was still physically male – indeed, I hadn't decided at that point whether or not I would transition – it was very much a lesbian relationship not a heterosexual one. In the end, Gilda ended the relationship because, she said, I wasn't female enough for her. That really hurt at the time and seriously challenged my developing conviction that I needed to transition.

Part 9. Coming Out

Chapter 34. Mission Improbable

In March 98, I was faced with a dilemma regarding my two oldest friends – as I wrote in my diary at the time:

On Sunday 29th March 1998, two of my oldest male mates — Hugh & Mike — phoned me to say they were planning to pay me a surprise visit the following Saturday. I warned them that they would have a shock if they did arrive without warning. "They didn't know what I get up to up here" I warned them. "That was the idea, to catch you at it" said Mike (the other mate). We had a lot of banter about this for half an hour. They were sure I was winding them up. I encouraged them to think that this was the case.

I have always been concerned that one (Hugh) would turn up unexpectedly. He has done so plenty of times in the past when I was living in Cambridgeshire — phoning from his mobile and saying "put the coffee on I'll be there in 5 minutes". If he were to do so now, he would be confronted with Helen.

Rather than risk a confrontation, I'd prefer to introduce the subject in a controlled manner.

We are supposed to be meeting at Stoke on Trent next Sat (11th April). Hugh wants to visit a big motorcycle dealer there. They then plan to stay at the flat Sat night.

I have prepared a series of four 'briefing papers' for them.

This is in 4 stages. If their response to any stage is negative; then I walk away and say that they can never visit the flat — but that I will meet them at another venue should they come to Manchester.

Up to the final revelation; they will almost certainly think I am still winding them up. They'll be able to walk away and not be sure that I do have a secret.

I shall attempt to retain this impression.

As you'll see, the last stage before the revelation is a form with a list of possible activities — some sexually based, some anorakish, some the truth. They'll believe that I could be involved in the anorakish ones (eg American line dancing, 60's music, model making/ radio controlled yachts etc) as I've done similar things in the past. I don't think they'll believe that it's bondage/S&M etc. I expect them to say they can't handle some of the anorakish activities — but that they'll go along with the gag on most of the others.

IF they say they can't handle the 'cross dressing' & 'Gay Village' activities. Then I'll just say "sorry guys, you've said you can't handle what I do — so I guess there's no option but for us to go our separate ways and for you to avoid my flat permanently"

If they don't tick those boxes, I give them the final revelation sheets. I expect them to still think I'm kidding until they see the photograph that's printed on the second of the pages.

So, next Saturday could be interesting.

It could back fire on me. They may not tick the cd & village boxes thinking it's still a gag. They may still not be able to accept this. Oh well — then I'll blame them.

Part 9. Coming Out

I could be about to lose two of my oldest male mates. But I don't see that I have any choice. Better to do it this way (I think) than to simply say "don't come and see me" or risking them just turning up on the doorstep one day and coming face to face with Helen.

One thing I am reasonably certain of is that they'll keep my secret. I hope so. Mind you I may be about to find out that they already know — and, perhaps, that my wife does as well.

There was one incident many years ago when I walked into our dining room to find Hugh saying something about transvestism to my wife. I didn't hear very much but what I did hear was accurate. I'm pretty certain Hugh will be OK with it. Not quite so sure about Mike. As Hugh has a full beard/ moustache, it's not likely that he is tv himself.

The 'Briefing Papers'

The actual paper to be given to them follow: some of you may be old enough to have seen the television series 'Mission Impossible'. If I had a small portable tape player, I'd probably have presented it THAT way:

Preliminary briefing notes

Preamble

Your jointly declared intention of penetrating the security zone hitherto known as Mike's Manchester Mess (MMM) has made it necessary to expose some, if not all, of the activities based therein.

It has been deemed far safer to your mental well-being to expose these activities in a controlled manner rather than risk a surprise visit and immediate unprepared confrontation.

The revelations required by this may or may not be significant. Nevertheless, any information revealed must be held in the strictest possible confidence regardless of whether or not you accept the challenge of visiting MMM and proceeding with this evening's mission whatever that might or might not entail.

The security classification is 'Eyes Only'. No information may be revealed about the activities in and around MMM and any other locations visited as part of the mission to any other person whatsoever. This specifically includes all who may have contact with any members of the family or in-laws of any participants in the activities.

You are free to withdraw from the mission at any time.

No photographs may be taken during the mission.

No sound or video recordings may be made during the mission.

No attempt may be made to identify others who may be encountered during the mission.

Stage 2 Briefing Notes

Mission Limitations

The Mission is to accompany me to MMM and other locations. You may participate in the activities or act as observers as you choose.

The conditions in MMM would inevitably have revealed the nature of the activities which take place there and in other locations to be visited as part of the mission.

Part 9. Coming Out

It would have taken substantial time and effort to have sanitised MMM for a visit to eliminate the risk of exposure of the activities based therein.

Even if MMM had been sanitised, it is likely that contacts made by others involved in the activities which occur at MMM would have resulted in my own 'cover' being blown.

For this reason, I have decided that I have no option but to give you the choice of learning of those activities and keeping them totally secret — or seeking an assurance from you never to attempt to penetrate the MMM security zone at any time.

The activities are NOT illegal. Some may, however, consider them subversive.

They will almost certainly make you reconsider your opinion of me.

The planned activities will not expose you to any physical risks other than those normally involved in a major city such as Manchester. I can offer no such assurances concerning your mental well-being.

It should be made clear that I have valued your friendships for some 35 years.

I do not wish to lose that friendship. I will, nevertheless, understand if you feel unable to contact me again in future should you proceed to stage 3 and learn of my activities.

Do you wish to continue?

Should your decision be positive, you may still withdraw from the mission at any time. But this is the last opportunity to do so without being exposed to the truth.

If your answer is NO, you should leave immediately.

You can then retain your current opinion of me and believe that I have been 'winding you up' — which could be the truth of course.

Briefing Notes

The Secret?

So, what is the secret?

What 'subversive' activities take place within the security zone at MMM?

Listed below are some possibilities. Consider them. One or more are true. Are there any you could not handle?

Subject	I can believe this	Sorry, but if this is true I couldn't handle it
Girlfriend(s)		
Orgies		
Bondage Parties		

Part 9. Coming Out

S&M		
Cross-dressing		
Nightclubbing		
Gay Village		
Folk Club		
60's music club		
American line dancing		
Wine making/ tasting group		
Model making club		
Scale model racing		
Radio controlled yachts		
Radio controlled aircraft		
Amateur Radio		

Warning.

If any of the subjects ticked as 'can't handle' are correct, then I shall have to ask you never to penetrate the security zone around MMM.

Should you NOT tick any box as 'can't handle', you will be expected to participate in the evening's activities — even if only as an observer. Think VERY carefully about your answers

If neither of them tick 'cross dressing/ gay village as 'can't handle' — then they get the following.

(What happens if one does and the other doesn't? Good question. I don't know) I guess I tell them that one has ticked a box that indicates that he can't handle my activities so in fairness they should go.

Stage 4

The Revelation

No, it's not a joke guys. I do have a secret that I've kept for 40 odd years.

Or, at least, I believe it's a secret — maybe you already know somehow.

I am a transvestite.

I visit tranny friendly venues in Manchester's gay village at least a couple of times a week. In fact, I am probably one of the best-known TVs on the Manchester scene and on the Internet. I am involved in support groups and am President of a major Internet based tranny club — Vanity Club UK.

I have been involved in helping dozens of trannies to accept that their condition is not a perversion — but an inherent medical condition which is caused pre-natally.

My flat is well known as a haven for trannies. It's far from unusual for a dozen or so to visit it at different times each week. This will include transvestites and transsexuals. When I said there were half a dozen girls around most weekends, I wasn't kidding — though perhaps not the sort of girls you'd fancy.

I am not gay — but have quite a few gay friends through mixing with them.

I didn't ask to be a TV. But as I am — I now enjoy it after years of guilt and shame.

Since my contract ended at Christmas, I've spent nearly all of my time living in female role other than when it's necessary to dress in male mode — signing on etc.

The computer course last weekend was for trannies. They give TVs an excuse to come to Manchester — which has the best TV scene in the UK (probably the world). You wondered why I wasn't devastated to be offered a job in Manchester Hugh — and why I stayed on here when the contract ended? Now you know.

No-one has a definitive answer about the cause of transvestism — but if you are a transvestite, it is an integral part of your nature and cannot be ignored. Try to fight it and it creates stress. I've stopped dressing several times in the past — for up to 6 years at a stretch. But it re-emerges eventually. I've now stopped trying to stop — and have come to terms with what I am.

It was during one of my denial periods that I met and married Jenny. I've fought it in the past; I've been totally ashamed of it and felt guilty as hell over it. I don't any longer — but I still have no wish to risk upsetting Jenny, Joanna or my mother if they were to find out as I am not sure that they could understand it.

I ask, therefore that you respect my request not to tell anyone. I would not have risked telling either of you if I thought I could not trust you.

I appreciate that this revelation may be difficult to come to terms with. If you prefer not to come to the flat, I'll understand — though I hope you will and give me a chance to answer any questions you may have.

This evening

Part 9. Coming Out

I would normally go out to the pubs and clubs in the Village on a Saturday evening. I'd like you to join me.

You may not feel comfortable with this idea. But I can assure you that whilst you will see some very strange sights, you will not be at any risk and you will have a very interesting evening. It will certainly be educational and I think you'll be at your ease fairly quickly.

Most of my TV friends are well presented — forget any idea of a load of Kenny Everett or Dame Edna Everage look alikes. (Though there are one or two around). TVs come from virtually every background. The conversation is not a lot different to other groups of friends getting together — perhaps with rather less emphasis on football.

You may find it strange hearing TVs calling each other by their femme names — and seeing me dressed as 'Helen'.

Well, it's up to you. Now you know my darkest secret. I hope it won't affect our friendship.

Ask what you like and I'll try to answer the questions as far as I can.

Well, that's it. That's how I propose to handle my coming out to a couple of old friends.

Without the picture — they'd probably still believe that I am winding them up. That SHOULD show them that I am not joking.

I may yet chicken out. But I intend leaving the flat as it is — and THAT would expose matters so unless I say sorry guys you still can't come to the flat, I'm going to force myself to go through with the revelation. Chances are that even if I was to clear it up and hide all my femme gear, I'd overlook something. I'd almost certainly get half a dozen phone calls during the time they were there. They'd probably want to use my PC to get onto the internet and I'd have to hide all my bookmarks.

In any case, as I've already said, Hugh IS likely to turn up unexpectedly sometime. At least this way I stand a better chance of him accepting things than if he was to just be confronted by Helen.

There is, of course, another scenario:

They may already be aware of what I am and do.

It's even possible that they are aware that I am Helen — and are regular visitors to my pages. Are you? If so, maybe I'll be confronted with the forms already filled in when we meet up!

Wish me luck.

Well, I did it.

We met in Stoke on Trent; visited a very large motorcycle dealership — which was the other reason Hugh wanted to come up this way, then went for a drink and some lunch in a pub.

Part 9. Coming Out

I passed them the various stages of the revelation documents — as expected, they thought I was still winding them up. The only 'can't handle' as far as possible activities were concerned was 'American Line Dancing' from Mike.

As I passed them the last envelope, I took a heck of a deep breath and said "I'm really not sure whether I should let you have this"; Hugh said "well, it's your decision". "Read it" I said — then watched his face. His eyes widened as he read the statement that I was a tv.

When they'd both read them, I asked "well?".

"Makes no difference," was the answer I got from both of them. "Why should it?" They asked

Pushing my luck, I asked how they felt about the planned evening in the village with Helen. "No problem."

We then went back to my flat, played a game of cards — then I announced that it was time for me to have a bath and get changed for the evening.

Even when I returned to the lounge dressed, there was just total acceptance of Helen. By the end of the evening, they were both calling me Helen (with occasional lapses through force of habit).

I could not have dared hope for a better response — or evening with them.

We went to Metz for a meal; then into Paddy's Goose, Dotz, Cafe Hollywood, Napoleons — then back to the flat with some of the other girls: Julie, Jane, Jacqui, Jackie, Susan, Kath; Sal & Martin also came back with us.

Mike was a bit reserved at times — but still had no problem chatting to some of the others. Hugh simply took it in his stride and thoroughly enjoyed himself.

There was an initial shock when they read the 'revelation' — and at that point I think both were convinced that it was still a 'wind-up'. As they continued to read the final pages, they realised that I was totally serious — but it has made no difference.

Neither of them had had any idea that I am TV. Hugh can't recall the conversation he had with my wife — so it obviously didn't relate to me — which eliminates the one possible question mark I'd had about my wife knowing about my transvestism. Now I am 100% certain that she doesn't.

Well, what else can I say. It went brilliantly.

I should be feeling over the moon — and I guess I do feel very very relieved. I'm also drained after the tension of the last week and knackered after a late night.

Chapter 35. Rocky Horror/ Coming Out to Family

In 1998, a group of us went to the Rocky Horror Picture Show. I was, inevitably, dressed in basque, stockings and high heels and made up to the nines.

During a phone call later with Jenny, I mentioned that I'd been to RHPS – which surprised her as I was, as far as she was aware, a total stick in the mud with totally straight values. "I didn't think you'd go for something like that" she exclaimed.

Part 9. Coming Out

"Well, it's sixties music and you know that's what I like." (It isn't 60s music really but Jenny didn't challenge me). That was the end of the exchange!

When I spoke to Joanna, I got the same initial surprised response but she followed up with more questions:

"So did you dress up?"

"What do you think?"

"No – I don't suppose you did," – sounding disappointed.

"Well, you are wrong!"

"What, stockings and suspenders and all that?"

"Yes."

"Did anyone take any photographs?"

"Yes."

"I've got to see them!"

The next time we met, it was for her graduation from University of East Anglia – and there was absolutely no way I was going to rain on THAT parade! So, it was only when we were all at her mum's place in Potton, Bedfordshire that the next step took place.

I arrived 'home' early afternoon after a fairly tiring drive.

After initial greetings and being provided with a cup of coffee, the subject of the Rocky Horror photographs was raised.

"Have you got them with you?" asked my daughter.

"Yes." I replied.

"Let's see them then" she demanded.

I suggested that they should go into the lounge and sit down to look at them.

Time had run out. With my heart in my mouth, I passed them both the pictures of me in my outfit – my hair and make-up done.

They laughed. And laughed and laughed.

"You think it's funny me being dressed as a woman?" I asked quietly.

"Of course," was the response.

I took a deep breath. "I do it all the time," I said, "I'm a transvestite, here's some other photos of me".

"What?" asked my wife. I repeated what I had just said.

Jo said "cool."

There was a longish question and answer session covering the usual topics:

How long had I been TV? — all my life — though it had been during a purge stage that we had met and married.

How had I hidden everything? — in the garage.

Part 9. Coming Out

Am I going to have the op? — maybe — I don't know at the moment what will happen.

Am I gay? — I don't fancy men, but have no idea how I will feel in the future due to the effects of hormones if I decide to go further. At the moment I'd probably turn out to be a lesbian.

Why hadn't I said anything earlier? Because I didn't understand it myself and could not expect her to accept something I felt disgusted about. By the time I realised it was nothing to be ashamed of, I was living away and I felt it was best to wait until our daughter had finished her degree. (Which my daughter thanked me for).

Is being TV why you don't want to move back here? Yes. I would not expect you to put up with me dressing around the house and wanting to go in and out as a woman. (She agreed this would not have been acceptable).

I also pointed out that we had effectively agreed to separate the last time I had been 'home'. She said that she had planned to raise the subject that weekend as well.

We agreed that there was no 'blame' to be attached to the marriage ending. We both felt our interests had drifted apart and that there was no point in pretending otherwise. We discussed splitting the property. I said I didn't want anything from her home other than personal items; I would keep what I had in Manchester and we agreed that there would be no ongoing financial commitments between us.

All in all, a very amicable settlement of the situation.

They both wished me luck in the future as 'Helen' whatever that involves.

I was actually amazed at the reaction I received — or lack of it. Both were extremely understanding of the situation — and seemed reasonably well informed. I am quite certain the fact that my wife and I were splitting up in any case helped her to accept my position and I have no doubt that if we had been trying to hold the marriage together then the outcome might have been different. I suspect that she would have accepted my need to dress — providing it was not around the house or local area.

My daughter later asked if I planned to have other relationships and said that she thought I should.

My wife agreed that there was no reason to tell her parents or family that I was tv — and that she didn't see any reason for me to tell my mother or sister at present and she wouldn't mention it either. Obviously, we have told the family about the separation. Nobody has been surprised about that.

Quite a weekend!

In fact, it didn't end there. As I wrote in my diary at the time, I realised I was facing a crisis:

As you will have seen from earlier diary entries, I have outed myself to my wife and daughter, friends and colleagues. The one person I have been trying to protect has been my mother — and, because of this, I had tried to keep the news of my transgenderism from my sister. It wasn't that I didn't trust my sister not to tell our mother — but there is always the possibility of accidentally letting something slip which then results in awkward questions. I

Part 9. Coming Out

was also conscious that if my sister knew, then she would share the responsibility of keeping the news from mother.

My wife and I are separating/ divorcing quite amicably. I had told her about my new lifestyle so that she understood why I was prepared to accept the end of our marriage — and to avoid the need for our daughter to have to keep quiet about my tgism. (I felt I had to tell her as she is quite likely to visit me in Manchester at some stage and would be faced with my new home being rather un-masculine).

By telling both of them, I felt that each could talk to the other and share any 'problems' they might have with my tgism. As it happens, neither appeared to have any difficulty accepting that I was tg.

At least, that's what I thought at the time.

My wife had agreed not to tell her parents nor my sister about me. (Her mother talks to my mother and I had no confidence that she would be able to keep quiet about my situation if she knew about it).

A couple of weeks ago, I received a letter from my wife stating that she could no longer agree to keep the news from her parents. It appears that they have been trying to persuade her not to go through with the divorce. Obviously, the fact that I am TG is a factor as she would not be happy if we were living together and I was going in and out of the house dressed.

Later that same day, I received a cryptic message on my answering service from my sister asking me to call her. When I did so, she asked if there was something I needed to tell her. I played ignorant — and asked what she was on about; she said she had written me a letter and I would have to wait until I received it.

Suspecting that my wife might have told my sister, I tried phoning her. Later that day, I eventually got in touch with my wife and asked if she had said anything about me to my sister. Her silence told me that she had and, when I prompted her further, she admitted that she had told my sister that I was TS.

The letter from my sister arrived a few days later. It was much more supportive than I felt it would be from the tone of our telephone conversation — and I then called her and explained what I could. I told her why I had not previously confided in her and said I would prefer to talk about things face to face and invited her to come up to Manchester. She asked if the invitation included her partner and I said it did; and that I would also probably have a new partner with me. I explained to her that I now have a girlfriend in Manchester. As I did not want my wife to feel that as soon as we had separated, I had found a replacement for her, I asked my sister not to tell her about Gilda. She said she would not deliberately reveal the news — but nor would she lie if asked directly. She said the same situation applied to telling our mother about me. She did, at least agree to let me know if she did tell either of them.

The following weekend, my sister's partner phoned me to say that my sister was too upset to talk to me directly but that she had told my wife about my girlfriend. (sh*t and fans colliding came to mind). I called my sister later that day and had another chat. I also spoke to my wife. As it happens, I think the overall outcome was probably OK. As my wife can talk to my sister about my tgism she no longer feels the need to talk to her parents — and my sister has agreed not to say anything to our mother. My wife appears not to be too upset over the fact that I now have a girlfriend up here — although both she and my sister are a little confused about the concept of me being potentially TS with a girlfriend ("Does that mean you are probably a lesbian TS then?" my sister asked.)

My problem now is that I don't honestly know if I can rely on them keeping the secret permanently. I'm not suggesting that either will deliberately say anything — but there have already been remarks which I know have set my mother wondering. If the news is going to come out — then it absolutely has to be from me and not any other source.

I am encouraged by a recent telephone conversation with my mother. During it she hinted that she knows that there is something about my lifestyle in Manchester; she has seen my longer, dyed hair and may have noticed other things about me. (My sister certainly had).

However, my mother has said that she has noticed that I am far happier in myself these days and whilst she may put this down substantially to Gilda, she has also said that we all have to live our own lives and I get the impression that she will support me regardless.

I still don't want to cause her any distress.

Even if she can accept the fact that I am potentially TS, I can't help wondering if she might feel in some way responsible for this.

Certainly, she might well feel guilty for the fact that I have been unable to accept my condition for so many years. I suspect it's a no-win situation.

I suspect that if I tell her, she will be upset either because of what I am — or because of the guilt and shame I carried for so long.

If I don't tell her and she hears it from someone else — then she will be even more upset.

Gilda and I went over to Alford to see her. On reflection, it was a mistake to take Gilda with me – especially as a partner. It created a 'double whammy' of potential change of sex and a lesbian relationship. Both challenged mum's religious beliefs.

After we left, mum took her phone off the hook for two days – not wanting to talk to anyone. She wrote me a letter effectively saying that she was concerned that I was making a huge mistake – that she'd never seen any feminine characteristics in me as a child or as an adult.

Mum did, however, organise a 'coming out' barbecue for me – so that other members of the family could get to meet Helen. I then sent a round robin letter with Christmas cards that year explaining what was happening. By then it was almost certain that I would be transitioning.

Chapter 36. On the Dole/ Wang End 98 – Mid 99

I spent most of the first six or seven months of 1998 unemployed, waiting for CEGELEC to contact me to start the next contract. My benefits came to about £198 per month and monthly payments for an outstanding loan were about the same. By the middle of the year any surplus I'd had from the CEGELEC contract was spent and I was left with just pence in the bank account.

Part 9. Coming Out

CEGELEC had been absorbed into GEC Alsthom and as there had been redundancies, they could not take on contractors so there not be a new contract in the near future.

When I next visited the Job Centre, one of the few times I still dressed as 'him', I was offered an 'open ended' vacancy in a computer workshop. It seemed to me that, although poorly paid – little more than I was getting on the dole after I lost council tax and housing benefits – it would be good experience in case another opportunity like the Philippines came up where there would be no second line support on call and I'd need to be far more self-reliant.

When I started at the Wang Global workshop in Trafford Park, I was told that I was required to fill in for an engineer who was on secondment for two weeks – a quite different situation to what I had been led to believe by the job centre. The two weeks work would mean I lose my benefits and I'd end up a lot worse off! Fabulous!

The workshop was part of a large store of equipment used in Barclays Bank branches managed by Allports. Our role was to check the equipment returned from branches, clean and service it and pack it up again ready for redeployment. Most of the kit was counter equipment with the occasional PC and HP LaserJet printer. There was no real training and no manuals for the devices. If something didn't work, we'd work out for ourselves what was wrong and fix it. Sometimes it wasn't obvious how to dismantle something – an HP printer for example. Trial and error was usually successful in the long run – albeit with the inevitable wastage (in one case 3 side panels before I learnt how to remove one without damaging it!)

The workshop team included a Team leader Mehdi, his deputy, George, Ian – a young committed Manchester City fan and another guy whose name I can't now recall. From time to tIme the fIeld engIneers would also spend tIme In the workshop.

When I'd learned that my assignment was only for two weeks, I wasn't very happy but I had fitted into the routine. On the Wednesday of the second week, Mehdi asked me if I'd seen a programme the night before on Drag Queens and their partners. Not particularly wanting to get into a discussion on this topic, I said that I hadn't. In fact, I had seen it while round at Gilda's.

"I'd take the lot of them out and shoot them," said Mehdi.

"Why would you do that?" I asked

"They're all raving poofs!"

"Actually, there is a difference between cross dressing and sexuality" (I didn't bother to add though that all the drag queens I've known have also been gay)

"It's the same thing" Mehdi insisted. Try as I might I couldn't get him to understand the difference between sexual orientation and gender identity. In any case, it made no difference to him, anyone falling in that category were beyond the pale.

I stood in front of him.

"How many TVs do you know?" I asked. He reeled back in horror at such a thought.

"I don't know any," he insisted – obviously not wanting to be associated with such creatures.

Part 9. Coming Out

"I'm one," I informed him quietly.

"What do you mean?"

"When I'm not at work, I live and dress as a female. That's why I know something about the subject and you clearly don't."

His chin hit the floor and he looked at me with total disbelief'

"I think I need a cigarette", he said and, with that, turned away and went outside.

I returned to my workbench, convinced I'd blown the job. Well, it wasn't too bad. I only had a couple more days to go in any case. I wondered if anyone else in the workshop had overheard our conversation. Again, it hardly mattered if they had.

About fifteen minutes later, Mehdi came back in and joined me at my bench. Here we go, I thought!

"I don't understand what you were saying and I don't agree with it – but as your supervisor, I have to separate my personal views from my professional ones. You are a good worker. Do you want a coffee?"

In fact, the assignment didn't end that Friday. It continued for quite a few months. Had I known that that would be the case I doubt if I would have revealed myself as I had done. I still didn't know if the others had heard so when Mehdi came over to me and started talking about the subject, I tried to keep my voiced down and wished he would do the same! This happened on several occasions before I turned round during one conversation to find all of the guys from the workshop and some from the warehouse standing in a semi-circle listening. I realised that I was 'out'.

Chapter 37. Decision Time

When getting up each morning to go to work, where I was known as male, I became increasingly aware that I really couldn't carry on like this. I was actually wearing female clothes at work: female t shirt, female jeans, female knickers, female pop-socks, I wore clear nail varnish and ear studs. The only male attire were my trainers – and then only because I couldn't get female trainers in my size.

I had signed up for an 'Introduction to Counselling' course at Salford University. It was only for twelve weeks of the Autumn term.

I only enrolled in time for the second evening — at which the tutor asked us all to say something about an item we were wearing or had with us and what it said about us. I'd gone almost straight from work — so was dressed rather casually in jeans, sweatshirt etc. As the others had their say, I wondered what I could say about myself.

Swallowing a lump in my throat, I said that my name was Mike — at least that was one of the names I use and that I was dressed casually because I liked to feel comfortable — and that the reason I was on the course was to learn more about counselling because of a section of the community that I was a member of that I wanted to help feel comfortable with what they are. I said they would probably have seen an example of this on Coronation Street —

Part 9. Coming Out

Hayley. I said the people I wanted to help were transsexuals and transvestites. I told them that I was also known as Helen.

You could have heard a pin drop. The reaction I've had since then has been quite positive — but I'd have been very disappointed if there had been any negative reaction from people training to be counsellors of course.

One evening we had a session of role playing — one acting as a 'client' the other as 'counsellor'. My partner was in fact the tutor. I decided to have some fun with her! Before this session started the tutor took the other 'counsellors' to one side to brief them on how to behave during the 'session'.

I used a genuine example from someone I have tried to help.

I have to say that the tutor was totally beaten by the challenge I presented her with. She had no idea of how to cope with the problem of a transsexual. She even forgot to try to 'throw me' with the reaction she had briefed the other counsellors with!

In the end she admitted that she would not know where to start if faced with the problem I had given her. I pointed out that I had some experience of the practical aspects of helping TVs and TSs — but was very conscious of my lack of training in counselling and that's why I was on the course. I also said that if she did encounter TVs/ TSs — then I could point them in the right directions and she said she would follow up on that if the situation arose.

Thursday 17th December (98) was, in fact, the final evening of the introductory course. I had been attending the course in male mode as I had been going straight from work. On the penultimate evening, I had asked the tutor if she had any problem with me coming to the final evening as Helen. She had assured me that she would be very happy for me to do so.

I left work early to allow time to change then get over to the college.

What should I wear? In point of fact, the previous few weeks, I'd been wearing female jeans and tops and Cuban heeled boots which were androgynous. I considered wearing the same — but with my boobs in place, hair in a feminine style and make up and jewellery; after some thought I rejected the casual look. I decided that I wanted to look smart — but not overdressed. I chose a burgundy, button through, dress which is just below knee length, a scarf which helps with the rather deep V neck and smart 3-inch-high court shoes.

I had a quick bath — then got made up and dressed and did my hair. How does that look I wondered? A glance in the mirror showed that I had done a reasonable job!

As I approached the door to the building housing our classroom, I saw Ros — one of my fellow students having a smoke before class. He glanced at me as I approached — then looked away again. As I reached him, I said "Hi!". A look of astonishment appeared on his face!

Several of the other students complimented me on my appearance "You look fabulous" said one! During the course of the evening, Anne, the tutor, said that she had felt 'chuffed' (pleased/ gratified) that I had felt able to attend as Helen. At the end, she gave me a hug and wished me the best of luck for the future. She even offered to have my certificate for the course made out for 'Helen Williamson' rather than the name under which I had enrolled.

Part 9. Coming Out

In January 1999, I started the next stage of counselling training at Salford College. On the first evening, we had to say two things about ourselves. One true, one false. One of the guys said that he had done a parachute jump dressed as a woman. I followed him and said that it was funny that he had done a parachute jump dressed as a woman as I'd also done parachuting and also dressed as a woman as I was Trans. The rest of the class had to vote which of the two options they thought was true. The votes were roughly even. Chris, one of the other students had however 'clicked' when I made my statements and had, she told me later, thought "Now I remember where I've seen you before!"

By now, I had made an appointment to see Russell Reid, the leading private psychiatrist in the UK dealing with gender identity issues. The appointment was for March 1999.

I was certain that I would have too many strikes against me to go the NHS route and expect treatment in a reasonable period. I was over 50; overweight, I smoked, I was much larger than most women and might be expected to have problems 'passing'' At that time, the NHS was believed to operate a three-tier system. If you were young, passable – including being 'average' build and didn't smoke, you'd be on the fast track. If you were like me, you were on the slow track – which effectively meant you'd have little chance of treatment.

So it had to be the private route. I didn't have the money for surgery yet – but I did have an insurance policy that was due to mature in a couple of years or so.

Russell's offices were near Earls Court, West London – so Gilda and I stopped with some friends of hers near the Edgware Road leaving us an easy final few miles the next day.

I was reasonably certain that RR would confirm my own diagnosis that I was transsexual but I needed a second opinion in case I was convincing myself as this fitted in with my theories. He did agree with me and prescribe hormones.

That initial visit would be followed by further consultations at three monthly intervals – although these were interrupted by later events! On one occasion, I had arrived near Russell's offices early so decided to have a coffee at one of the local cafes. It was a lovely morning so I sat at one of the pavement tables. I then realised that the individual at the next table, reading the Financial Times, was Adam Faith – a pop star from my teenage years, now a financial pundit.

Russell Reid provided a letter that I could take to my GP. When I received the letter, I met up with a couple of transsexual friends in Churchill's bar in the village. When I arrived, they were deep in conversation about hormones.

"Can anyone join in?" I asked.

"Sorry, it's girl talk," Kym   said – meaning 'we' are transsexual, 'you' are transvestite. (There was no malice in this it was just a bit of banter).

"Read it and weep," I told them – passing over Russell's letter.

She only had to see the headed notepaper to know what it would say.

"About time!" said Kym. "You kept quiet about going to see him, didn't you?"

This was an awkward time. I had been diagnosed as transsexual and was undergoing treatment, but I still had to be seen as male at work and college. The constant switching to

Part 9. Coming Out

and fro is painful. Knowing what potentially lay ahead in terms of rejections and difficulties finding work also took their toll. At one time I had even looked out of the window of my kitchen at the ground 12 storeys below and thought, for a moment, about ending it there and then.

When I'd come out as trans at college, I'd said that I would want to attend the residential weekend as Helen. There had been no objection to this at first – but two weeks before the weekend, I was called into the office and told that the tutors had not thought that this was a good idea. They thought it might disrupt the other students.

I made it quite clear that I did not accept their stance; that I had now been diagnosed as transsexual and was, therefore, protected against discrimination by the Gender Reassignment Regulations which covered employment and vocational training. I advised them that if I could not attend the weekend as Helen, then I would not be able to attend at all and that would prevent me from passing the course, result in potential losses and I would sue the college. Their faces made it clear that this had taken Liz and Lyn, the two tutors, by surprise. They pointed out that I attended the evening classes as male so what was the difference. I told them '46 hours'. I explained that it was difficult enough to present as male during the working day but at least I had most evening and all weekends as the real me. To have to live back as male constantly for a whole weekend would be intolerable. They said they would discuss the issue further with their colleagues and get back to me.

It was then time for the first of the evening's sessions – where we were split into 3 smaller groups for personal support and discussions of issues. I raised what I had just been told by the tutors and was hugely gratified by the level of support from all of the other students. They were as horrified as I had been by the suggestion that I would not be allowed to be Helen for the residential weekend – and very offended by the suggestion that they wouldn't be able to cope with a different 'me'.

As it happens, that evening the course was being evaluated by the accrediting authority. As we all gathered for the second session of the evening the tutors introduced the assessor and then left the room again. The assessor started by outlining the purpose of the visit – then asked what we thought of the course and the tutors.

Several students said how good they thought it was and that the tutors were excellent.

I then said that until a couple of hours ago, I would have shared their opinions – but that a meeting I'd had with them earlier had changed the situation. I explained exactly what had happened. Once again, there was total support from the others and disgust at the suggestion that I not be allowed to attend the residential weekend as Helen.

There was utter uproar! I did say that I appreciated that some fellow students might feel reluctant to express different views with me present – so I said I would leave the room while they discussed whether they thought I should be allowed to attend the residential as Helen. After a few minutes the door opened. "We have a question" said one of the class. "Are you the same as Helen as you are as Mike?" I replied that most people seemed to think I was nicer as Helen than as Mike. "Thank you!" the door closed – leaving me to ponder my fate.

Part 9. Coming Out

If I didn't have my classmates' support, it would not be possible to continue the course. I needn't have worried. The class backed me 100%.

After the assessor had finished, it was time for our coffee break. As I was about to go into the refractory, Lyn and Liz asked if they could have another word with me. They said that they had discussed the situation with their colleagues and had a proposal to put to me. "Was I prepared to re-contract with the class as Helen and only be regarded as Helen in future?". "Of course, that's exactly what I want – the only problem is that due to the time the course started, I would struggle to change clothes before class". That wasn't a problem for the tutors. In that case I could attend the residential as Helen and I would only be referred to by that name in future.

As I entered the classroom with the two tutors, they were immediately attacked and accused of being judgmental, discriminatory and other descriptions that should not be applied to counsellors. "I am feeling very defensive" protested one. "So you should! How dare you decide that we couldn't deal with Helen being herself? Isn't it an essential part of counsellor training that we ARE at peace with ourselves? How can you even think of stopping her doing so?"

The class had had their chance to vent their feelings and it was time to step in.

"Can I just say that the tutors have relented and have agreed that I can attend the residential as Helen?" "So they bloody should!"

From that day onwards, I managed to leave work half an hour early, dash back to my flat and change and attend the class as Helen. The weekend wasn't too bad – apart from one session where we had to discuss our childhood. It's often difficult for a trans person to discuss their childhood – it can bring back memories that we want to hide. I managed to deal with it by saying that if I'd been born with the appropriate body parts, I'd probably have been a bit of a tom-boy – probably joining in many of the boys' games rather than playing with dolls. We'll never know of course.

When we'd first enrolled at college, we should have been issued with identity cards – but the machine had broken. By the time it was repaired and a new session organised, some months had passed. As we went along the corridor for our photographs, one of my friends remarked that it was a good job the photos hadn't been taken at the start of the course as she had changed her hair style. "Mmm – I've changed a bit too", I reminded her. "What do you mean?" "I started the course as Mike!" – "Oh yes" she laughed "I'd forgotten that". Now THAT demonstrates what most trans people want – just total acceptance and transition being just something that happened.

I completed my level two course and went on to do the two-year Diploma. At the end of the diploma, we had to do an assignment on the Issues and Counselling Needs of a part of the community. Not surprisingly, I chose transgendered people.

The assignment was supposed to be about 2,500 words. The body of my assignment **was** limited to 2,500 words – but there were probably ten times that of appendices – including pages and pages of results from some questionnaires that I had posted on the internet. I'd had thousands of responses from transvestites, transsexual individuals, friends and families of trans people and from others with no direct link to trans people. I created a power point presentation based on my assignment which I gave to the class. Sadly, the tutors didn't deem it worthwhile attending this unique presentation. I think this said something about their own lack of awareness of their own developmental needs.

That presentation formed the core of many others that I have provided over the years.

By the middle of 1999, things felt quite stable. I was studying counselling which might be an opportunity for future employment, my transition treatment was going OK and I was in a relationship. At work, I had been told I was the best worker in the workshop and that Mehdi, the supervisor was going to have the guy I was covering for moved permanently to the role he was doing elsewhere and I would be appointed in his place. I had, however, also been told, by one of the field engineers, a friend of Mehdi's manager, that if I did change sex, it would make it difficult for the other engineers. They would have to moderate their language and take down the 'page 3' style posters off the walls.

A week after being told I was the best worker in the workshop, I was told that my contract was being terminated. Obviously, this had nothing to do with the conversation with the field engineer – or my plans to transition!

I was offered a few weeks work visiting Barclay Bank branches to upgrade the memory in counter devices so they could cope with updated software for Year 2000. That meant attending a briefing on the Friday afternoon so I had to go into the workshop on the Saturday morning to get my timesheet signed off. Weekends were Helen's and I sure as hell wasn't going to pander to anyone else's prejudices by dressing as male in my own time! His face when he saw me was a picture – it was as though this was the first time he realised that I really was serious about transition and what it meant.

I was back unemployed, but now I had a real dilemma. Did I apply for jobs as the person I had been (and was still legally) or as the person I had finally accepted was the true 'me'.

If I applied as Helen, the chances were that I wouldn't even get an interview. If I applied as Mike, I'd have to put my transition on hold for goodness knows how long. By now I'd probably known around three hundred individuals who had transitioned. Of them only nine had managed to stay in the same jobs. Some, it was true, had decided to change jobs because they didn't want to stay in the same macho environment, they'd chosen to prove they were men! Most, however, had been forced to leave – either dismissed or just made to feel so uncomfortable or accused of not performing to the required standard.

The Sex Discrimination Act Gender Reassignment Regulations made it clear that discrimination due to gender reassignment was illegal. The problem was always proving it – and if you were new in a job, they just had to say you hadn't passed the probationary period.

I decided to apply to small/ medium private companies as male – but to larger organisations and any public bodies as Helen. I felt it was more likely that larger companies would have policies in place and, perhaps, they'd be less likely to circumvent the law. Almost certainly a naive assumption – but there you are.

Part 10. Probation

Chapter 38. GMPS interview

Amongst the first batch of vacancies for which I'd applied as 'Customer Services Manager' for Greater Manchester Probation Service – a posh name for the help desk manager. I didn't hear anything back after sending off the application so assumed it was a non-starter. Then I got a letter apologising for the delay but they'd been going through a reorganisation and asked if I was still interested. Nothing else I'd applied for had come up – I'd had just one interview with a small computer company. I wrote back to say that, yes, I was still interested and was invited to an interview. My first as Helen.

On arrival at reception on the sixth floor of a large office block, I was taken into a small office and given a paper. "What would you do as Customer Services Manager if you were faced with the following". It then outlined a department in disarray with staff who hadn't been there long, dissatisfied 'customers' systems that were out of date etc etc. Please prepare a short presentation of your ideas.

My initial reaction was that this wasn't hypothetical. This is what I WOULD be facing if I got the job. I didn't honestly expect to get the job – I was here for the practice. The advert had said they needed good network experience – which I lacked.

Then it was time to meet the panel. Susan Wildman – Head of PR, Ray Weingenz, Manager of one of the District Offices and Sulieman Baiyai – Technical IT Manager. The line manager for the actual role wasn't present due to a family emergency.

I gave my presentation and outlined my ideas from a couple of flip charts. I was then subjected to some questions. I waited for the technical ones that I was convinced would trip me up. Apart from "What is the difference between a WAN and a LAN" – which I could answer, there were none. But no-one had mentioned me being trans. The application form had asked for two references so I had provided names but added that if they asked for references it would have to be as J.M. Dale as I was transsexual – so they must know. Or had they just missed it?

At the end of the interview, I was asked if I had any questions of my own. I replied that I hadn't but that I wanted to check that I had given them all the information that they needed and hadn't left any gaps in the answers I'd given. I was assured that they didn't need to clarify any answers. I then said "In that case, I'd just like to add one final point. It seems to me that this job doesn't just need someone with experience of computing – which I have, it also needs someone with experience of marketing and PR to promote the department to the rest of the organisation's staff – and I have that too. I am, therefore, perfect for the job".

It seems the panel agreed with me. I had only been back home for about an hour when I had a phone call offering me the position. I don't think they'd have needed the phone to hear my scream of delight! I later learnt that the panel had nearly offered me the job on the spot – but decided they did need to discuss their views.

The next morning, I had another phone call – this time from Stan Cook who was to be my line manager. He was sorry to have missed the interview, could I call in and see him

Part 10. Probation

sometime. "Certainly, when?" "How about later this morning?". I got dressed and returned to Oakland House.

Stan is a Geordie and would sometimes refer to me as 'man' — but that was just the Geordie expression and no offence was meant at all. On the wall of his office were the flip charts I'd used for my interview presentation. While we were chatting, there was a knock on his door and one of my future colleagues, Linda Cook (no relation to Stan), offered us some cake as it was her birthday. We were briefly introduced. Linda led the IT training team, the other half of Stan's department.

For the next hour or so we continued to discuss the job; yet there was not one word about me being trans. I couldn't believe it. I knew I didn't pass successfully at this stage – and they MUST have seen it on my application form in any case.

Then Stan said "There is something else we need to discuss. How do you want to handle it?" "What do you mean?" "Do you want to keep it confidential; do you want us to tell people or will you tell people?"

I'd seen a Staff Bulletin in reception the previous day so I said I would do something for the bulletin. And that was about it!

I had to undergo a medical before I could join – and the doctor was on leave at the time. We agreed, therefore, that I would come in again on 15th and see the doctor and if all was OK would be deemed to have started that morning.

That afternoon, I had an appointment at the job centre. The devil in me came to the surface and I attended as Helen. I pointed out that being trans was undoubtedly affecting my chances of getting work although I was hopeful of an interview I'd had with Probation.

I then had another phone call from Stan. Penny Jones, the Diversity Manager would like to meet me. Could she come to my flat?

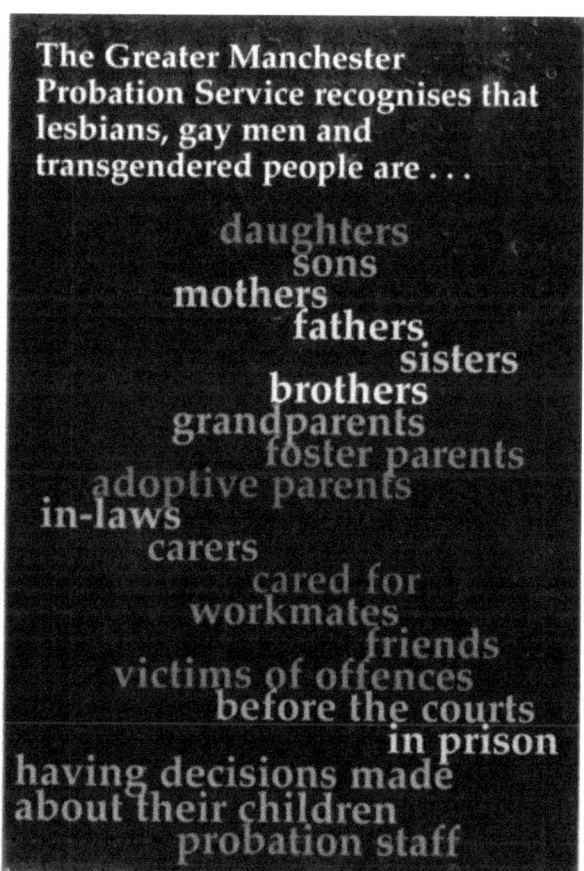

Cover of GMPS LGB&T handbook

Part 10. Probation

She brought with her a folder that GMPS had produced on LGB&T issues.

Although there had not previously been any transgendered staff, section 13 of the handbook was all of the Press For Change material on trans issues.

To say that I was impressed is an understatement!

During our conversation, I raised the question that seems to cause the biggest problem for trans people – that of which toilets I would be expected to use. "The ladies, of course" said Penny. I later learned that one person at HQ had asked which loos I would be using and had been told it would be the female ones – it was pointed out that there were two sets of ladies' toilets at HQ and if anyone did have serious problems – then they could use the other ones.

Chapter 39. Starting on the Service Desk

As planned, I started on 15th after being given a clean bill of health by the doctor. I was taken down to the Service Desk on the fifth floor and introduced to my team. There should have been three support staff – but one was off on sick leave. He had been on the shortlist for my job – having been acting up for a few months. It appeared that he had assumed that he would just walk into the role and had not prepared for the interview.

One of the team was a young lad with a multi coloured Mohican haircut. He apologised for the hair – but I pointed out that as a trans person, I would hardly object to anyone else's freedom of expression. The final member of the team was Graham – almost a George Forman double.

I was given my log-on details and started work. I felt that one of the first things I needed to do was get out to the district offices and introduce myself – and to work out what the problems were and how to resolve them.

I was also taken round Headquarters and introduced to people. I encountered nothing but good wishes and welcomes. We then called on the Chief Officer, Christine Knott. She asked how I was settling in and I said it was fine, I said that I anticipated that there might be some issues but if so, I would deal with them and make allowances. "No, you won't" she said very forcibly. "If you have any problems, you are to let me know and they will be dealt with"

In fact, the worst that happened was being called he instead of she – a slip that was immediately corrected by the individual. There may have been some jokes behind my back – but I never got to hear of them.

I wrote the article for the Staff Bulletin and posted a message on a Lotus Notes LGB&T issues message board. This effectively said, you've undoubtedly heard on the grapevine that there is now a transsexual working for the organisation – Hi! That's ME! I did a bit of an explanation about what trans is and offered any help I could to anyone with issues relating to trans.

Part 10. Probation

Also on the LGB&T notice board was the announcement of a LAGIP[17] conference in Norwich. I joined LAGIP and booked a space.

Linda Cook and I had regular meetings on Monday mornings with Stan. One week he wanted an update on some work that we'd been asked to do. Linda had completed hers but, due to significant problems with the IT system the previous week, I hadn't done my report. Stan asked why I hadn't done it – though he must have known the reason. I felt that saying I'd been busy would really sound weak; so, I said I'd been skiving!

Chapter 40. LAGIP

While I attended the LAGIP conference, I was challenged by one of the other members.

"What are you doing here?" she demanded.

"I identify as lesbian."

"That's ok – because this isn't a place for trans people."

"Well, maybe it should be."

"No. We've had that debate before and decided it is only for Lesbians and Gays."

Now that's just the sort of statement to make me think 'Really? We'll have to see about that.'

The next day was the Annual General Meeting. LAGIP had been a very unstructured organisation with just two elected officers a convenor and a treasurer. Its roots could be traced back to 1976 when a group of lesbians and gay men had gathered together at a NAPO[18] conference in Harrogate because of heterosexism and homophobia at the conference and in the workplace. Two Gay men succeeded in a motion which committed NAPO to support the campaign for the equalisation of the age of consent and getting NAPO to affiliate to CHE[19]. In 1982, this informal group formed LAGIP at the NAPO Conference in Southport and a year later it had been recognised as an autonomous group. After a couple of decades informal existence, there was a move to put in on a more structured basis in 2000.

There was a request for volunteers to join a steering group. I offered to help. There was also a request for someone to lead on the next conference in two years. Having managed several conferences in the past, I put my hand up again.

Over the next couple of years, I worked with the other steering group members towards a more structured organisation. I also started to raise the question of extending the membership criteria. There was significant resistance and as I was the only trans person working in probation and as I still identified as lesbian, it wasn't really a significant issue.

One day, I had a message that someone from Bedfordshire Probation Service had been in touch. They had heard through the grapevine that Manchester had a transsexual member of staff and one of their officers had decided to transition. Could they talk to me to get some

---

[17] Lesbians and Gay Men In Probation
[18] National Association of Probation Officers
[19] Campaign for Homosexual Equality

Part 10. Probation

advice? I arranged to go down to Bedfordshire to meet with the individual and some of her managers and see how I might help.

A few days later, I was making a coffee in the kitchen at work when Chris Knott, the Chief came in. I mentioned that I'd been in touch with Bedford and had booked a day's leave to go and meet with them. "No, you're not" she said very firmly. This took me totally by surprise – she had always been so supportive until now. "This is Probation business. You go down in our time and at our expense!" she continued.

The meeting was at Bedfordshire's HQ in Bedford and included their HR Manager and their Chief Officer, John Scott. I agreed to go back down and do some presentations to colleagues on transgender issues and work with them on a plan for Ashley's transition. This included having a 'safe house' (my flat) in case there was unpleasant press interest in the story of a probation officer 'changing sex'. In the end there was a storm in a tea cup with 'Beds on Sunday' newspaper featuring it on the front page for one week.

During one of the presentations, Bed's Chief jokingly said that it was one of his claims to fame to know me! Due to the numbers attending, he ended up sitting on the floor – but not before making a joke about Manchester United having lost a match the previous weekend. When I started talking, I did point out that I hated football – so rude comments about Man U didn't worry me at all; and I did ask if Bedford even have a football team – aware that they are better known for rugby. I said, in any case that I wasn't a Mancunian and having lived in and around St Neots (about 12 miles away) for nearly 30 years, Bedford had been the nearest large town so I felt more at home there than in Manchester.

Ashley was the first of about four individuals that I helped support through transition at work within probation and the prison service.

Chapter 41. Surgery

In mid-2000, I had a further appointment with Russell Reid. He said he was happy to refer me for surgery and asked who I wanted to see. At that time, there were two main options in the UK for private surgery: Mike Royle and Tim Terry. Whilst it was by no means the most important factor, MR was significantly more expensive than TT. It seemed to me that TT now had as much experience as MR had had when he was first acknowledged as the no 1 choice. I hadn't heard of any problems with TT and he was much closer than MR so I decided to speak to TT first.

I would also need a second psychiatric assessment and knew that there was a specialist working at the Nuffield Hospital where Mr Terry operated (Deenesh Khoosal) – so I made appointments with both for the same late afternoon.

I saw Mr Khoosal first then Mr Terry. Both consultations went well – Tim did say that he would want me to get a second psychiatric assessment and was pleased to hear that I had just had this with Deenesh. So, it was all systems go for surgery in November.

The big downer that year was that Gilda had dumped me. I wasn't sufficiently woman for her. That hurt. Oh, did that hurt. I don't know how many packets of tissues I got through crying my eyes out.

Part 10. Probation

At Pride weekend that August I saw Gilda with another woman snogging. That pissed me off no end. The next day I went round to her house and told her what I thought of her – throwing a ring that she had given me back at her.

Later that afternoon, I was walking up Bloom Street, just opposite New York New York, when three guys started calling me names. There was one in particular so I crossed the road and faced him from a distance of about four inches. "What did you say" I demanded, looking him straight in the eyes. "Keep away from me; keep away from me" he whimpered. I SO wanted him to touch me. I had so much pent-up anger that I am sure I would have knocked him senseless – but I was still sufficiently aware that I might get away with self-defence but not assault.

I turned on my heels and started to walk away.

"Fucking tranny," he called.

Spinning round, I went back to him. Looked him up and down as though he was something I'd picked up on the soles of my shoes and said: "You don't even know the difference between a tranny and a transsexual do you. This is OUR area and if you don't like what you see around here – then fuck off".

When I went back down that way a bit later, there was no sign of them, so maybe they took the hint!

Surgery itself was a piece of cake.

It had been planned so that I could use sick leave from 1999-2000 and 2000-1 – plus some leave to cover the time off work – though Stan had made it clear that something would be arranged to cover me.

I drove over to Leicester on the Thursday (2nd November) with Joan, one of my friends from college. She would then take my car home and have the use of it while I was unable to drive. I stopped in a B&B on the Thursday night and smoked a last cigarette that evening as I'd been advised to ensure that there was a gap of 36 hours before surgery to avoid coughing due to the effects of anaesthetic on any carbon monoxide in my lungs. I was admitted to the hospital on the Friday morning and given a dose of Picolax and warned not to wander too far from a toilet. The laxative was designed to ensure that the bowel was empty before surgery in case any of it was damaged.

My room was better than many hotel rooms I'd stayed in. I had a television and, of course, private en suite bathroom (not that I'd get to see much of it for several days after surgery). Tim Terry was doing two GRS[20] operations per week at this time; Wednesday's at Leicester General for the NHS and on Saturdays at the Nuffield. At the Nuffield, we would go into the hospital on the Friday morning for surgery on the Saturday and generally be discharged the following Sunday. This meant that on the Friday and Saturday nights there would be two of us in the ward. On the first Friday, I went along to see the girl who had had surgery the previous Saturday. She had a friend with her who was intersexed. Soon after birth she

---

[20] Gender Reassignment Surgery – often referred to as "Sex Change Op" in the gutter press.

Part 10. Probation

underwent surgery to make her male; she later decided that this was not what she wanted and had GRS to give her female genitalia. She had now decided that this wasn't right either and she wanted to have both sets of genitalia – as she had been born.

Saturday morning, I was prepped for surgery.

The next thing I knew, I was waking up. I wasn't in any pain – so wondered why they hadn't gone ahead with the surgery. Then I realised that I was clad in a 'teddy bear' as we called it – lots and lots of padding below the waist held in place by a giant nappy to all intents and purposes – and various tubes from different parts of my body and arm. So, maybe they had done 'the op'. This was soon confirmed for me by the nurse. All had gone well. She asked if I was in any pain and I said there was a bit of discomfort but not what I would call pain. She pointed out a switch suspended from the ceiling that would allow me to self-administer some morphine if I needed it and told me to let them know if I needed anything else.

I had a couple of phone calls later that afternoon, I'm sure I wasn't at all coherent but at least the callers knew I was OK.

The first three days post op you are only allowed water – nothing solid; then you can start to have fruit juices in the water, then tea.

If you are squeamish, you may want to get behind the sofa for the next bit – or just skip the next paragraph.

In simple terms, the surgery entails creating a cavity for the neo-vagina, removing the testes and the inside of the penis, re-routing the urethra, taking part of the head of the penis and the attached nerves and repositioning it to create a clitoris; then inverting the skin of the penis into the cavity to produce a neo-vagina. The scrotal skin is used for the labia.

It is necessary to pack the inside of the neo-vagina to stop it closing up – which would largely negate the purpose of the surgery! This 'pack' has to stay in place for up to four to five days during which time you have to stay in bed virtually immobile. You must not bend more than a few degrees at the waist to avoid putting pressure on the surgery and must not, under any circumstances, cross your legs – even at the ankles or you risk deep vein thrombosis.

The day after my surgery was bonfire night – and I was entertained by firework displays through the window. But apart from that, laying there was boring. Daytime television is boring. Holding a book above your face to read is tiring. I did also, I am glad to say, have visitors almost every day and phone calls. I also had loads and loads of cards and flowers.

And, there was no pain. Every time the nurses came to give me my medication, they asked how much pain I was in on a scale of 1-10. My response was always "I'm not".

Then it was time for the pack to be removed.

It had been held in place by stitches. One of them had been missed as Tim Terry started to remove the pack. Now THAT did hurt!

From then I could start to have proper food from an attractive menu.

It was horrible! My tongue was coated – possibly in salt from the forced detox of nothing but water. Everything tasted vile and even seemed to burn my mouth. Those appetising lamb

Part 10. Probation

chops were evil. Anything sweet was turned sour. Tea was just about tolerable. This wasn't fair. Part of the deal of going privately was being able to avoid NHS hospital fare!

With the catheter removed, I was finally able to use the toilet myself. I passed water during the night without any problems – but the next time I sat on the loo I hadn't the faintest idea how to do it. How do I urinate? What muscles do I use? I was on the verge of panicking when I thought "calm down, you did it during the night so let nature take over". I stood back up then sat down again and just relaxed. Thankfully it worked. But no-one tells you these things in advance!

One thing we are warned about is the helicopter effect.

Instead of going down when you wee, the urine often sprays out sideways like the rotors of a helicopter. Chances are it finds the gap between the seat and the toilet bowl and unerringly finds anything down around your ankles! Take a tip, girls, put some toilet paper in the way to stop the spray escaping!

On the Friday evening, one of the nurses came to see me. The next patient had checked in but they had a leg injury so wouldn't be able to undergo surgery as planned the next morning. The nurses knew I was studying counselling – would I have a word with the individual who I'll call Kay.

She sat next to my bed and we started to chat. I rarely judge whether or not an individual is transsexual; that's up to them to decide, but alarm bells started to ring within the first few minutes. The person facing me was involved in a relationship with a woman who had children. Kay intended to undergo the surgery – but then live as a man to give the children a father. This, and other bits of information, seemed to suggest that surgery would be totally wrong for Kay.

After about an hour, I told Kay that I was feeling tired and needed to get to sleep – so she went back to her own room.

The nurse then came to see me again and apologised for having subjected me to Kay's problems. I told her that I'd been happy to help but I asked her what Kay was doing at the hospital as she was not, in my opinion, transsexual. The nurse said she couldn't comment.

The next afternoon, Tim Terry came to check up on me. He said he'd heard that I'd had a chat with Kay and thanked me for having done so. I then asked him what she was doing here.

"What do you mean" he asked.

"There's no way that she is transsexual" I said – and explained why I had reservations.

"The problem is that she has had two psychiatric referrals and I'm not in a position to challenge them – so what can I do?"

"If you don't know the psychiatrists she has consulted, you could insist that one of them is Deenesh Khoosal; she is clearly well over the optimum weight for surgery – so you could say you want her to lose a couple of stone; and she smokes – she must have got through ten cigarettes in the hour she was with me last night"

"That's good advice" Tim replied patting me on the shoulder.

Part 10. Probation

He later came back and said that he had told Kay that he wanted her to have another consultation with Deenesh; that she needed to stop smoking and lose two stones. "I'll put my bill in the post" I told him.

The next day, I was collected by Joan and Gilda. I semi reclined in the car while sitting on a rubber ring. Part way home, I needed the loo and realised that the one (and only) disadvantage of GRS is that you can't nip behind a bush at the side of the road!

Back at the flat, Gilda had organised a task force to give it a spring clean – though I had already repainted the bathroom and bedroom – new paint being a very effective disinfectant. I'd also bought a supply of white cotton knickers as being the most hygienic.

Gilda had also prepared one of my favourite meals for my welcome home.

Although I'd been told not to exert myself and certainly not carry anything heavy, I made an appointment to see my GP at his surgery – it was only a couple of hundred yards from the flat. There were a number of issues I needed to discuss. After the first couple of items the GP complained that I should have made a double appointment booking if I needed to discuss so many items. I told him that I HAD mentioned to his receptionist that there were several things I needed to discuss. I pointed out that so soon after major surgery; I would have been within my rights to ask him to call rather than getting to his surgery. He clearly wasn't at all happy – and I was disgusted with his attitude. He hadn't appeared to have a problem with me pre-op but now that I was physically female, I felt that he saw me as such and, therefore, a second class being.

I lost no time in switching to a different surgery where I've had nothing but polite and sympathetic and supportive treatment.

Time to get back behind the sofa – or skip the next paragraph if you are squeamish.

As I mentioned earlier, it is vital that the neo-vagina doesn't close up. To prevent it trans people need to insert dilators regularly. The sets provided by Nuffield contain four different size dilators and you should use them four times a day for at least fifteen minutes. This is far from comfortable and it's usual to apply generous amounts of KY jelly to ease the insertions. Immediately after surgery, my GP was giving me prescriptions for three month's hormones at a time and, having checked how much KY jelly I was using per week added that as well.

I then took my prescription to the chemist who turned to go into the pharmacy section – starting to read the prescription as she did so. She then stopped and looked back at me to query the amount. I nodded and said – it's right! I don't suppose it is every day that someone asks for 39 large tubes of KY jelly at a time.

While I was recuperating from surgery, there was a meeting at my flat involving Stephen Whittle, Paula Stephens and Ashley M from Bedfordshire Probation to discuss some work that Stephen and Paula had been commissioned to do by the Home Office on the needs of transsexual offenders.

Chapter 43. The 'Gerbil'

2002 saw a milestone judgement for transsexual people in the UK. Two trans individuals won their cases in the European Court of Human Rights against the UK Government on the grounds of rights to privacy and marriage. I was driving into Salford Quays one afternoon when the announcement was made on the news. My hand punched the air and I yelled "YES!" much to the surprise of nearby pedestrians.

In 2003, the government published the Gender Recognition Bill – popularly known as the 'Gerbil' amongst trans people. There was considerable opposition to the Bill especially from the extreme right and from the Christian Evangelical Alliance.

The Bill proposed to give transsexual individuals recognition in their 'acquired gender' 'for all purposes'. There were some exceptions and some conditions to this recognition and it hasn't satisfied all trans people – but it was still a huge leap forward for most of us.

In spite of the opposition and, at times it seemed touch and go, the Bill was passed and entered into law as the Gender Recognition Act 2004 (GRA). Applications for recognition didn't start for some time and, even then, for the first six months was limited to individuals who had transitioned at least five years earlier. I came into this category and successfully applied for recognition and received my certificate and a replacement birth certificate. I was now, for all purposes, legally female.

Two main criticisms of the GRA have been that some trans people could not obtain recognition unless they were divorced or annulled their marriage. Where partners had stood by the individual through the transition, this seemed very poor thanks and left them in very difficult positions. Thankfully the Same Sex Marriage Act does now mean that trans people can remain married – though it has done nothing to rectify cases where the individuals did, reluctantly, separate in order to allow the trans person to gain recognition. They can, of course, remarry but that's not really the same. The other criticism is that the act only gives recognition to those who are going through gender reassignment – not the wider trans community — including those who identify as neither male nor female.

The Civil Partnership Act also became law in 2004 – another important step forward for LGB individuals.

Chapter 44. From Customer Services to IT Project Manager

After returning to work, I was asked to undertake some projects as well as managing the service desk. These included an asset audit – organised by the main IT contractor to the probation service at that time known as Bull. It was clear from their initial plans that they were poor at project management. A number of the sites that they planned to visit no longer existed, new sites were not on their lists and the times they had planned for sites bore no connection with the work that needed to be undertaken.

There was also a reorganisation going on in the service affecting the IT Support Officers in the district offices. It was proposed that these would be absorbed into the district structures but that two could be managed by me as part of the service desk. When Stan told me about this, he said that one of the affected individuals considered me to be arrogant. My reply was "So".

I was then asked if I would join a team that was reviewing bids for the future support of IT throughout the probation service. I was given the criteria against which the bids were to be judged and copies of the bids to evaluate. It was clear to me that none of the bids complied fully with the criteria so I said so.

In spite of this, a winner was selected. I was then asked to attend two of the 'walk-throughs' where they would provide more detail about the proposed services. The two I attended were on 'Project Management' and 'Quality Assurance'. Perhaps my training in PR should have influenced me but I did remark during the Project Management presentation that I had seen no evidence that they were capable of organising a piss up in a brewery. At the meeting on 'Quality Assurance', I asked them to look at pages 36 and 37 (or whatever the pages were). Someone had copied and pasted the same page twice. "Who Quality Assured this document?" I wanted to know. There were red faces around the table.

Sadly, my poor opinion of Bull, later known as Integris then Steria was justified over subsequent years. Not that I think it was entirely their fault. There was clearly inadequate management of the contract by Probation head office.

Another project I was responsible for included an information security audit – which was assessed by the audit unit as 'well controlled' (the highest classification). As part of this project, I had to visit a number of sites used by probation for its work. One of these was the Pankhurst Centre. This organisation had adopted a rule that their facilities were for 'women, born women and living as women'. This clearly and deliberately excluded transsexual people. A member of Inner Enigma had also been a member of a poetry group which had moved to the Pankhurst Centre. The group was told that the transwoman could not continue to attend. I arrived at the Centre one morning to undertake the information security review. I knocked on the door. As it opened there was a horrified person on the other side. I explained that I was Helen Dale from Probation and had an appointment with XXX to do a review. "You'd better come in" she stammered.

At this time, I was acting as Project Manager but still retained my Customer Services Responsibilities. It was then agreed that there should be a formal 'Acting Project Manager' role – which would be advertised internally. The intention was to make this role permanent in which case, I was warned that I would have to reapply. I didn't think this was fair – but was assured it would be on the same basis ie internal candidates only.

Following the 'acting' role interview, the Head of IT Owen Bristow (who had taken over from Stan Cook) advised that I had not answered a diversity question adequately. As I was sitting on the NPS National Diversity Board at the time, I found that hard to believe! The problem lay, I was certain, in how the question had been asked. I sent the question to the NPS Head of Diversity who agreed with me. Owen had, in any case, sought dispensation from HR to appoint me in spite of not having passed this 'essential' question.

The largest project at this time was 'Technology Upgrade' – replacing all of the IT equipment in some 40 odd offices and replacing servers in each main office with a centralised 'Area Data Centre' at HQ. The basic planning and organisation was done by the national team – but this didn't take account of the fact that Manchester was far larger than most of the other probation services – only London and West Midlands were the same size or bigger. Project timings had been based on an 'average' service – which meant a third the size of

Part 10. Probation

Manchester. For our purposes, we needed to allow longer preparation time – though not necessarily three times as long. I struggled to persuade the Project Director in London of this.

Eventually, I managed to arrange a meeting with him after one with the Head of Diversity related to the staff associations. It was late morning when we eventually met. As we went into his office he said "Roles" which I heard as "rolls". I thought it was still a bit early for lunch! "No, roles – what's your role on the project?". "Oh, I see, I'm Project Manager. It's my job to ensure that it is implemented without problems in Manchester. In that respect the buck stops with me". "Right, well I am Project Director. I don't 'manage' the project, I 'direct' it" – arrogant sod!

He was about the most patronising individual I have ever encountered — when he spoke to me, I could feel a fatherly hand patting my head and hear "don't you worry your pretty little (female) head about things it's all under control".

That wasn't how it appeared to me.

Thankfully, I was attending a 'Service Review Forum' that December involving IT managers from Probation Areas around the country chaired by Janine Williams, the 'Head of Live Services' from Probation HQ. Janine was going through her update and she came to a new topic. A new Project Director is being appointed for Technology Upgrade. My ears picked up. "Does that mean that XXXXX is no longer with us", I asked. "Err, Umm, err, hmm, err, yes Helen that is what I'm saying". "Hallelujah! There IS a Father Christmas!" I exclaimed – a view shared by several others around the table who had been as impressed as I had with XXXX.

I learned later that my nickname at HQ was the 'Exocet'. Well, if that meant I went to the heart of problems – that was fine with me.

My planning work continued with the project. We needed to identify how many new machines there would be; what the arrangements would be for deliveries, where kit would be stored during the update and when the old equipment would be removed which order to upgrade the sites, who would need training on the new systems – and who would provide it and when; it would be necessary to extend the server room at HQ and arrange for the new data centre to be installed; the air conditioning would need to be upgraded and new alarms fitted. Data on the local office servers would need to be extracted, securely transported then loaded onto the data centre and checked.

At last, everything was in place and the first of our sites was due to be migrated on the Monday morning. Mid-afternoon on the Friday, our Head of IT – Owen Bristow came into my office. "I'm glad you're still here Helen, I've got some bad news for you. Technology Upgrade has been postponed". NPS had run out of money for that financial year! Fabulous organisation!

Having issued some emails advising the offices that arrangements had been cancelled, I went home for the weekend.

Monday morning Owen came to see me again.

"Are you OK?" he asked.

"Yes, why wouldn't I be?"

Part 10. Probation

"Well, all your work has been wasted."

"Not really – they'll have to do the upgrade at some stage. I had every last detail sorted to the nth degree – nothing would have gone wrong – every site would have been upgrade exactly as planned. Now if there are problems, it will be because of the delay. Prove that I'm wrong!"

Owen looked at me "I can't".

"Well, there you are. I'm in a no-lose situation" I said triumphantly!

Taking advantage of the delay, I re-worked the project plan over the next couple of days – building in a safety margin. I then took it to Owen and told him that I would need six weeks from the date the project was reinstated to the date of the first site upgrade. Nobody could argue with me and I got my six weeks' notice.

In the end, one site, Oldham, was later than planned coming back on line – reloading the data took longer than expected. In fact, it completed moments after we had taken the decision not to bring the site back up until the following morning. The overall project had involved more than a hundred staff – not counting the end users of the system. We celebrated the successful implementation with a party at HQ (albeit with soft drinks only).

There was an incident at one of our offices where there was a break-in after the new kit was delivered and installed. It seemed likely that offenders attending appointments had seen equipment clearly marked as computer related being taken into the building. As it happens, they stole devices that needed to be linked to the network before they could be used – they'd have been better taking the monitors instead. It was a lesson for the future and when equipment was delivered thereafter, we insisted on it being hidden in black bin liners or similar.

TU was followed by a stream of projects over the years – often with several running simultaneously.

An IS/IT Strategic Programme Manager was brought in to manage the Project Team. As part of their interview process, I was asked to show candidates around HQ. One of the candidates cut me dead at the end of the guided tour when introduced to someone who was involved in the interviews. I didn't even get a 'thank you' or a 'hope to see you again'. After the interviews, I told Owen that if they appointed him – then there would be another vacancy in the team as I wouldn't work with him. I was assured that he was not being appointed. Instead, Elaine Hayton became my line manager. We soon established an excellent working relationship.

When the Acting Role was made permanent, I had to face another interview. At first it was advertised internally only; but the then local Unison Chair stuck his oar in and said that it needed to be advertised externally as well. I felt that as he was the Greater Manchester Branch Chair his responsibility was first to GMPA members – not the wider public. As I felt that he had acted against my interests, I returned my membership card to him with a letter explaining why I was resigning from the union.

When Elaine had explained the situation and asked if I was prepared to defer an interview already planned. I felt that I was in a invidious position. If I objected to the interview being postponed, I would be seen as difficult. If I agreed to it I was making it harder to win the position – and it put me at risk of another incident where an inappropriately worded question could cost me the job. I gave her a letter expressing my concern and why I felt entitled to refuse to agree to the postponement. Having made her aware of the depth of my feelings, I took the letter back and tore it up in front of her. I told her that I would agree, very reluctantly, to the delay.

On the day of the interview, we had to provide a presentation 'the application of Project Standards to work in Greater Manchester Probation'. Having co-written the GMPA Project Standards with Elaine, I was well placed to provide this presentation. At the end of my PowerPoint show, Elaine turned to her colleagues on the interview panel and said "you've just been given a talk on the elements of project management in ten minutes".

After the questioning had been completed, I returned to my office to await my fate. As the time passed by I started to wonder if the competition had been stronger than I'd hoped. Was there a debate over which of us to appoint? Was it too close to call? Eventually Elaine came in and congratulated me. "You wiped the floor with the opposition" she assured me. The second placed candidate was offered a temporary position a little later and told me that he had been assured that the interview had been a close-run thing. Well – close or having wiped the floor didn't matter – I'd come first and that was what counted. My position was permanent – the other was a temporary role.

Chapter 45. LAGIP 2 / National Diversity Involvement

Running parallel to my official job, I became increasingly active with LAGIP and in national diversity work.

LAGIP
Lesbians, Gay Men, Bisexual and Transgendered Individuals in Probation and Family Courts

Having effectively acted as unofficial vice chair to Michael Lloyd, the role was made official. As such, I joined him at national meetings – initially turning up uninvited but as though I had every right to be there.

I was then invited to provide a presentation at the first National Diversity Conference on working with transsexual offenders and to take part in a debate on whether or not information about sexual orientation should be monitored. Presenting the opposite case was my own Chief Officer, Chris Knott.

I had also volunteered to lead the organisation of the next LAGIP conference. At this time, LAGIP received no funding from NPS – so all events had to be self-financing. We wrote to the Chief Officers of each of the Probation Areas asking that they agree to fund a number of their staff to attend the conference at a cost of £250 per person. Due to confidentiality reasons, they would not be given the names of those attending. Most probation areas agreed to fund staff; in some cases, just one space, in others up to ten places. LAGIP didn't take advantage by charging for staff who had not attended even when all of the sponsored places were not taken up.

Part 10. Probation

As we couldn't know how many people would attend, we had to budget carefully and planned, initially, to use a low-cost gay hotel on the edge of the village. As bookings came in, we were able to move the venue to the Manchester Conference Centre – though we retained some of the rooms at the original hotel for those who preferred to use a gay venue.

As part of the agenda, we had a number of breakout groups – one of which looked at whether or not trans should be included in LGB organisations. I mentioned that I had a presentation on trans issues and was asked to add this to the agenda at the end of the day for those who wanted to stay and see it – nearly everyone did stay. At the end of the presentation delegates wanted to vote on whether or not to extend the membership criteria – but I insisted that this wait until the AGM the next day.

That evening, we had organised a buffet and some entertainment in Taurus – a bar at the top of Canal Street. We'd wanted exclusive use of a venue but as it was a Saturday night, this had seemed unlikely. I had, however, approach Ian and Polly in Taurus and explained what we wanted and got the reply "For you Helen, anything!" – they had added the proviso that we could have exclusive use until 10 pm at which point they would open up to other customers. They certainly did us proud with a fabulous buffet; we also had a DJ and karaoke on a raised area at the front of the bar.

Throughout the evening, LAGIP members came over to me and congratulated me on a great conference and bought bottles of wine. They assured me that I'd won the argument about membership criteria. There were so many bottles of wine that I was giving them away as fast as they were delivered – though I did manage to consume my fair share. Someone then dragged me up to the stage and we belted out 'I am what I am!' delegates then started to drift off around the gay village and, by about midnight, I was the last one left from LAGIP. Polly then came over and offered me a brandy, I told him I didn't drink brandy – but was persuaded to settle for a Tia Maria. Not just a normal measure – but half a wine glass full.

Taurus can't be more than a quarter of a mile from the Conference centre hotel – but I swear I must have done two to three times that distance wandering from one side of the road to the other as I weaved my way back. Once in the room, I just stood with the backs of my calves next to the bed and flopped backwards onto it.

Next morning was the AGM. Routine business completed; we reached the motion to extend the membership criteria. I was aware that there were some members, probably about six, who did not want to extend the criteria to include trans; I also estimated there were about six that I was sure would vote to extend the membership. That left more than fifty that I couldn't predict – although the previous evening's reaction was cause for optimism. In the end, one person abstained and everyone else voted for the motion to extend the membership to include bi and trans members.

In 2003, LAGIP received official recognition by NPS as a Staff Association and funding for NEC members and for an annual conference. In 2004, the Society Guardian wanted to feature LGB&T individuals in the public sector as part of an article about the founding of Stonewall. I was put forward to represent LAGIP – and was interviewed and photographed for the article.

Part 10. Probation

The National Offender Management Service was also set up in June 2004 within the Home Office to combine the Prisons and Probation Services. The Director General, Martin Narey, was from the Prison Service with a new National Offender Manager reporting to him – this was Chris Knott the former GMPA Chief.

Soon after his appointment, Martin Narey visited a number of probation areas, including Manchester, to meet staff and outline the plans behind NOMS. I attended the meeting at our Moss Side Office. NOMS had been created in response to the 2003 Carter report 'Reducing Crime, Changing Lives'. A response to the report had been produced but didn't mention equality or diversity at all. I challenged Martin Narey over this. He agreed that it should have been addressed and they had overlooked it in their response to Carter.

Society Guardian

'It's far more difficult in the private sector'

Helen Dale (below), 57, is acting IT project manager at the National Probation Service.

I spent 30-odd years working in advertising and PR and was living as a male heterosexual. I was married and have a grown-up daughter. I've been working in the public sector as a woman for the past five years and I really believe it's the best environment for a transgendered person. It's far more difficult in the private sector.

There is a lot of unemployment among transgendered people and although as a group they are a lot more visible, there is still a lot more to be done in terms of wider acceptability. My job for the probation service was the first job I ever applied for as a woman. Although colleagues in previous jobs were aware that I was considering living and working as a woman, I had been working as a man.

The interview for the probation service was a real non-event actually. I think they take their equality and diversity policies really seriously. I had a meeting with the man who was to be my line manager after I was offered the job. He said: "Right, let's think about how we handle this. Tell me how you would like to handle it."

It was impressive. A few days after getting the job, the equality and diversity officer came round to see me at my flat with the diversity manual. Greater Manchester Probation Service have been first class. I'm not saying they are perfect, but in my view they take things seriously.

In 2004, the Home Office LGBT staff association, Spectrum, was helping to set up a pan-civil service transsexual and intersex support network. The initial meeting of this group was in Manchester and I attended. We decided on the name a:gender for the group. The Civil Service Diversity Champion at this time was Martin Narey – the Head of NOMS. Three of us, a:gender's Chair, Dee, another member of the committee Louise and I went to see Martin at his office. When he met us, he apologised to me for having poached our Chief Officer. I assured him that I was only too happy to know that someone with Chris' commitment to diversity was working with him. We all then went into a conference room where Dee explained what we hoped to do with a:gender and why it was important – especially in view of the recent passage of the Gender Recognition Act.

He was completely supportive and asked what we were after. Dee informed him that we needed £50,000 for the first year. He told us he would cover that from his own budgets. He did, however say that membership would have to be limited to the civil service – not

Part 10. Probation

members of the armed forces, NHS or police etc. As he was also responsible for Probation, he agreed to extend membership to us in spite of the fact that we were not part of the civil service.

The following year, we invited Martin to be Guest of Honour at the LAGIP conference in Brighton. When I'd introduced him, he said that he had first met me just after he'd been appointed as Director General of NOMS and was visiting probation services. He said that I had challenged him over diversity and, when he had answered me, I'd given him 'that' look!

During a coffee break I asked Martin what he planned to do when a prisoner serving a sentence for attempted rape obtained her Gender Recognition Certificate and became legally female – although she was unlikely to have had surgery by then. Later that year, he resigned and became Chief Executive of Barnardos.

In 2007, there was further reorganisation with NOMS being moved from the Home Office and combined with the Department of Constitutional Affairs to create the Ministry of Justice. The Minister was Lord Falconer who had been responsible for talking the Gender Recognition Bill through parliament. When he came to visit us, I took the opportunity to thank him for the GRA. I also questioned a statement in a message that had been distributed to staff that said that the MoJ would aim to comply with legal obligations in respect of diversity. I said I didn't think compliance with the law was optional and surely the Ministry of 'Justice' should aim to set the standard for work in this field. He agreed with my comment and said that the MoJ would be an 'exemplar' with regard to equality and diversity.

Preparing for conference

Michael Lloyd stood down as Chair of LAGIP and the former membership secretary and I took over as co-chairs. Sadly, this arrangement didn't work out as there were major difficulties between us. Tony eventually resigned leaving me as sole chair. The following year I was, again, co-chair this time with Libby Wrighton – which worked much better but she then left probation. Rosanne Ferber then acted as my vice chair but her term of office was restricted by ill health. I felt it was vital to ensure continuity for the chair and vice chair roles so proposed to an AGM that we elect a vice chair who would serve in that role for one year then, subject to ratification by the members, would automatically become the Chair – serve in that role for two years – then revert to vice chair. This meant that the new vice chair would be supported by a chair in their second year of office, as they became the new chair, they would switch roles with the former chair who would continue to support them as the vice chair.

Part 10. Probation

A side consequence of this was that no-one would be able to serve as chair longer than I had.

When I had first joined LAGIP and we were talking about extending the membership criteria, there had been concerns that trans people would ride on the backs of Lesbian and Gays without contributing to the work. In reality, a far higher percentage of trans members served on the committee than lesbian or gay members. At one time nearly half the committee was trans. We didn't just work for trans rights either – we fought for LGB&T across the board.

Throughout my time in various chairing roles (and afterwards), I served on National Probation Service and NOMS diversity boards in its various manifestations. We also met with different Ministers.

On one occasion, Jack Straw called a meeting of the Chairs of the different staff associations to emphasise the need for the various associations within the MoJ to work together. At that time there were typically three associations for the strands of diversity: race, LGB&T & disability (though prisons didn't have the latter as they had no disabled officers!). For LGB&T there was the Rainbow network for the former DCA, GALIPS for Prison Service and LAGIP for Probation.

We three were already holding joint meetings and working together so when we attended the meeting, we all wore T-shirts bearing a 'working for justice' logo that I had designed. I think we made our point!

One of the initiatives I implemented as Chair was an Honorary Membership scheme – for individuals who supported the aims and objectives of LAGIP – but were not, themselves, LGB or T. We attracted a high number of senior managers as well as other staff through this scheme.

LAGIP continued to hold conferences around the country. Membership grew from about 80 in 2000 to 300+ full members and 200 honorary members in 2014 – before the Probation Service was dismembered.

One of the sad realities of being trans is the number who are murdered or commit suicide. Each year we hold Transgender Days of Remembrance for those that have died with vigils such as that in Manchester's Sackville Park on the edge of the Gay Village.

Part 10. Probation

On one such occasion, I attended a joint event in Birmingham with colleagues from prisons and the police service. After the event I needed to get back to New Street station for my train back to Manchester – and was offered a ride in a police car. When the car stopped, I was very tempted to jump out and run away just to see what onlookers' reactions might be! In the end I didn't – but I can now claim that as well as having been in and out of every prison in Manchester, the police in Birmingham put me on a train out of their city!

Chapter 46. Work with Trans Offenders

When I first joined Probation, I posted on the Lotus Notes LGB&T bulletin board that if anyone wanted support on trans issues to let me know. I provided some briefings for trainee probation officers and other members of staff.

I then learned that one of our officers was dealing with a trans person who had just been sentenced to five years for manslaughter. I was concerned about some of the comments made in reports about this individual by the previous officer and offered my help to the person taking over the case.

This offer was declined at first. This may have been because the officer was very new to the job so didn't want to seem inadequate. After her first visit to the case, she called me. She would appreciate my help after all.

I arranged to visit Hindley YOI with her and we met K. There were significant questions over whether she was transsexual or transvestite. This would make a major difference to the way she should be treated.

She went through her story which had been an awful history of abuse. As I listened to what she had to say, there was no question in my mind that K was transsexual – not transvestite. As we walked out of the prison, the PO[21] asked me what I thought. I said that there was no doubt in my mind that she was transsexual.

The local trans community arranged for someone to befriend her and visit her while in prison – a role I could not do as I worked for Probation. She did, however, ask if I could visit her on one occasion in relation to the befriender. This would not be an official Probation visit – though I did inform the PO dealing with her and make a note on the case management system of my visit.

When I arrived at Hindley, I went to the visitor section and explained that I was there to see and gave K's surname and number.

"Oh yes, HE's in the hospital wing isn't HE?" sneered the Prison Officer.

"Yes, she is." I replied

"Right. You got a mobile phone on you SIR?"

"No. And it's not 'sir'!"

"Oh, sorry ma'am – whatever," he responded as though I was something he'd picked up on his shoes.

---

[21] Probation Officer

Part 10. Probation

He had clearly identified me as another weirdo – like K. He didn't realise I worked for Probation. He clearly started to become concerned when he saw me writing down his number.

When I returned to the office, I went to see Stan Cook and I explained what had happened. "You have to make this official" he advised. We contacted the Senior Probation Officer (SPO) based at the prison. He then went to see the Prison Officer's manager. The officer had already anticipated a complaint as he'd told his manager that he may have 'inadvertently offended' a visitor. My stance was that I wanted to ensure that the individual and other staff were made aware that such treatment was totally unacceptable – no matter whether the visitor was on official business or a friend or family of a prisoner.

I remained in touch with K over the next couple of years until 2003 when she was paroled at the halfway point of her sentence. During this period, she telephoned me on a number of occasions at the office from the prison and we exchanged Christmas cards. On release, she was admitted to the GMPA women's hostel in recognition of her self-identified gender.

Unfortunately, the following Saturday she got drunk and went to the Transformation shop in north Manchester where she attacked a woman assistant[22]. She then went on the run.

There seemed a possibility that she might get in touch with me as I had been supporting her and arrangements were made in case this happened – the authorities ensuring that I was not put at risk. I was totally convinced that K would not harm me but others were less certain.

K gave herself up and was returned to prison. She was certainly facing having to complete the rest of her original sentence. A further sentence for assault would probably not add to this sentence. There was little chance of the Prison Service dealing with her gender issues during those thirty months. I have always wondered if she decided to plead guilty to a more serious offence to ensure that she was sentenced for a much longer period and force the Prison Service to provide treatment. Whether or not this was the case, she did plead guilty to attempted rape and was sentenced to an indefinite sentence with conditions that she not be released before her anger management and gender issues had been dealt with. When K was due to appear in court for sentencing, her solicitors asked if I could speak for her. This was clearly out of the question as it would be a conflict of interests.

Inner Enigma attempted to arrange for Gilda to provide counselling for K while in Manchester Prison – but the Prison Service refused to allow this as she was not accredited. Instead, she befriended K and has visited her over the intervening years.

K, of course, is the case that I was referring to when I asked Martin Narey what he would do when such an individual obtained their Gender Recognition Certificate.

The Prison Service seemed to be reluctant to risk adverse publicity in the Daily Mail or Express. They seemed scared of those papers' reaction to a prisoner with a penis and serving a sentence for attempted rape to be moved to a female prison. It seemed to be a vicious

---

[22] All of the information was published at the time – so I am not disclosing any confidential details.

Part 10. Probation

circle. She could not have surgery while she was in a male prison but could not be moved to a female prison before she had surgery. Nobody seemed able to accept that there was a simple enough solution: take her from the male prison to the hospital for surgery then take her to a female prison on release from hospital.

This went on and on for years until she eventually took the Prison Service to the High Court in 2009. Being ordered to move K to the female estate by the High Court gave the Prison Service the defence they may have needed against the Mail and Express and she was moved initially to Holloway. She was eventually released from prison in 2017.

If her aim in pleading guilty to attempted rape had been to get treatment quicker than she might by serving out her remaining sentence then getting on to the NHS system on release – then it certainly didn't work.

I am not, by the way, in any way defending K's actions. I have no doubt that the woman she brutally attacked was traumatised and felt that she was about to be raped. K clearly had anger management issues – though, knowing her history, that's not surprising.

Primarily as a consequence of what happened with K, Greater Manchester Probation commissioned Inner Enigma to provide support to trans offenders. I recruited Gilda and my friend Chris, both qualified counsellors as volunteers on the contract.

Staff also involved me in a few other cases involving trans offenders. In one case, a transvestite had been supported by a woman who had helped with cross dressing, make up etc. When she got involved in a new relationship, her partner asked her to stop supporting the TV. The TV then started going through the telephone book and ringing women at random to try to find someone else who might help. The individual was eventually caught and put on probation. I met the individual who was able to see that being trans was nothing to be ashamed of and they were given details of support groups they could attend. End of offending behaviour!

Similarly, I was asked to meet an offender in North Wales who had been stealing clothing from hotel bedrooms to avoid the embarrassment of going into shops to buy it. They'd been caught when a guest was in the room they had entered. Again, a chat to show that being trans is OK and, as far as I know, the individual didn't re-offend.

Some cases were more difficult. There was another trans offender in prison for a serious offence. To cope with the problems of being trans and unable to get treatment, they used drugs. This would put them back on the system that might eventually lead to release. They'd come off drugs again and get closer to consideration for release – then relapse.

Frustration that trans people face can often overflow – as it had with K. It also applied in two other cases I became involved in. In one, a transwoman had attended A&E as she had been injured. She noticed the staff laughing and making inappropriate comments and lost her temper – scattering equipment around the place. She was sentenced to unpaid work supervised by one of our offices.

Another of our officers asked me to meet a prisoner M due to be released from Styal prison just outside Manchester. During our conversation M revealed that she was just a few weeks post op but that the prison had taken away her dilators – preventing M from ensuring that her neo-vagina did not close up. This was potentially disastrous for her. I called the Nuffield Hospital where I'd had surgery and obtained details of where to get some replacement dilators – ordered them on my credit card and had them delivered to the hostel that M was about to be released to so they were waiting for her when she arrived. Thankfully, there were no long-term problems. (I was able to claim the cost of the dilators on my expenses but, frankly, would not have cared if I hadn't been able to).

Between the work that I had done and that undertaken by Inner Enigma, we had dealt with around twenty cases. On average, it would be expected that about half those cases would reoffend within two years. As far as I can tell, only three of those that we dealt with reoffended. It was clear that providing support had been very effective.

I also continued to be involved supporting staff who were transitioning and providing awareness training for their colleagues and for other staff interested in trans issues. On one occasion I was asked to do a presentation for North Wales Probation. Their Chief introduced me but apologised that she would only be able to stay for about ten minutes as she needed to get a report ready for a Board Meeting. She was still there half an hour later as she'd become engrossed in the presentation.

GALIPS, the Prison Service's equivalent of LAGIP, asked me to provide presentations on trans issues at their annual conference. I involved Gilda in the presentations. She had just encountered some discriminatory comments when visiting Manchester Prison which she related as part of the presentation. Following one of the four workshops, we were approached by some delegates who wanted to talk about Gilda's experience. They were from Manchester Prison and asked if Gilda would give them full details as they would deal with the matter for her.

Chapter 47. Diversity Awards

14.40 Individual Communication Award
Winner: Helen Dale
Contact E-mail Address:
Helen.Dale@manchester.probation.gsx.gov.uk

Elaine Hayton in her nomination wrote that 'Helen has developed her counselling skills and been instrumental in setting up a charity (Inner Enigma) which provides a point of excellence for TS knowledge in the North West of England.'

Gerry Hindley, Board Chair of Staffordshire, presented Helen with her award. In his presentation Gerry outlined how Helen 'Used communication tools including presentations, training, one to one counselling, group development, and management briefing...to make a very significant contribution to the wider understanding particularly of trans-sexual issues within the service...The judges were impressed by the wide coverage of her work, involving students, hospice staff, NHS, and help line volunteers, and her provision of specialist support on trans-sexual issues across the service as a whole.'

In 2004, NPS announced that they were seeking nominations for Diversity Awards in a range of categories. Elaine told me that she wanted to nominate me for one of the awards. I had to tell her that there could be a problem as I was one of the judges!

Part 10. Probation

Elaine contacted Diane Baderin, Diversity Manager for NPS who was leading the awards and was assured that this would not be a problem as there were seven categories to judge and each member of the panel would only be involved in a couple of them. I would, obviously, not be allowed to judge the category I was entered in.

When we came together to judge the submissions, I was very impressed with one that dealt with trans issues. I thought the individual must have done a significant amount or research and her conclusions seemed eminently sensible. When I reached the end of the paper, I found that she had credited the reference for a lot of the work. It was me.

At the end of the day, the panels got together to confirm that we had winners for each category. The original idea had been that the ceremony would be like the Oscars – with none of the nominees knowing whether or not they had won until the names were announced. I had planned to leave the room before the team said who had won the Communications category – the one for which I'd been nominated, but they made the announcement before I could leave.

On the day of the awards, Elaine and I travelled down from Manchester to the Swiss Cottage Holiday Inn in London. When they got to the Communications category, I put my papers on the floor so I was ready to stand up. Elaine still did not know that I knew I was the winner. As the compere started to provide details of the winner and it became clear that it was me, she gripped my arm and said "It's you, isn't it?"

Chapter 48. Butler Trust Award,

In 2008, I was nominated for a Butler Trust Award. These were in honour of RAB Butler, a progressive Home Secretary of the 1950s. They were for Prison and Probation staff for innovative work with offenders.

The initial nomination was prepared by the Diversity Manager on behalf of the Chief Officer. The initial written nominations were assessed and a short list prepared. The next stage involved an interview by the panel in London. My interview was in Westminster just after I returned from leave. The train to London was delayed and as we were arriving into London, we were advised that Victoria Line services were disrupted. I called the Butler Trust and explained the situation and said that I was on the way but I might be a bit late.

Fortunately, I knew my way round the tube network having lived in London for so long and in the end managed to get to the venue almost on time. The interview panel was chaired by England footballer Trevor Brooking – I didn't like to say that I hated football!

The interview went as well as I could have hoped for so if I didn't win then I had, at least, done my best.

A few weeks later, I was having my regular supervision meeting with Elaine and the subject of the award came up. I said "you do realise that if I was to win, I'll need to be given about a month to do a project for the Butler Trust – perhaps involving an overseas trip". We were quite busy at this time and Elaine's face reflected her sudden realisation that her team might be halved for some weeks. "You did read the small print on the nomination form, didn't you?" I added. In fact, it hadn't been Elaine that had signed the nomination – it had

Part 10. Probation

been the Chief. She could take it up with him! "Well, we will have to face that if it happens" I said as I gathered up my papers and returned to my desk.

The first thing I noticed was an envelope bearing the Butler Trust logo. As I opened it my heart was in my mouth. I read the first paragraph and walked into Elaine's office. "You know what we were just discussing?" and handed her the letter. All concerns about having to lose my services for a month or so were lost in her obvious pleasure at my being honoured with an award as she hugged me.

The awards would be at Buckingham Palace and presented by HRH Princess Anne. I would be able to take one guest with me. That would have to be Joanna.

Before we could be trusted to meet the Princess Royal, we had to be briefed at a meeting at the prison Service College at Newbold Revel. This included being instructed in how to address royalty and how to bow or if the ladies preferred, curtsey.

Earlier that year, before I even knew I'd been shortlisted, I'd been shopping at the Lowry Outlet Mall near my house and had come across a lovely brown jacket and a skirt and top – all separates but they went together well. The jacket had a mandarin style collar and was café au lait; the skirt was calf length and flared with contrasting materials one smooth the other slightly rougher in chocolate – while the top was short sleeved and beige with crystals around the neckline

I had no reason to anticipate ever having an occasion to wear the ensemble bit, after some umming and erring, had bought them. They were ideal for the trip to Buck House!

I needed a hat though so it was back to the Outlet Mall where I was able to find something that would go with the rest of the outfit. I'd need shoes and a handbag too! And organise a hairdressing appointment and for my nails to be done. Then, disaster, a broken tooth. When I explained why it was important that my smile be as perfect as possible, I was fitted in.

At the weekend, I pressed my unworn jacket and hung it on the back of the door so it wouldn't get crushed.

Part 10. Probation

Jo and I had decided to travel down the day before so we had booked a hotel near Victoria. After being shown to our room, I opened my suitcase to hang up my jacket. My heart sank. It wasn't there. It was still hanging on the back of the door at home.

There was only one thing to do. Head for Oxford Street. We started at Marble Arch where I knew there was an Evans and a large Marks and Spencer's. They had nothing suitable. On to Selfridges – nothing; well, nothing within the amount I was prepared to spend. There was one jacket in Etam that was just about useable though it was more suitable for evening wear but I bought it in case it was the best I could find. Then, close to Oxford Circus, I saw some dark brown blazers being taken into a shop. We dived in and I asked if they had one in a 22 or 24. They did. I tried them on and immediately bought one. My heart could stop racing now.

Jo and I then went over to the London Eye where we took a ride and could see the palace at the other end of the Mall – over the tops of the buildings along Whitehall.

We met up with Hugh for dinner that evening – then it was a reasonably early night ready for the big day.

We caught a cab outside the hotel. "Buckingham Palace please" "Going to get an award are you" asked the cabby (I imagine the hat had given me away). He dropped us off near one of the gates and we found where we were supposed to go. We were to be admitted from 9.30 – though there was some question whether this included guests. I persuaded the Police Officer on duty that this was what the invitation letter said and he finally agreed. We were admitted and allowed to walk through the arch into the inner courtyard then up the red carpet and into the building.

We climbed the impressive stairs led up to our left. I came across Craig Houllihan from Leeds – a regional coordinator from GALIPS that I knew who had also won an award. After a rehearsal and a brief comfort break, guests were allowed into the throne room used for the presentations and we all took our seats.

When it was my turn to go forward to receive my award, I'm glad to say that I didn't 'fluff it'; HRH congratulated me and asked if I felt

Receiving my certificate from Princess Anne. Photograph © John Prater Photography

supported within the Probation Service (yes) – after a "good" she took half a step back – my signal to curtsey again and withdraw.

Part 10. Probation

After a group photograph, we were served lunch (not particularly impressive) before ten-minute sessions with HRH in small groups for informal chats. Unfortunately, our little group was dominated by guys talking about sport so I didn't have any chance to say anything.

Then it was outside for individual photographs on the red carpet on our own and with our guests.

Instead of each winner undertaking a project, which Elaine had been concerned about, the Butler Trust arranged for us to undertake an NVQ in 'The Development and Dissemination of Best Practice in a Correctional Setting' involving four one day sessions at Newbold Revel and other 'homework'.

Jo and me on the red carpet at Buckingham Palace

Chapter 49. Oldham Pride

In 2005, I had a call from Susan Wildman, formerly Head of PR for GMPS and one of the panel that had interviewed me and now Communications Manager for Oldham Council, to ask if I would speak at the opening of the first Oldham Pride.

I felt honoured to be invited to be one of the opening speakers and really pleased to note that the Prairie Dogs line dance group were also participating in the ceremony. When I realised that I recognised one of the dances they were doing from my time with the group, I joined in.

Looking round the displays, I came across the Police LGB association stand staffed by a former neighbour!

Chapter 50. Back to Highpoint

I've done a lot of presentations on trans issues at probation and prison venues. One that gave me particular pleasure was the Eastern Region 2008 Diversity Conference being held in the training centre at Highpoint. When I was originally invited, I was asked if I needed directions to the prison. I said I didn't think so as I've lived there from 1962 to 1965 when it had been RAF Stradishall.

It did seem strange waling into the Conference Centre which had previously been the Officers' Mess (dad had been a Warrant Officer so we would have used the Senior NCOs mess – now part of the prison). The central area had, of course, been massively changed during the conversion. The runways had been dug up and used as hardcore for the M11 motorway and returned to farm land – although you can still see where they used to be on aerial photographs. The quarters we lived in are still there, however, and seeing them again was nostalgic.

Part 10. Probation

Chapter 51. Inner Enigma

Inner Enigma was a support group set up in Manchester for Transsexual individuals. There were other TV/TS groups but the founders wanted somewhere where they could focus on issues relating to transitioning from one gender to another. Originally called Rebirth, it was formed in 1999 and met in the upstairs bar in Julia Grant's Showbar in the gay village.

The name was changed after Pam, one of the members, registered the domain name of Rebirth and offered it to the group. The leaders didn't want the domain to be held by any one individual and accused Pam of trying to make money out of the registration. This wasn't true – she only wanted to be reimbursed for the costs incurred. Nevertheless, the name was changed to Inner Enigma.

For a while, the group was affiliated to the LGF and run by a steering committee that any member could attend. LGF then suggested that IE should float off from the charity and exist as a separate entity. It later became clear that this was part of LGF redefining its own mission and becoming an LGB only organisation.

The original founders had, by then, moved on. Those of us who were left on the steering group set up a committee – and I prepared proposals for the organisation to register as a charity so that we could apply for funding. We organised a meeting that was publicised as far as we could. At that meeting, I put forward ideas of what we could do and what it would cost. It amounted to about £5,000 over about three years. Most of those present saw this as a bit of a pipe dream. In fact, having been set up as a charity, we did get grants from the Lottery and from Pride towards a befriending service and were successful bidding for the Greater Manchester Probation contract to support trans offenders. My knowledge of the service and of dealing with trans offenders obviously gave us a head start – but I made no attempt to influence the evaluation process.

By the end of the first year, we had well exceeded the pipe dream target of £5,000 and, in fact, our main problem was finding people to undertake work to provide services and activities that we could easily afford to fund. This was an issue that dogged the organisation all of the time.

With TV/ TS groups, transvestites often need permanent places where they can go to dress and mix with others on a regular basis. Transsexual individuals, in contrast, often start the transition process and need substantial support at that stage. Eventually, they are likely to go through surgery and complete the path they'd been on. Many then just want to disappear into the woodwork and get on with the rest of their lives as the gender they always felt themselves to be. They don't usually want to continue mixing with other trans people – they no longer need the support. Some, it is true, remain to provide support for the next generation of those transitioning. This tends to mean that there is a constant flow of people through a TS group – mainly of inexperienced individuals.

By now, IE was meeting in Taurus – using a room downstairs in the cellar. This was clearly not disabled friendly – a fact pointed out by one of the on-line members. She made the point that this stopped her from attending. We looked around and the only premises we could find that would be free of charge and available and disabled friendly was the International Hotel – another of Julia Grant's ventures. We could, however, only use it on Sunday afternoons.

This had its pros and cons. It meant that potential members would have more time on a Sunday to travel to and from meetings – but it would then exclude some who attended an LGB&T friendly church that met at the same time. Unfortunately, numbers started to fall away and instead of the thirty to forty that had attended early meetings and even the ten to fifteen that had attended Taurus, it often fell to fewer than five – including the organisers. To make matter worse, the member who had pressed for disabled access never ever attended a single meeting.

We eventually decided to return to an evening meeting as these had proved much more popular – but the damage had been done. We had also tried to organise social events – but trying to find an activity that sufficient people would support proved impossible.

I took several members to London for a protest outside the Royal College of Nursing – where there was a meeting discussing changes to the way in which trans people would be treated by the medical professions. When we got there, I think there were about eight to ten of us outside the venue – we were certainly outnumbered by the police! It was a very peaceful and good spirited protest.

At lunchtime, a group of the delegates attending the meeting came out to talk to us. I spoke to a short dapper guy who had introduced himself as being with South Staffordshire NHS. I asked how many GRS procedures they funded each year and he said "one". I started to have a go at him over the inadequacy of that service at which point he said "hang on a minute; I'm one of us!" I hadn't realised that he was female to male transsexual – why would I?

On several occasions I tried to hand over the Chair of IE to other members but each time something happened and I was faced with watching the organisation collapse or stepping back in. I stepped back in on three occasions – twice as Chair and once to complete overdue accounts for Companies House. Sadly, the pressures of being trans can cause mental illnesses and depression that impacted on their work for the group. This would have been far less critical if we hadn't been a registered charity and a company limited by guarantee. Those formal statuses place obligations on the official officers and directors.

The first time I handed over the Chair, 'R', my successor, failed to submit accounts on time and the group was fined by Companies House. The Chair then just disappeared from the scene and I was asked to take over again. When we were faced with a similar situation after the next time that I handed over the role, and being threatened with a £1,500 fine, I had sorted out all of the accounts from the mess they'd been left in and handed them over to 'A' the new Treasurer. They were effectively ready for submission and just needed sending off to Companies House. I then left on holiday. On my return, I found that the accounts had not been submitted.

I had been trying not to be involved in the committee meetings as I thought it was fairer on 'S', the new Chair, if she didn't have the old guard breathing down her neck. I felt I had to attend the next meeting however so that we could get things sorted out.

Part 10. Probation

'A' arrived late and the committee meeting had already started and had discussed various items including a proposal to extend the membership criteria to include non-binary individuals. I had pointed out that whilst this was fine, it would entail changing the constitution (which would require a vote at a General Meeting) and the registration with the Charities Commission as it did alter our objectives. 'A' then started to speak about her personal problems. To some extent, I felt it was OK to allow committee members to 'check in' and get things off their chests – but there has to be a limit for Committee meetings – which should, after all, be focussed on the operation of the group rather than individual problems. Those were more appropriately dealt with at the support group meetings themselves – or have a dedicated period before the 'business' meeting for committee members to raise issues of concern.

As 'S' was making no attempt to bring the meeting back to the business agenda – and we absolutely had to deal with the issue of the accounts, I felt obliged to interrupt A's report of the problems she was having. I was, by then, quite frustrated and probably sharper than I might have been when I asked if the accounts have been submitted and, when told they had not, asked why. A then became agitated and said she was leaving. I insisted that she leave the accounts with us so that I could deal with them.

My views were supported by other committee members including SH. S, the chair then also became agitated and said she wasn't at all happy with what had happened and asked the committee to leave.

The next day we received a four-page rambling tirade of an email claiming that SH and I had behaved like Rottweilers. In it she made serious allegations about SH and me – which I asked her to withdraw. She did not withdraw the remarks but resigned from the committee.

She had also pointed out that she had participated in the Pride parade that year and asked where I had been on that day. Well, the answer was simple, I'd been on the Probation Service float as I had almost every year since I'd joined Probation. It was so sad to see someone who had worked hard for the group suffer such a breakdown – which it proved to be.

We called another committee meeting to elect a replacement chair. As no one else was prepared to take on the role, it fell to me once more.

In April 2012, we held a committee meeting at my house. At the end of it, I advised the other committee members that I planned to retire from the Chair when I reached 65. I was asked when that was and I looked at my watch and announced "two hours fifteen minutes". I stuck with that decision and, sadly, IE is no longer functioning.

Chapter 52. Counselling

I have continued to provide a counselling service since I first qualified with interruptions only due to ill health, focussing on individuals with gender identity issues. Over the years, I've dealt with around 100 individuals.

For a number of years, I did it mainly as part of the Lesbian and Gay Foundation's face to face team – even when they abandoned support for trans people. However, when they

Part 10. Probation

proposed limiting counselling to just six or twelve sessions per person, I felt I could no longer continue with them. My experience had shown that many trans people need support over much longer periods of time as they go through the transition process.

I've also worked with a couple of other venues.

In 2002 I was contacted about a client by Maundy Grange in Accrington. Whilst seeing this client, I saw that Julie Hesmondhaigh – who played the transsexual character Hayley in Coronation Street, and a supporter of Maundy Grange, was attending a coffee morning one Saturday.

If they were having a screen transsexual person – they could have the real thing as well! So I went along. I joined the queue for autographs. When I got to the front of the queue, Julie looked at me questioningly and asked "we've met before haven't we?" "Yes, at Annie's. You made us cups of tea" I reminded her. Annie Wallace had been Corrie's transsexual advisor and a few of us had met up for tea one afternoon. (Annie is now headmistress Sally St. Claire in the Channel 4 soap opera Hollyoak.)

Probably the most difficult case I ever had to deal with was Cassie, an individual in a hospice who had MS and had come out as transsexual only when terminally ill. I was warned from the start that it was unlikely that she would see Christmas that year. Cassie had already lost most of her power of speech. All she could do was make sounds that only the nursing staff understood and nod or shake her head. One of the basic lessons in counselling is that you never ask 'closed' questions; you always use open questions. But the usual rules didn't apply here. It was only by asking questions that Cassie could answer with a nod or shake of the head that we could communicate. Because of my personal experience of being transsexual, I was able to ask her questions and say things that showed that I understood and shared how she felt. I honestly believe that it was SO important that she knew that she had been understood.

She was the hardest client I ever had to deal with. I would go out to my car afterwards and just cry. Even now, as I remember her, there are tears in my eyes.

As predicted, she died before the end of the year. I received a phone call from the nursing home while I was talking to a member of Inner Enigma who had self-harmed. Gilda, who had also visited Cassie with me on one occasion when we gave a talk to the staff on trans issues, came with me to the funeral. As so often happens, Cassie was referred to as 'male' during the service "because that's how most of those present knew 'him' – although he had identified as transsexual at the end". How about how Cassie felt? It seemed totally disrespectful to the person whose life they were supposed to be celebrating.

Since my split with LGF, I have continued to work on my own. I have the use of a room at a council owned venue one evening a week. Clients are asked to contribute a small amount towards costs but, if they can't afford anything, then I won't turn them away.

I did have one client who pleaded poverty in spite of being a smoker but then asked if I could use my credit card to pay a private psychiatrist in London a significant amount for a consultation – which they would give me. That felt like they were 'taking the proverbial'. I

Part 10. Probation

felt that if they could afford £300 for the consultation and travel costs, they could afford to contribute £5 towards the supervision costs that I had to pay out every few weeks.

As well as being a counsellor, I qualified as a Counselling Supervisor and have undergone training as a mentor. I haven't actively sought supervisees, I did the course originally to support other members of the Inner Enigma committee who might be counselling or otherwise supporting members.

Part 11. Moving on

Chapter 53. New Start

In 2001, the insurance policy we'd taken out to cover the mortgage when buying the house in Little Paxton matured. I'd already taken out a loan from it to cover my surgery – but there was still a significant balance with which to pay off the remains of the business loan – and put a deposit down on a house.

I'd realised that my probation and state pensions would mean that I'd be receiving too much to qualify for any housing benefit – but probably leave me short if rents kept rising. By buying a place, there was a reasonable chance of increasing my equity and, eventually, paying off the mortgage.

My budget did rather limit my location options. I also wanted to avoid being stuck in rush hour traffic for several hours each day.

Then I found a place that had potential. It had been repossessed and had been left unoccupied for a while – with inevitable vandalism as the result. But it was cheap. Even allowing for repairs including new back door, new patio doors – completely refitting the kitchen and redecorating throughout, it was still within my budget.

The house was a three bedroomed semi-detached. The style was mock Tudor at the front – with false beams painted black above the ground floor and white plaster between the beams. The side and back of the house were plain brick.

The entrance hall was almost non-existent; just room for two doors to open up to left and right and stairs up to the first floor directly ahead. Well, I say doors to right and left – but all of the doors had been removed. The stairs were a vivid blue – far too powerful to face first thing in the morning.

To the left of the hall was the lounge that ran from the picture window at the front to what should have been a patio window at the rear. Unfortunately, the patio window was broken and boarded up. There had been a conservatory at the back leading out from the (missing) patio doors – the base was still there but the rest was missing. I later heard that someone had turned up early one morning and removed it!

The lounge was a challenge. All of the woodwork and the radiators had been painted silver. Skirting boards, false beams, door frames (all of the doors were missing) and a plate rail with numerous wooden block brackets were all silver. Stripping the paint from the skirting boards, ceiling beams and door frames was bad enough – but the nooks and crannies of the plate rail would have been a nightmare so I simply removed it and filled in any holes!

Part 11. Moving On

There was wooden flooring too – but paint had been spilled around and there was a cooker standing in front of a fireplace. The chimney breast was brick faced and there was space for a gas fire.

On the other side, the hall led into the dining room – then into the kitchen. The ceiling in the kitchen was blackened and the windows broken. It looked as though someone had set off a firework on the window ledge. A door led into the back garden. The kitchen would clearly need completely refitting.

Upstairs, to the left led to the principal bedroom at the front and a smaller bedroom, which would serve as an office, at the back. To the right was the bathroom and toilet and a third bedroom. There was access to the loft from the landing.

While negotiating, further damage was done – and I managed to get the price reduced even further.

Once it was mine, I redecorated throughout; about the only places I missed were the cupboard under the stairs and inside a wardrobe in the bedroom. I had the new kitchen installed and a wardrobe and dressing table in the bedroom.

Unfortunately, the bedroom furniture had not been made in accordance with the design I'd submitted. Each place there were drawers, they had put in one less that I had asked for. The centre section of the wardrobe should have had four drawers, there were only three; each of the bedside cabinets should have had three drawers, there were only two and the side section of the dressing table should have had four and there were only three. The wardrobe itself hadn't been made to fit and they had planned to block off and waste the excess space along the wall. I had quite a dispute with the suppliers and told them I was only prepared to pay for the percentage of the work that I considered they had done.

At one point they instructed the fitter to start removing the furniture that had been installed. He was about five foot nothing. I was ten inches taller and twice his weight. I stood in front of the wardrobe and said that if he wanted to remove it, he would have to get me out of the way first and if he touched me, it would be assault. He decided against any physical confrontation.

Once the place was redecorated, new doors installed and carpets laid, and the new kitchen and wardrobe and all the tiling in the bathroom had been done, I didn't want to leave the property vacant so I moved in.

Chris and her then husband Steve helped with the move. Getting my stuff down in the lift from the twelfth floor of Albion Towers took longer than we'd hoped but we got some of my stuff down to the house on the first day. There was still quite a bit to shift the next day but we'd had enough.

Chris and Steve went home and Gilda was due to come over with a takeaway for us to eat. When she arrived, I realised that all my cutlery was still up at the flat. Gilda suggested I go next door to borrow some what we needed – but I was filthy from shifting stuff all day and didn't want the neighbours' first impression to be of such a scruffy and very unfeminine person. She then said she would go round.

Part 11. Moving On

She was gone quite a while and I was concerned that the take away was getting cold by the time she returned.

"You don't have to worry about your neighbours," she told me, "It's a couple of lesbians who have been worried about who was moving in next door to them!" That was certainly a relief. I had, indeed, been concerned about who would be next door – it could so easily have been some thuggish chavs who might have caused me nothing but trouble.

After moving in, I had the conservatory replaced and a decent size garage built to give plenty of space for the car and for garden implements.

Until the garage was built, the side of my property butted onto the backs of a couple of semi-detached and a bungalow on a road leading off mine. Most of these were unoccupied at the time and youths from the area played football in the back gardens. Their ball came into my garden and one of the kids scrambled over the fence to retrieve it. I was at an upstairs window and yelled at him – overlooking the fact that my voice dropped an octave or so as I shouted at him. My cover had been blown!

There were a number of incidents after this – with windows being broken and verbal abuse. Some of the kids would call to me from down the road; they'd also knock on my door and ask if I was a man or woman and when I responded with why do you ask, they'd say "You've got very big hands"; I'd look at my hands and say "I suppose they are"; "Your voice is very deep" "Yes, it is isn't it". Some very young children then started ringing my bell and running away. I eventually had words with them – and some of the parents.

The next day they were down the road and called to me and waved. I waved back. A few minutes later there was a knock. When I opened the door three of the children were standing there. We started to talk and I sat down on my doorstep.

The following day they waved again and called "Hi Helen". I'd made some friends.

The plastic sheeting installed to protect the windows from being broken

Not everyone was friendly though and I had several broken windows and 'tranny' scratched on the front door. In the end, I planted a hedge of Pyracantha and some Twisted Willows to provide a screen. While these were growing, I set up a trellis in front of the lounge windows with Clematis and covered the downstairs windows at the front with plastic sheeting on wooden frames to block the stones. The effectiveness of this was demonstrated by the fact that,

Part 11. Moving On

by the time the planted screens made them superfluous, there were nearly twenty holes in the plastic sheets.

I reported the incidents to the police and was amused when two officers came to see me. It seemed that they didn't dare come singly!

Eventually, I established a good working relationship with the local community police officer and had his mobile number in mine. I also volunteered to join the Salford Police division Independent Advisory Group as a transgendered lead. I later joined the Greater Manchester Police Strategic LGB&T IAG – but this folded just as I was joining.

The area I'd moved to was just across Trafford Road from a notorious estate. It was a collection of cul-de-sacs but there was a rat run from the corner of Trafford Road and Eccles New Road – just behind the old church steeple standing on its own near the Regent Road roundabout at the start of the M602.

The street lighting in the area has large globes on the top of each lamp post and these, with the church steeple peeking over the rooftops of the half-timbered houses, gives the impression of being in a small country town. Or, rather, it would if it wasn't for the frequent police, ambulance and fire engine sirens and the sound of India nine-nine[23], the police helicopter, circling over the nearby estate. It's not where I would live by choice – but it is convenient for work and for the Village. The price is not only the personal abuse I've faced – but the general level of incidents in the vicinity since I moved to the area: four lots of shootings (including 2 murders) – one of which I heard from my flat and prison van escapes. Four local pubs have been closed down by the police.

One of the things I really did notice after transition was the way you are treated as a female compared with being seen as male.

When I wanted to replace my car, I had a pretty good idea what sort of thing I wanted. I was used to decent performance and road-holding and they were important to me. The Cavalier SRi was, I felt, too masculine and I wanted something with a bit more style.

When I visited one car lot, the salesman tried to convince me that a Rover 213 would be appropriate. "At least try it" he said. I just wondered what out of 'stylish', 'decent performance' and 'good road-holding' he hadn't understood from my requirements! All three by the look of things! I did test drive it. He asked what I thought. I could have told him that it didn't meet my requirements but I just said "I don't like the colour".

I sold the existing car to some youths who had beaten me down on the price. They'd originally called a couple of weeks before and had been rude about my voice but when they called again, I agreed to show them the car. By then I was aware that the wipers were beginning to play up and I just wanted to get rid of it. We negotiated a price and they offered to pay all but £20 and come back with the rest the next day. I was quite convinced that this wouldn't happen but told them I would hang onto the log book until they had paid in full. They then asked if they could have some of the money back again as there was no petrol in the tank.

---

[23] I — India being the ninth letter of the alphabet so the call sign becomes 999.

Part 11. Moving On

A day or so later, I had a call from the police.

"Was I the owner of Vauxhall Cavalier registration D******?"

"I used to be but I sold it earlier this week. Why".

"It's been found in the vicinity of an incident. Can you tell me where you were at 11.30 this morning?"

"I was at the headquarters of the West Midlands Probation Service in a meeting with about forty other probation service staff. Is that a good enough alibi for you?"

It was – but I would be required to make a statement – could I call in to the police station to do so sometime.

It seems that the youths had bought the car to avoid being in one that was stolen and possibly being watched for by the police. They would then use the car for several robberies in one day.

That seemed a reasonable approach – but I think in their case it was flawed as one of them had given me his gran's address as his own!

When I went to the police station to make a statement, I was asked if I'd had any previous names. I said I had but when they asked what they were I asked why they needed to know.

"We need to check whether or not you have a record."

I pointed out that I was a witness not a suspect and that I worked for the Probation Service who would have checked my record before offering me a job and if anything had happened since, they'd presumably have dismissed me so I wasn't prepared to give my previous names.

Chapter 54. Eliminating the Male

In transitioning from male to female, it can be useful to portray an unambiguous image. In my case, I invested in skirt suits for work – in spite of the fact that many female colleagues wore trousers or even jeans. My make-up was as immaculate as I could make it – my nails manicured, eyebrows trimmed. I was complimented on my appearance by staff at my local Sainsbury's.

I rejected any 'masculine' interests and tried to interest myself in feminine pastimes. I SHOULDN'T be interested in male things!

I still see this as a valid approach up to a point. Anything that helps those around you to accept you as female even if it involves fitting in with stereotypes can help.

Gradually, however, having established myself in other people's minds as female, I could wear trousers rather than skirts. If other women near me didn't wear make up all the time — perhaps I'd fit in better without so much. Some of my female friends enjoy Formula One – so why shouldn't I?

If you want to blend in, I also realised that you need to adjust your presentation to others around you. Most of the folks round where I live tend to dress very casually – very few dress up to go shopping for example. My local Sainsbury's, for example, is right on the edge of an estate that is regarded as rough. It was just opposite there that Indian student Anuj Bidve

Part 11. Moving On

was shot and killed on Boxing Day 2011 – and just up the road that a gang attacked a prison van and released a prisoner. On the other hand, stars from Corrie and other TV shows shopped there regularly.

These days I wear what I like and do what I want and, if some of those things don't seem particularly feminine, I can live with that.

Chapter 55. Flotilla in Greece

A flotilla holiday – cruising in a yacht on crystal clear waters under a brilliant blue sky broken with just the occasional fluffy white cloud was my idea of heaven. Now, at last, I was making that dream come true.

I had walked down from my house to Anchorage tram stop and was on my way to Piccadilly where I'd catch the train to Manchester airport – then on to Nidri in Greece. I'd already dropped my case off at the airport and checked it in the previous day so only had my hand luggage.

I wrote the following account for an internet diary 'Ms Dale's Diary[24]' I kept at the time – this was, in fact from the final 'episode' published in 2003:

An experience of a lifetime

(other people's names have been changed to protect me! Or have they?)

On 22nd September 2002, I walked down to the tram, which I then took to Piccadilly; caught the train to the airport for a flight to the Greek Islands for a sailing holiday.

As I was on the tram, I was wondering what the hell I was doing – and about the risk I was taking. The holiday involved a week in a hotel at a beach resort with dinghy sailing, windsurfing and cycling as part of the package plus other beach facilities from other operators; the second week would be on board a Moody 31 yacht with strangers. I had no idea who those strangers would be – nor even whether they'd be men or women or some guys some girls. I did know that there would be up to 4 of us on the yacht. We would be part of a flotilla with a dozen or so other yachts in the company of a 'lead crew'.

I'd booked some 'brush up' training as much to meet some of my fellow sailors as for the actual tuition. That, I discovered on arrival, would be the Friday and Saturday of the first week. In the meantime, I had the use of the beach facilities.

My main concern was around how long it would take people to suss out that I was TS – and what their reaction would be when they did. Would I cause a rift with some of the flotilla accepting me while others were uncomfortable around me? Would those I was to share a yacht with kick up a fuss? It was with some trepidation, therefore, that I headed out to the airport. Would I end up spending all the time on my own – excluded from the festivities? Even if the others didn't suss me – or had no problem with me being TS, would they all be couples/ groups or (very likely) much younger than I?

The sailing itself would be no problem; heck when you've yacht raced across the Channel in a Force 9 gale – the Southern Ionian's usually light winds would be easy to handle; I'm also

---

[24] An obvious take off of Mrs Dales Diary – a popular radio soap opera of the 50s and 60s

Part 11. Moving On

an experienced dinghy sailor with a couple of thousand of hours of sail time. The social side was a different issue – and it was about this that I was apprehensive (scared ****less more like!).

When sailing, you are likely to get wet. Make up and well-groomed hairdos don't last long. You are usually in unisex type outfits in dinghies: T-shirt, shorts, etc – and lifejackets soon conceal any other differences. It wouldn't be easy trying to maintain a feminine image.

BUT, I'd earned this holiday. It was very much MY sort of break. So I was on my way.

The flight was nearly an hour late but caught up 20 minutes en route. We eventually got to Prevekas where the Neilson rep met about 20 of us; led us to the bus for the 45-minute trip to Nidri on Levekas. There was bottled water on the bus for us (Neilson's attention to detail was superb). We checked in to the hotel at about 11.30pm; I dumped my bags and wandered out into the grounds and the 'tree bar' (built around a tree). I got chatting to a couple of guys, had a couple of drinks then headed for bed.

This holiday is not for those that like to laze around all day. Briefing the next morning started at 9.30am! Some of the new arrivals were on 4-day training courses, while 5 of us had decided we only needed an improver or brush up course. The 4-day course was mainly the Monday – Thurs while we were scheduled for Friday and Sat. So much for my plan to use the training to mingle with my fellow flotilla sailors! The rep then told us about the planned evening excursions. I told him to put me down for everything! I'd mingle somehow and try anything (almost).

The five of us doing the two-day training later in the week then walked up to the dinghy/windsurfing area where we joined one of the groups – in my case the advanced dinghy sailing. That afternoon, I sailed with a girl from Scotland called Angela. At my encouragement, she pushed the boat harder than she had previously tried. Eventually, we overdid it a fraction and capsized – no problem, this is normal in dinghies and the water was so warm and buoyant. I did receive a heck of a bruise as a consequence – all of the inside of my upper arm was covered.

That evening, there was a meal for those involved in the flotilla groups. I met a young couple who introduced themselves as George and Chas; Chas being short for Caroline – George then explained that Chas had been her name before the change!! I was very tempted to say something – but didn't. (Does anyone need me to clarify that George had been joking?) I got to become friendly with George and Chas over the course of the holiday –but more of that later.

Tuesday, more sailing in the morning — practising race starts. I'm a bit beyond racing dinghies these days – certainly single-handed Lasers (I sold mine nearly 20 years ago). So, I decided to take the afternoon off and laze by the pool. George and Chas turned up later and I asked if they had any plans for dinner that evening; we arranged to meet up. Angela was in the room next to mine and she knocked on my door to ask what I was doing for dinner so she joined us – as did about 6 others (the others seeing me as the social secretary!). So much for my fears of having to eat on my own! All that week, I had very little time on my own; I went on planned excursions on the Wed, Thurs & Friday evenings. Saturday, another group

Part 11. Moving On

of us got together including the guy I had just trained with and his wife. It really was a matter of if you saw anyone on their own, they were invited to join you. Fabulous atmosphere.

There were a few other incidents I didn't mention in the diary which I thought were quite amusing: Angela and I were practicing 'man overboard' drill. I threw over the dummy and called 'man overboard'. She then asked me to deal with the jib – but I reminded her that I was now in the water and unable to help. After a couple of attempts when she kept forgetting that I was not supposed to help, I called 'man overboard' again as I rolled backwards off the boat into the water. Then she had no choice but to deal with everything herself while I just lay on my back in the warm water, my buoyancy aid keeping me afloat.

One of the training sessions was in the use of trapezes. The instructor explained how you should put one foot on the side of the hull – push out with that leg then bring the other to join it. You then leant outwards relying on the trapeze wire connected from about two thirds of the way up the mast to the harness around your waist to take your weight. He asked for a volunteer to try it – so I stepped forward. As I smoothly hooked on then pushed myself out the instructor asked if I had done it before. I told him I sailed Fireballs – which explained everything. In fact, I hadn't done much trapeze work as that had been Hugh's role as crew.

Another time we were out on a Hobbie catamaran. As we came back into shore, we were supposed to turn up into wind just as we got to the beach – but my crewmate who was helming timed her move a little too early. We were head to wind – but too far from shore. There was a breakwater preventing us from going forward so our options were limited. I took the helm and pushed the sail out against the breeze and we started to reverse – allowing me to steer us to the beach. I think even the instructor was surprised.

Back to the diary:

Sunday afternoon I met the two guys I was to share a boat with – I'd already met Kathryn, the other girl. We were due to move aboard that afternoon but, at the last minute, Kathryn backed out leaving me on my own with the two guys. I took the aft cabin; Tony had the fore cabin and Rich used the fore cabin for changing and slept in the saloon. Adequate sleeping space – if Kathryn had been with us, it would have been a push. It was pointed out to me that Tony and Rich had done 5 previous flotillas in the Ionian Sea; Tony had trained as a 'competent crew' Rich as 'Day Skipper' Rich, therefore, was nominally skipper of the yacht Lia. Fair do's, they had nearly 70 days sailing experience each in the Ionian where they would usually encounter winds up to force 4 or 5 (anything more forecast and the flotilla is usually 'storm bound' in port). My 50 years' experience (about 17 of which had been spent owning the equivalent of Formula 3 racing dinghies compared with the family saloon of a Moody 31) only added up to about 400 days plus 30 on the tidal Solent, 2 on the Bristol channel, a Round The Island race and 3 cross channel races – in winds up to gale force 9. Clearly their male 70 days flotilla beat my female 450 days in a wide range of craft. (Memo: must get my Ocean Yachtmaster certificate! – well, at least Coastal Skipper (next up from Dayskipper) PS: I've started the training for this!)

The flotilla crews had a meal that evening – then slept aboard the yachts.

Part 11. Moving On

Monday morning, we had a briefing then set sail. The plan was to sail to a harbour about 9 miles NNE of the main base. We were free to make our own way there and stop where we liked for lunch, we opted to anchor in a small bay and had a swim from the boat before lunch. Tony's incessant chattering was a bit irritating – but not impossible. Then we had a message over the radio to say that our overnight stop had to be changed as the original destination was full. We had to head for a different port south of our start point. Those familiar with compasses will realise that this is the opposite direction. As we approached the harbour (Sivota), crews began calling up for mooring instructions. "Listen to those plonkers" said Tony "they haven't a clue what they are doing". This went on every time one of the flotilla called the lead boat. I eventually pointed out that the crews were doing what we had been told to do. I then went below. I suspect that my tone of voice may have indicated a degree of irritation. I was beginning to suspect that Tony was the plonker – not the other crews. I'd also been a little concerned about Rich's navigation and seamanship when calculating the distance we had to sail when he measured the direct route over land rather than keeping to water.

Tuesday, we sailed from Sivota to Kioni – a lovely little port. On the way in to the harbour we picked up a nice wind. The others were about to reef the sails – it really wasn't necessary – all we needed was good boat control. A yacht, with the wind from any direction other than dead astern does not go quite where it is pointed; the sideways effect of the wind pushes you downwind. So, if you want to get somewhere you aim upwind and anticipate drifting down to where you want to be. This is very basic stuff. Where did Tony keep aiming? At the point he wanted to get to. Err, 'competent' crew? And where was the official 'skipper' (the 'day skipper')? Well, they said they had done the course, not that they had passed. With a bit of coaching, we got the boat sailing well and aimed roughly in the right direction. Funnily enough we went faster that afternoon than they had achieved all the previous week!

That night I was a bit annoyed when the guys went off without taking the rubbish ashore to the waste bins. (In Greece, toilet paper does not go down the pan – it goes into a small bin in the bathroom and is then thrown away).

The next morning (Wednesday), after briefing, they decided they would visit the local museum; no invitation to me to join them; no discussion about the impact this had on our departure time. Nothing. I expressed my feelings that there were two crews on the boat – the two of them and me. Made no difference.

We left Kioni about 11.30 and sailed and motored around to Friskado on the next island – anchoring in a little bay for lunch and a swim. That evening was a repeat of previous ones as far as tidying the boat was concerned – so I decided to leave it to them and remind them to take the rubbish with them when they went ashore.

Thursday, we sailed for Vasiliki – a resort renowned for its own local wind 'Eric' that usually springs up in the afternoon. We stopped for lunch as usual in a little bay. Another of our flotilla 'Wendy Rose', sailed by a couple on honeymoon, was near us and I dived off our yacht and swam over to theirs for a chat – what a fabulous experience! I got out of the water before the two guys and was rather tempted to hoist the anchor and leave them there!

Part 11. Moving On

I didn't. We had trouble with the anchor winch and found that our radio wasn't receiving. Wendy Rose passed messages for us to the lead boat. As we left the bay, the wind picked up and we had a good sail into Vasiliki. The two guys were chatting on the fore-deck and I was left to handle both sails and helm. No problem. I had the sails trimmed as I wanted them and the boat on an ideal course. The entire rig started to 'hum'.

I can remember, to this day, Tony turning to me and asking in a very condescending tone if I still had the motor running.

"No Tony."

"What's that noise then?"

"Tony, that's the sound a yacht makes when it's being sailed properly!" (I can also do 'patronising').

As we approached Vasiliki, Tony and Rich who had remained at the bow, Tony clearly sulking, suggested that we drop the sails and motor the rest of the way. I was feeling mischievous and told them that I intended to sail right up to the quay. I could see the terror in their eyes!

When we had halved the remaining distance to the quay, I started the motor and told them to drop the main while I furled the jib.

We reached the moorings and backed up to the quay as instructed. That evening there was a 'flotilla dinner' – I had a drink with George, Caroline, Sue and Geoff beforehand. When we reached the taverna for the dinner, there were 4 seats at one end of the table and some at the other end near my crewmates. I was (thankfully) separated from Tony by Matt the flotilla skipper. As usual, Tony was his usually entertaining self (not). At the end of the meal, the other boats simply divided the bill between the number of people. Tony and Rich were quite happy to do the same (especially as they'd had a starter and I had not) – until they realised that my main course had been rather more than theirs! Almost everyone then went on to a bar for another drink. By then I'd had a couple of cocktails and half a bottle of wine – so I was starting to relax!

Others asked me where my crew were. "Don't know, and I'm just glad they aren't here" I told them. Some, including Caroline asked how I was putting up with them. I remarked to Caroline (introduced as Chas 'before the change' – on the first night) that I was very tempted "to freak them out by telling them I'd had a sex change!" She laughed at the thought! I then said "want to know the funniest bit? "What?" she asked. "I have" I told her. "Wow" she said.

I didn't tell Tony or Rich. They didn't deserve to be privileged with that information.

That night they returned to the boat – making a hell of a noise – at 1.30am. They came down to the saloon and started to talk. Rich told Tony to keep his voice down – but this had no effect. I opened my cabin door and said "can't you two show some f****ing consideration for other people and not come crashing back on board at this time like a herd of elephants". They continued talking (somewhat quieter) until I fell asleep. I could hear them moaning about 'snide remarks' and 'being excluded' by other members of the flotilla.

Part 11. Moving On

The next morning, I went into the main saloon and Tony asked how I was. I told him that I was unhappy and would be asking the lead crew to remove me from the boat as I wasn't prepared to share with them any longer. I pointed out that I could not bear the thought of being on my own in a harbour with just the two of them for company that night. (The flotilla had a 'free sail' that day and could go where each crew wanted so long as they were back in Nidri the next day).

I returned on the lead boat 'Siva' to Nidri where Neilson put me up in a hotel for the last two nights of my holiday without any extra cost. As we were leaving Vasiliki, the couple on Wendy Rose (Natalya and Mark) called up to offer to take me out with them the next day.

On the Saturday, I sailed on Wendy Rose – a Beneteau Oceanis 361 (a rather more luxurious boat than the Moody 31); superb fittings, so much more space, longer, wider and more headroom. As we tacked for the first time, I realised that I was sailing with a crew who knew what they were doing. Now, to be fair, the Ionian is not a challenging area and attracts beginners so it's probably unfair to judge Tony and Rich against experienced crews (well, it would be if they hadn't boasted of their 5 previous flotillas and competent crew/ dayskipper training).

Returning to Nidri that afternoon, we passed Lia. I couldn't quite work out the course they were sailing and the way the sails were trimmed. For the sailors amongst you, they were close hauled and 'tacking' (well – gybing) across the wind. This would have made sense of the wind hadn't been from astern over the starboard quarter! I MIGHT have understood if they'd been broad reaching rather than running – and sails trimmed accordingly. The truth was, I suspect, that they thought the wind was blowing from the opposite direction. And Tony called the other crews 'plonkers'!!

Several times during the fortnight people remarked on my sailing and asked if I'd been doing it long. I told them I'd been sailing on and off for 50 years; each time the comment was along the lines of "15 years – that's quite a while". "No", I'd reply, "50, 5-0 years". No one believed that this was possible – everyone put my age as early to mid-40s (or at very worst 47).

Apart from Caroline I told 3 other people about my past; this was during a conversation that started with the aggressive effects of testosterone; went through the differences between men and women (including the Mars and Venus books); and eventually led onto transsexualism as a kind of interface between the two. (One of the guys had said that his brain mapping seemed to be more typically female than male). He asked how it would be possible to tell if he was TS – I'd mentioned by this point that I had some experience of counselling transsexual people. Eventually he asked how I would help someone to decide if they were TS or not. It was the last but one night of the holiday so I said: "It's based on a good understanding of typical feelings experienced from conversations with more than 300 transsexual individuals and personal experience". The two guys didn't pick up on this at all as far as I could see – but as we walked up the street Angela said "I must be very naïve. I hadn't realised you were TS". This in spite of sharing dinghies most of the first week; meals together, talking etc.

Part 11. Moving On

The major watershed for me was being in close proximity with 50 other people for two weeks with no comments about my history. When I did mention it to a couple of people, a reaction that showed that they hadn't even considered it – followed by total continuing acceptance of me as an individual. This in spite of being in swimming costumes/ T-shirts and shorts most of the day, no make-up, hair messed up from the wind and spray.

Far from being shunned and having to spend most of the time on my own, I made so many friends and only had two meals on my own and one of those was an early breakfast. Both Caroline and Angela (the ones I did tell about being TS) have asked if I'm interested on joining them sailing next year.

While on the holiday, I met a guy called Keith who told me that if I enjoyed sailing, I might be interested in a group he belonged to called SPICE. He tried to explain what it was – but I didn't really get the message. He said he would get them to send me details when he got back to UK. Which he did. The outcome was a new chapter in my life which we get to later in the story!

I did return to the area some years later, by which time I had qualified as a Day Skipper and was in charge of the yacht.

Part 12. Riding the Roller Coaster

Chapter 56. Relationships: to Tell or Not to Tell?

As I joined an online chat room one evening, I saw that someone had posted "No mate, if I wanted a crew to sail round the Med with me, it would have to be female"

Sailing? The Med? Hmmm

"Hello, I'm female and I sail," I posted.

"Really? What sailing have you done?"

"Flotilla in Greece, weekend in Anglesey, bits round the Solent, a Round the Island Race, three Cross Channel Races, 20 years dinghy racing."

"Oh, ok. Yes that's proper sailing."

We chatted a while longer and he eventually asked if I wanted to see a photo. I told him I'd love to see what his boat was like!

After exchanging some emails, we spoke on the phone and I arranged to go down to Weston Super Mare where he kept his yacht up the River Axe. The problem with his mooring was that it was only possible to get in and out one hour either side of high tide and not always then. He said the next time he'd be down there was the following Friday but that high tides were 12 noon and midnight.

I told him I couldn't make the lunchtime due to a hospital appointment in the morning but could make it for midnight. He questioned the fact that I was offering to meet someone I didn't know at midnight in a secluded boatyard! "It's OK" I told him "I'm used to dealing with murderers" "F****ing hell Helen, what do you do?" "I work for Probation".

In fact, it wasn't midnight that we met. I drove down after my hospital appointment and would have arrived mid-afternoon if I hadn't had a problem with the car en route. I had just passed the Frankley services on the M5 motorway near Birmingham when my engine just died and all the instruments failed. I was in the outside lane doing seventy miles per hour at the time; traffic was busy; both inside lanes had traffic – so I put on my hazard warning lights and slipped the car out of gear and coasted across the two inside lanes onto the hard shoulder.

I called for the AA who arrived after about half an hour (useful to be able to say you are a woman on her own). The mechanic said it wasn't safe to work on the car where it was so he would tow me to the next exit. As we drove the couple of miles to junction 4, I noticed that the ignition warning light kept coming on and then going out again. I mentioned this to the patrolman and suggested it might indicate a bad connection. He agreed and we were both proved right. The earth strap from the alternator had snapped. The patrolman disconnected the battery while he worked on the car. Having repaired the earth strap he asked if I would try starting the car again. I asked, in my sweetest voice, if it wouldn't help to reconnect the battery first.

The delay cost me about an hour which wasn't too bad.

When I arrived at the boatyard it was about half past four, I guess. I met John and he took my kit and led me down to his boat.

Part 12. Riding the Roller Coaster

"I won't be at all offended if you text a friend with my vehicle registration and where you are" he told me.

"What makes you think I haven't done so already?"

"Have you?"

"Oh Yes".

Chris and I had an arrangement, previously only used by her, for us to do just that!

That evening we went out for a meal – then back to the boat. The sleeping accommodation was in the forepeak and cramped. It was little more than a triangular shelf in the bows – with very little headroom. John made a comment that he wasn't sure whether to come on to me or not – to which I replied "not on a first date".

The next day, we waited for the high tide and watched as the water level in the river rose gradually, eventually starting to cover the bottom of the rudder. That was as high as it got. High pressure was sitting over the country at the time – giving sunny settled weather but also stopping the high tide from getting as high as it would normally do. As the tide stalled then started to ebb, we decided to drive along the coast to Watchet where there was a classic boat rally.

When I logged onto my emails back in Manchester, I found one from John that he had sent some days before raising the possibility that I might be transsexual. I replied saying that I assumed that the previous night had answered his question.

I went back down again a week or so later and we did manage to get the yacht out of the river and onto the Severn Estuary. The plan was to sail over to Cardiff, have lunch there then come back over to the Somerset side and have tea somewhere like Watchet before returning in time for the next high tide to allow us to get back up to the mooring.

As we set course for the Welsh shore, I asked if we were heading for Cardiff, what the town or city off our starboard bow was (I could see what looked like a large sports stadium). "No idea," said John. I thought I might have an idea! As we pulled into the marina in 'Cardiff', I looked up at the sign on the jetty. It read 'Barry Island Yacht Club'. Never mind, it didn't really matter. We moored the yacht then went ashore for lunch. When we returned to the yacht, we found it was high and dry – and would remain so until the tide came back in several hours later. We spent the rest of the afternoon in the Yacht Club bar – playing snooker.

Once the yacht was refloated, we sailed back to Weston with me on the helm. John had seemed nervous when I first took the tiller but seemed to relax when he realised I wasn't a total novice.

As we reached the mooring, John took a line and jumped onto the pontoon to secure the bow then came to the stern to throw me a line to secure the back of the boat. As he threw it to me, it would have been much better if he had let go instead of coming with the rope. As he fell into the muddy water, I tried not to laugh. I did; honestly. But it was impossible not to.

Some weeks later John asked if he could come and see me in Manchester over the August Bank Holiday. I said it would be fine but I would be on a float in a parade on the Saturday.

Part 12. Riding the Roller Coaster

Probation had been the first public body to take part in the Manchester Pride Parade and I'd been involved in the floats since joining the organisation – I had only missed their first time which had been 3 months before I started working there.

As the floats gathered for the parade, John looked around him then said "do I get the feeling this parade is something to do with gays?" "Yes – not a problem is it" "Not at all – you just didn't tell me".

Next morning, I turned to him and said "you do realise what I am don't you?" "Yes – I do now".

The relationship continued for a while after this but John would make arrangements to come up – then just not arrive. I wouldn't hear from him for weeks or even months then he'd be on the phone chatting as though we had been talking an hour earlier. Eventually, when he rang to arrange another visit, I told him that I enjoyed his company but I wasn't prepared to keep planning weekends around him and for him to not turn up. I told him to call me on the Friday and if I was still free, he'd be welcome to come to Manchester. That was the last I heard of him.

Telling or not telling and, if so, when, is a perennial problem for trans people. If you say something right at the start, there is a very good chance that you will not see them for dust. I had two profiles at one time on 'Plenty of Fish'. On one I said nothing about being trans – on the other I did mention my history. There were ten to twenty times more enquiries to the profile where I hid my past.

On another occasion I had been chatting to a guy who was a school governor in Gloucester; I mentioned that I had been to Elmbridge – and he knew the school well. I mentioned that I had moved just as the eleven plus exam results came out but that I would have been accepted for Sir Thomas Riches Grammar School. He pointed out that Tommies was a boys only and I would have gone to the High School for Girls. Well actually ……. He thanked me for telling him and said he needed to think about it. That, again, was the last I heard of him.

Sometimes it might work the other way. I had come across a guy, working in IT for Manchester University, who was a fellow Neil Diamond fan. I went round to his place to listen to the latest CD and we got on ok. I then invited him on a SPICE American Pool night as my guest. Also there was another trans friend and SPICE member, Paula. As I drove him home afterwards, he enthused about Paula – what she had been through, how brave she was etc etc. I wanted to shout that I had done the same – but, of course, I hadn't been open about things from the start!

One of the dangers is that if you don't tell someone and they find out later, they may feel disgusted by having had sex with someone of the same sex and there is a risk of a violent reaction. There has even been a case in Scotland where a transguy has been imprisoned for 'obtaining sex through deception'. Having spoken to someone (senior) from the Crown Office Scotland, I gather that there were specific circumstances in this case but it is, nevertheless worrying for trans people in Scotland.

Emotionally, there is also a real risk that you don't tell someone at the start of the relationship and they then felt that they had been misled and they can no longer trust you. It really is a total minefield. By then there is a risk that the relationship has become very important to you and if it ends, you can be devastated.

For some trans people, the answer is to have relationships with other trans people – sometimes one who has transitioned in the opposite direction, sometimes with another person who has travelled the same route. Some transwomen find it easier to establish relationships with other women.

At the moment, I am not looking for a relationship. I'm not sure that I could fit someone into my life if I found someone to be honest – although I suspect that if I did find someone else who was important to me, I'd then be prepared to give up my independence or at least some of it. I certainly don't want to get into another relationship where I give up all of my needs and interests to fit in with a partner's. Maybe I'm just taking the easy option and avoiding the difficulties involved with a new relationship. I do have plenty of friends to mix with – mainly through SPICE; plenty to occupy my time and I quite like my own space as well.

Chapter 57. Transphobia & Ignorance

Being insulted is common for trans people (and other minority groups). Sometimes it's deliberate abuse, sometimes it's due to carelessness sometimes because of ignorance – just not realising that one's actions may be offensive.

I've mentioned my visit to Hindley YOI – but there have been lots of other incidents too. It's particularly difficult for transwomen on the telephone. Our vocal chords are thickened during puberty and our voices tend to be deeper and flatter than other women's. Some trans people have the vocal chords shaved to increase the pitch but there is a danger of this producing a Minnie Mouse sound and limiting tonal ranges. Pitch is, in any case, only part of the story – harmonics, the words used, how men and women say things or ask for something are different and women typically use many more tones when speaking.

Most of us undergo speech therapy to try to feminise our voices – but the telephone is nearly always a killer! Telephones always cut off the top frequencies and without the visual clues of us standing before them, most of us are probably called 'sir' at some time. Usually, a polite correction "it's not sir, it's madam" does the trick. Sometimes, however, there is a bigot – or a fool on the other end.

I was calling our Stretford office one day to speak to the office manager. The receptionist (a temp) asked who was calling and when I said "Helen Dale" he replied "You don't sound like a Helen." I suggested that he read some material I had posted on the organisation network to see why my voice may not be typically female. I also had a word with his office manager.

Another time, I had a problem with my PC and had a call from a technician at Steria – the national support company. He kept referring to me as Sir in spite of numerous corrections. Eventually I put the phone down on him. He called me back and continued to call me Sir –

Part 12. Riding the Roller Coaster

even when apologising for calling me Sir. I put the phone down again and he called back again – still calling me Sir and getting more and more flustered.

After the call was over, I called the Head of Live Services at Probation HQ (responsible for managing the supplier) and asked how I should go about making a formal complaint. I explained what had happened and he spoke to his opposite number at Steria who called me to apologise.

The very worst call, however, was with the Burlington Macdonald Hotel in Birmingham. We had used the hotel for the LAGIP conference – but there had been delays settling the invoice by NOMS. I was trying to resolve the issue and called the hotel Accounts Manager to update her. One of her team answered the call and I asked to be transferred. As he did so I heard him say "Helen Dale, the man who thought he was a woman". When I spoke to the manager I asked "did I hear that correctly?" her response was "no". That confirmed that I had heard the comment correctly or she would have asked what I meant. It was clear to me that there was an ethos that permitted transphobic remarks within that department at least – otherwise the individual would not have dared to make such a comment.

I complained to the Chair of the Macdonald Hotels group and eventually received a reply from the Regional Managing Director. I was assured that they took diversity very seriously and that the remark "had not been intended to offend". I challenged this and asked how it could be taken any other way – but have never received any satisfactory explanation and, frankly, an apology tempered by such a statement is no apology at all.

Another incident that should never have happened was a letter sent to me by Hope Hospital (now Salford Royal). It was a copy of a letter to my GP and showed my name and address with 'diagnosis Gender Reassignment' clearly visible through the window of the envelope.

After the trouble that I had previously encountered locally, I was scared that this disclosure would result in even more trouble for me. I had weeks of feeling on edge waiting for another stone through the window – or something pushed through the letterbox.

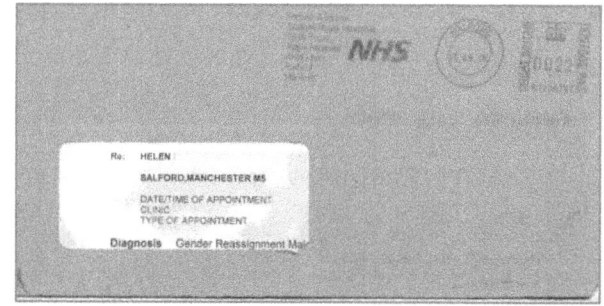

The letter from Salford Hope Hospital (now Salford Royal) unlawfully disclosing protected information

The Gender Recognition Act 2004 prohibits the 'disclosure of protected information' – which includes the fact that someone has gone through gender reassignment. This letter clearly breached the GRA and I could have asked the police to prosecute the Endocrinologist who had asked her secretary to deal with the letter. Unlawful disclosure is a criminal offence and is subject of a fine of up to £5,000.

Part 12. Riding the Roller Coaster

The consultant was aware that I had a Gender Recognition Certificate – I had told her during the consultation covered by the letter. There are some exemptions where disclosure is not unlawful – but none of them apply to consultants disclosing to administrative staff. It may be convenient for them to do so and, providing the staff are trained in their obligations under the Act, most trans people would agree to this being done – but, in law, without our agreement, it is illegal. We would also expect the staff to be trained to protect the information – and carelessly folding a letter so that the diagnosis is visible through the window of the envelope is unacceptable for any medical condition! It also breaches the Data Protection Act.

I complained via Patient Advisory & Liaison Service and, when they were unable to resolve the matter, to the Healthcare Commission then the Ombudsman – and to the Data Commissioner.

All agreed that Hope were in the wrong – but none would order compensation in spite of the distress I had been caused. Local solicitors weren't interested in helping – they did too much work with the NHS themselves and probably didn't understand the issues in any case. The Data Commissioner agreed that Hope needed to amend its processes to prevent recurrences – but, they told me, they couldn't order any compensation. The Ombudsman said that Hope needed to amend its processes but that the Data Commissioner had dealt with the issue of compensation – so they wouldn't.

I had offered to train the staff at Hope on the issues – but this was declined. One of my recent projects had been implementing 'Information Security' practices in Greater Manchester Probation so I was something of an expert by then on the Data Protection and the Gender Recognition Acts. I asked them to implement proper safeguards; I'd written some for Probation Staff to ensure that offender records were protected in accordance with the GRA – but, it seemed, it would be too inconvenient for the hospital. I still have a letter from the Chief Executive, David Dalton, telling me that I should go elsewhere for gender related treatment!

Chapter 58. Affirmations

In my experience, almost all trans people struggle with other people's acceptance (or not) of them. Many constantly wonder if they are being set up and if others are actually laughing at them behind their backs. Such doubts are, typically, much more common when starting out on the transition road but can linger for many years thereafter. It really doesn't matter how many times other trans people or counsellors etc. reassure you, for a transwoman you know that they are biased.

When you are invited to something in your 'acquired' role by other women, it can be hugely reaffirming.

Part 12. Riding the Roller Coaster

For me, the biggest affirmation for me was when Chris asked me to be her Chief Bridesmaid when she married Steve. It was a very special day. During the reception, I was at the bar with Kirsty, another trans friend of ours, who was bemoaning the fact that we could, if we were honest, never really expect to pass completely in public. A few minutes later we were sitting at a table – with another couple on their own on the next table so I invited them to join us. The other couple asked how we knew Chris and where we'd met. I'm not sure how it happened but something came up about transsexualism – perhaps I mentioned that I counselled trans people. They may have said something about never having met anyone who was transsexual, I glanced at Kirsty. The other couple caught my look and asked what was up. I think that I may have said that I was transsexual and they refused to believe me. Kirsty then said that she was too. "Now we know you're kidding" they said. In the end, they did believe us. I then turned to Kirsty and asked "what was it you were saying earlier about never passing?"

Best friend (& adopted sister) Chris (left); me (centre) and another brilliant friend Liz (right) preparing to do the Timewarp at Ribby Hall, Blackpool

Part 13. New Adventures

Chapter 59. SPICE

Keith had been true to his word. He emailed me to say he had asked SPICE to send me details. A couple of days later, there was a knock on my front door. When I opened it, a guy said "Hello, I'm Martin from SPICE. Keith has asked us to send you the brochure but as we live only three doors away, I thought I'd drop it round"

When I had bought no 7, their property was also on the market – but I could never get an appointment to view. I suspect, in any case, that I'd have gone for no 7.

Amongst the brochures was a catalogue of events planned for the current month or so. As I looked through the events, I spotted a number that had me thinking "that looks good" "that would be exciting" "I'd enjoy that"

Keith had been right. SPICE looked very interesting!

I filled in the application form there and then together with my first event few bookings and wasted no time in walking round to Martin's House/ SPICE office and posting them through the door. The events I had chosen were Line Dancing; a 60s weekend and some regular badminton sessions. I had previously been a member of Prairie Dogs LGBT line dance group – so doing it with SPICE seemed to make sense. I'd also played badminton on and off since my teens and 60s music is my era.

Joining SPICE did present something of an issue though. What did I do about being trans? The flotilla holiday had given me the confidence to mix socially with 'normal' people; they clearly didn't 'read' me – or, if they did, they simply accepted me. Nevertheless, I knew that there was a risk that if I was known to be trans from the start, THAT's what people would pre-judge me on. I really wanted to be known as Helen first and if the fact that I was trans came out later – at least they'd have judged me on who I am not what they thought I might be due to preconceptions about trans people.

The line dancing proved to be a bit of a disaster. It was a club that SPICE had booked a few slots with. In fact, I was the only SPICE member attending. They also expected dancers to pick up the moves from a very quick run through – and I wasn't at that level!

The badminton, on the other hand was an excellent mix of social and exercise and I found I was generally able to hold my own with most of the group. There were some who would regularly beat me at singles but, in spite of being one of the older members, I found I could make up for a lack of stamina with experience of placing shots.

In the thirteen years since joining, I've done more than 200 different events with the group. Lots of them have been regular monthly events such as Badminton (usually followed by a visit to the pub) – which I did almost every Friday until I injured my calf muscle on a holiday; local pub meets – I hosted the Worsley meet for some years; SPICE Hits Town – where we'd gather once a month in a club in Manchester. Others were 'one offs' or at longer intervals.

Part 13. New Adventures

The latter included:

Social weekends

The social weekends involve all of the SPICE groups from around the country and have been known to attract four to five hundred members in the past – though numbers have tended to fall off in recent years.

'Spicefest', in particular used to be huge and we would take over an entire holiday camp such as Pontin's in Southport. The accommodation was nothing to write home about – but we didn't tend to spend much time in the chalets so this didn't matter. We were basically like a bunch of kids – I often describe SPICE as a Youth Club for adults.

Chalet mates at Centerparcs Whinfell

As with all SPICE social weekends, there was a fancy-dress dance on the Saturday evening – but two of the main highlights for me were a giant water fight and a wrestling match. The water fight involved everyone armed with water pistols including some massive hand-held water cannons. I don't think anyone worked out who was on what side – or who won. It was just mayhem. I thought I was clever at the start by wearing all of my sailing waterproofs. I was

The Spice "Spice Girls" at Spicefest Southport

convinced that I would be invincible in my kit. I didn't take account, however, of two facts. First that it would make me the prime target for almost everyone else (that is how it felt); secondly, running round in trousers that reach up to the chest, a jacket that extends to mid thighs and boots was tiring and HOT! I eventually gave up the protection and changed into shorts, T shirt and trainers.

The wrestling match was organised by Andy, one of the members who is also a referee. We had the works – proper wrestling ring and wrestlers like those who appeared on Saturday afternoon television back in the 60s. I took my place in the front row and when any of the wrestlers fell out of the ring, I would pounce and hit them with a 'handbag' (actually a washbag with no heavy contents). I was told later that the wrestlers themselves loved the fact that we'd entered into the spirit of the display.

One of my first events with SPICE and where I shared with other members was a 60s weekend at Pwllheli in North Wales. Two of the ladies with whom I shared reappear later in my story.

Part 13. New Adventures

Other weekends included the Edinburgh Festival – where I noticed that there was a trans comedienne performing. Unfortunately, when I arrived at the venue, she had finished the previous day and the programme was incorrect.

SPICE's signature weekends have to be those at Centreparcs. When I first joined, they used two of the parks – Winfell near Penrith and Sherwood Forest. The Winfell site was also known as Oasis. When I first saw 'Oasis Weekend' my reaction was that I really couldn't sit through a weekend of listening to them! When I found out that it wasn't anything to do with the pop group but that the weekends offered a huge range of activities, I booked future events.

At this time, SPICE had 'message boards' where we would participate in forums about all sorts of topics. MBA's (Message board addicts) tended to use nicknames on the boards. I had started as 'Salford lady' but I later needed a name for the scoring system for a Laserquest evening and that was too long. During my days using CB radio, my handle had been 'Fireball' after the sailing dinghy we owned. 'Ball' no longer seemed appropriate so I changed it to Firebird – and that also became my MBA name. One of the other MBAs was Naomi whose board name was 'Glitter Girl'. She and some other female friends in SPICE suggested that we had a 'girls only' chalet at the spring Centreparcs weekend and invited me to join them. That was one of the most important steps for me – being accepted by other females as 'one of the girls'. We formed the 'Glitter Gang' – I was, as I said on my Message Board heading 'the shy retiring member of the Glitter Gang'.

I continued to attend the Centreparcs weekends, particularly Winfell, for about ten years – eventually stopping because I was concerned about walking between the lodges and the centre in the cold after a heart attack. It could be quite a walk and up and down steep slopes.

The other regular national weekend is Dragon Boat Racing on the River Avon at Pershore. The racing, one of the few times the SPICE groups compete with each other, is on the Sunday – after a party on the Saturday night (you can see where most members' priorities lie). Most of the members tended to camp for the weekend – and I joined them on my first event.

Part 13. New Adventures

Now, I have camped since the age of about 11 with the Scouts. When I did a 2-day hike for my 'first class' badge, Reg and I woke to find snow on the ground and on the tent (and later hiked through a blizzard). I'd camped in the Brecon Beacons and Norfolk as an Officer Cadet in the RAF. We'd spent many family holidays camping in Devon and Cornwall and Wales – and in France and Germany. The Dragon Boat weekend was in the summer; but I froze! The showers were dreadful as well – so I decided that for future events it would be B&B for me! I had obviously gone soft.

The following year, I booked a B&B. So too, did Chris. I had managed to get the last of the en suite rooms – Chris and Steve would have to use the shared facility along the corridor. Except, Chris and Steve got to the B&B a couple of minutes before me and persuaded the owner that it would be OK to swop our bookings! I never trusted Chris again as far as hotel bookings were concerned!

Driving things

SPICE events provide an opportunity to drive all sorts of different 'vehicles'. I've had a go at hovercraft, quad bikes, off road go karts and even tanks. A group of Spicers also went away for a weekend outside of SPICE where we had experience of 'green lane driving' in a Land Rover – including driving down the path of a mountain stream. I also had a chance to drive, or is it ride, a Segway – quite an experience.

Dinners, Parties and Balls

SPICE started as a purely adrenaline-based activity club – but has developed over more than 30 years into more of a social group. It still does adrenaline activities but it also offers more relaxed events such as black-tie balls. Most of the groups run their own Christmas and Summer balls – but there have been a number of national Anniversary Balls in my time. These really are spectacular. Dave Smith, SPICE's founder, also took a table at a 'Supersonic Dinner' held in the Concorde hangar at Manchester airport. This was in aid of Manchester Pride – so, of course I joined the table.

Not all of the events are Black tie – some of the other events that I've attended included

All dressed up at the Spice 25th Anniversary Ball

Supersonic Dinner — under the wings of Concorde

Part 13. New Adventures

Bavarian Nights at Rivington Hall, Barn Dances, Ceilidh and a Fawlty Towers Dining Experience at the Lowry Centre restaurant in Salford. Dinner is served by Fawlty Towers lookalikes – with various incidents livening up proceedings. I won't reveal their secrets – so get along one of them and discover it for yourself!

Shows

Amongst the shows I've attended with SPICE have been amateur and professional theatre presentations – including SPICE's own Pantos (which is where I first met Naomi). Then there is the Rocky Horror Picture Show. You may recall that it photographs from a previous visit were involved in me coming out to Joanna and Jenny. SPICE are very fond of fancy dress and RHPS is an ideal opportunity to go wild. I do warn the guys that dressing as Frank-n-Furter can be the first step on a very slippery slope!

With Spice at Funny Girls in Blackpool

Also on the trans theme, SPICE have also been to Funny Girls in Blackpool and the Birdcage in Manchester.

I was a bit bemused by the claim of one of the waitresses at Funny Girls that she only dressed as a female for the job. I did wonder why you'd take a job that required you to cross dress if you were not already that way inclined.

During our first visit to the Birdcage (which may not actually have been with SPICE – I think it was a hen party) there was a Lily Savage lookalike acting as compère. I'd known someone who lived in Albion Towers at the same time as me who was a Lily Savage double. I went up to the DJ box and asked if she had lived in Albion Towers – but was asked to wait until the next dance break as the cabaret was about to start again. At the next break I went back up and was greeted with "hi Helen – sorry didn't recognise you earlier". We managed to get several messages for the bride to be and the rest of our crowd.

Workshops

On a quieter note, SPICE also organise a wide range of workshops. One of the first that I attended was 'When Venus and Mars Collide' – based on the book by John Gray about the difference in mental approaches of men and women.

We were split into groups of four and asked to complete a questionnaire that indicates brain sex on a scale from -40 to +320. At the bottom end of the scale tends to be male responses – then an overlap – then typically female scores. I'd come across similar 'Cogiati' questionnaires before. When one of the other women said she had finished and scored her responses, she told us it was (say) 225. I said that's what I would have expected – and one of the other two women was dubious about my claim and asked how I could know. I said it was from what she had been saying earlier and the sort of comments that she'd made. I

Part 13. New Adventures

was then challenged to say what I though her score would be so I estimated 185-200 (or whatever it was). She seemed surprised to find that her score was within what I suggested.

Cogiati tests have been used as diagnostic tools to identify if someone is or is not transsexual. This is extremely dangerous as they are usually far from conclusive. I have only ever used them once in my counselling practice when I was dealing with an individual who claimed to be TS but displayed none of the symptoms or views that I had come to expect from someone who was transsexual. I had asked them to complete the 'brainsex' test and they came out very much in the male range.

When chatting over coffee with two of the three ladies who'd been in our quartet, I asked where they were from. "Stoke," they replied, "Where in Stoke?"; "Newcastle," they told me, "My dad's from there," I said. "Yes, we know. We've had this conversation before. You shared a chalet with us on the 60s weekend!" Oh well, you can't remember everyone you meet and if you encounter them again in a different environment, it can be difficult making a connection. That's my excuse anyway.

I am currently involved in the Creative Writing workshops presented by Lynn Trotter who has been very supportive of my efforts – these have really kick started my writing including this autobiography.

Sailing

Sailing has been one of my sports for as long as I can remember – and SPICE has given me the opportunity to take part in various events.

One of my early sessions with SPICE was a weekend out of Oban – quite a trek from Manchester. The yacht was moored outboard of another working boat whose deck we had to cross before boarding the yacht. As I grabbed the shroud and swung my legs over the guard rails, the skipper who was watching remarked "You've done that before". "once or twice" I told him.

That night we left the harbour and anchored near Calf Island – not far from another yacht. The next day we had some basic instruction and safety briefing. As

Spice Easter Sailing Trip

there was next to no wind, we started to motor – planning to head up the Sound of Mull up to Tobermory.

We were about to head up the Sound when there was a screeching sound from the engine compartment. When he opened the cover, he was enveloped in a cloud of smoke.

Part 13. New Adventures

We switched off the engine and he asked me to take the helm and keep the yacht where we were. With little wind or currents, this wasn't a problem. We might drift gradually towards land but, if so, it would then become shallow enough to drop the anchor. In any case, what breeze there was may not be enough to get us anywhere quickly but probably enough to provide some control.

The skipper found that one of the two alternators connected to the engine had totally seized up and the smoke had been caused by the drive belt rubbing on the locked pulley. There was, obviously, no spare alternator on board. The drive belt would be too long if the seized alternator was left out of the drive loop. He could jury rig a drive belt but there was no knowing how effective it would be – probably not reliable enough for any significant journey.

By now the wind had picked up so we decided to sail up to Tobermory where we might be able to obtain a replacement alternator. As we made our way up the Sound, the wind continued to increase – giving us a nice close hauled[25] sail. At Tobermory, we had to turn to port (left) and head down a channel – with the wind over our quarter; then turn port again downwind before turning into the wind and (hopefully) stopping with the bow next to a mooring buoy. The turn downwind took us very close to a moored yacht and the wind swung from one side of the boat to the other – a manoeuvre known as a gybe. This can be a violent manoeuvre as the wind is constantly pushing against the sail – so it needs to be handled carefully with the crew watching the boom as it swung across ensuring that their heads were well out of the way!

In the event, the manoeuvres went well, we missed the moored yacht by a couple of feet and stopped close enough to the mooring buoy for one of our crew to catch hold and secure us.

The skipper did remark that we had been a bit close to the moored yacht. I pointed out that we had missed it and, in fact, in my dinghy days we'd have been a lot closer.

Unfortunately, the skipper was unable to get a new alternator in Tobermory – one would need to be sent over from the mainland and that couldn't be for a day or two. What was worse was that there was a gale warning in force and if we were on the mooring buoy, we'd be stuck on board – so we were given the option of moving the yacht onto the pontoon which would cost a little more. The skipper decided he could trust the jury-rigged emergency alternator belt for the hundred yards or so to the pontoon and started the motor. As we reached the pontoon, he misjudged it and we hit a pillar on the pontoon carrying the power and water supplies! (At least I hadn't hit the moored yacht that he had accused me of getting too close to!)

We were stuck in Tobermory for about two days – most of which was spent in the pub. Even the brightly coloured houses along the quayside did little to cheer us up.

---

[25] Close hauled is where the wind is sufficiently from the side – typically about 45 degrees off the bow so that the sails can power the yacht

Part 13. New Adventures

A few years later, I decided to join the SPICE yacht in the Round the Island race. The plan was to meet up on the Thursday, practice on the Friday, take part in the race on the Saturday and head back from the Isle of Wight to what the locals call the 'North Island' on the Sunday. I drove down to Gosport stopping overnight en route and visiting Beaulieu Motor Museum on the way. After stowing our gear on Kelana, we went for dinner. Over drinks, the skipper asked if any of us had done anything like the Round the Island before.

"Yes, I have," I admitted.

"Good – what have you done?".

"This. The Round the Island race."

"When was that?"

"About thirty years ago."

Competitors are split into different groups – either all one class of yacht like the Sunsail 37 or yachts of similar performance and everyone is given a handicap rating to try to even things out.

On board Kilena for the Round the Island Race 2011 — I'm wearing the red hat.

The fastest yachts – typically multihulls – go off first with progressively slower classes heading off at ten-minute intervals. We were in the white group – about the ninth to start with just two behind us.

We were judged to have been over the line at the start which meant we were penalised and ended up in the bottom half of our group – which was a pity.

The wind was quite strong, about force 5 or 6 from memory and we had reefed sails to reduce the pressure. As we hit the waves, the wind picked up the spray and hurled it at us crouched in the cockpit, those nearest the bow taking the brunt and sheltering those further back.

The race course took us down from Cowes, through the narrows at Hurst Castle where the wind blows against the tide flowing in the opposite direction causing a nasty 'chop'.

Then the fleet rounds the Needles – turning more down wind.

Going along the southern side of the Island, the waves hit us from the starboard quarter giving us a corkscrew motion – but also allowing us to surf down the front of each wave until it passed under us and we dropped off the back to wait for the next wave. We tried to stay surfing for as long as possible – constantly adjusting our course the compensating while waiting for the next wave. The wind is never constant in either direction or strength; with the boat adjusting its course and the wind direction varying it's easy, too easy, to end up with the wind on the wrong side of the sail resulting in a potentially dangerous and disastrous involuntary gybe. I was on the helm at this stage and did get caught gybing first one way then the other – fortunately without injury or damage. Other yachts were not so fortunate and we saw some which had been dismasted and we could see the Coastguard and Air Sea Rescue

Part 13. New Adventures

helicopters being kept busy. There were even some multi-hulls that been turned upside down.

As we passed St Catherine's point, the southern tip of the island, we were sheltered more from the wind and continued up to Bembridge Ledge where we turned north west for the final leg past Ryde to the finish line off Cowes.

Crossing the finish line, we noted the number of the yachts immediately ahead and astern of us and our time and texted these to the race organisers.

It can be a gruelling – but very satisfying day. I had told the skipper that I had had a heart attack less than three months earlier so wasn't supposed to do physical exercise that involved exerting myself without first warming up. That tended to exclude hauling in quickly on sails and quick work on the winches. I was fine helming though (and did lend a hand on the winches in any case).

The following year, 2012, I decided to take part again. This time SPICE had two boats in the race Kelana and Par Excellence. I was allocated to Par Excellence. I was anxious to avoid being over the line at the start and perhaps be a bit more forceful when it came to close quarter encounters with other yachts. It had seemed to me the previous year that Mike, our skipper, had tended to use cruising tactics based on safety rather than the cut and thrust of racing that I'd been used to in Fireball dinghies. I felt that there was a middle ground that might be beneficial. I was appointed tactician for Par Excellence – and found myself matched against another former Fireball sailor on Kelana. The scene was set for another duel!

The weather in 2012 was even rougher than it had been in 2011 with gale force winds at times. In fact, around a quarter of the entries didn't even start the race and even Ellen MacArthur retired. To be fair, she was skippering a yacht with some disabled young people on board so she was, quite rightly, being cautious – but I can claim to have finished a race from which she retired!

We didn't see much of Kelana as we fought our way round the island – but, in the end, we finished ahead of them and a creditable sixth in our class three places ahead of Kelana. Overall Par Excellence was 179th and Kelana 200th out of 822 ISC rating system boats.

In complete contrast to the Round the Island Race, a long weekend sailing in Malta was about as perfect conditions as I've ever experienced. A good breeze to power us along under a cloudless blue sky reflected in the crystal waters. What more could you ask?

As I had booked with Easy Jet, I had flown out to Malta the day before we were due to join in case there were problems with the flight. I also arranged to stay on the island for a few days after the sailing to have a look around. The flight out was in contrast to my earlier visit to Malta. Then we had been en route to Iraq in a noisy RAF Transport Command DC3 Dakota via a refuelling stop in France. This time we were in a modern jet doing the flight in one hop and in a fraction of the time.

Being May, the Mediterranean hadn't had time to warm up – so the water was chilly for swimming but we still managed a few dips.

Part 13. New Adventures

Adrenaline

SPICE started as an adventure/adrenaline activities group and still does such events. Amongst these are two that I've tried: Diving with Sharks and Fire Eating.

I had avoided the Fire Eating for some time but won a voucher for it as part of the raffle at a preview night that I helped with. When I said that I'd been avoiding it, Martin said he could always put it back in the draw. I then said I hadn't said I wouldn't do it – effectively backing myself into a corner. Oh Well! On the day, we started with events designed to build trust in the other participants and with your partner for the actual Fire eating/Breathing later. These included falling backwards off a table onto the arms of the other members; allowing your partner to lead you while you are blindfolded – including up and down steps and other obstacles.

A "signature" Spice event, Fire eating!

Finally you are taught to 'eat' the fire and 'breath' it.

The thrill and sense of satisfaction you get from successfully doing both is quite amazing!

The Diving with Sharks was at the Blue Planet Aquarium near Ellesmere Port. This was voted as the tenth best place in the world to dive with sharks due to how close you get to those teeth. (The number one venue is Gansbaai in South Africa where you can cage dive with Great White Sharks).

I wanted to dive with sharks in a controlled environment because I anticipated meeting them while diving in the open sea – and I didn't want my first encounter to be such a shock that I panicked. Clearly the Blue Planet wouldn't be allowed to run these events if they lost too many visitors – so they OUGHT to be reasonably safe. I'm not sure my boss was that convinced as she came

*Diving with Sharks at Blue Planet Aquarium;
I'm on the left!*

Part 13. New Adventures

along to watch me – probably so that she would set wheels in motion to replace me if things went wrong.

Very few sharks are dangerous of course and these were well fed before we went into the water! Sadly, humans are far more of a threat to sharks than they ever have been to us. It is disgraceful how many are killed just so their fins can be used for soup.

Following a briefing, we entered the tank. We wore scuba gear – but not fins as we walked around the tank rather than swam. We then knelt down and allowed the fish to swim around us. I was watching one fabulous ray swim from my front and over my head; as I followed its path, I saw a Sand Tiger Shark coming from behind me and gliding just a couple of feet over my shoulder. Its razor sharp teeth looked quite menacing but it was an awesome experience.

Holidays

SPICE also do a range of holidays each year. Soon after joining, I saw one for two weeks in Kenya. A week in Mombassa where you could learn to dive followed by a week on safari. It had to be done.

Then it seemed that it might all go wrong. I had a phone call one evening from Dave Smith, the founder and owner of SPICE who said he had heard that I might be transsexual. He explained that this might make it difficult for anyone I might share with on the holiday. It was not an easy conversation for either of us. I didn't want to lose the chance of this holiday but nor was I happy with being pre-judged in this way or having to tell someone that I was TS before they had a chance to meet me.

We reached a compromise that evening that I would, if necessary, take a single room but that I would only pay half the supplement.

That night, I tossed and turned – really annoyed with myself for having agreed to share information about me. This was against my strategy of trying to let people get to know me before they learned I was TS. I had no problem if someone didn't like me because they found me unpleasant or disagreed with my views etc – but I really didn't want them pre-judging me based on misconceptions.

The next morning, I sent Dave an email asking that he didn't do anything until I'd spoken to him face to face. Fortunately, his office was near where I worked so I could easily go round that evening.

We chatted and it became apparent that Dave had thought I was pre-op and still had a penis. When I made it clear that this was not the case, he accepted that it was not unreasonable for me to share with other women.

We did, however, agree that we would organise a get together for the women from Manchester going on the Kenya trip. This would give them the chance to call the office and say that they didn't want to share with someone – if that was the case.

In fact, one of the other ladies did ring the office and told them that she preferred to share with me.

Part 13. New Adventures

In the end, on the return trip, we were discussing a reunion the following year and I mentioned that it coincided with an anniversary for me. No-one was at all concerned about my history – and Dave and I have become friends.

The holiday was all I hoped it would be. We arrived in the dark having changed aircraft in Nairobi and were shown to our rooms. A late supper had been prepared for us after which most of us crashed out. The next morning, I peeked through the curtains of our room and just exclaimed 'wow!' My roomie asked what it was and I said just come and look at this view. We looked out over a grassy area, then a swimming pool to the Indian Ocean. Paradise!

The view from our room

The first week was very hectic with the Dive Training. Each night we had to prepare one of the theoretical modules and be tested on it the next day before the practical sessions. Then, at the end of the week, we had a final theory test – in which we had to score 80%. Lynn, one of the other girls and I had established a friendly rivalry. Each day both of us had been scoring perfect results in the theory tests. When it came to the final day, Lynn finished a moment of two before I did and handed in her paper. When it had been marked, I mouthed "how many did you get wrong" and she held up two fingers – very good out of 75 questions. Then my paper was returned and she looked at me questioningly. I touched my forefinger to the tip of my thumb as I held up my hand – zero wrong! "Bitch" she mouthed, smiling.

The next day was our first 'open water' dives. There had been a storm at sea and visibility was appalling. The instructor had assured us the conditions were good – but I could hardly see my hand in front of my face as we descended the guide line to the bottom. I was disorientated as we descended and experienced equalisation problems with my ears. "If these were good conditions" I thought, "then diving's not for me!" Once we got to the bottom and could see things, it became easier. We didn't stay down long but resurfaced where we carried out a buddy tow – pulling a partner along.

The second open water dive was much better. Visibility was far clearer. As we swam along, we could see lots of fish heading in the opposite direction. I remember wondering if they knew something that we didn't and if we were about to meet something with lots of sharp teeth! By the end of that dive, I was hooked.

Part 13. New Adventures

We left Mombasa at the end of the week in three minibuses, heading inland for Tsavo game reserve. As we drove north we passed through small ramshackle towns. The contrast between our hotel and the locals' homes was incredible. Our bedroom was probably larger than the entire houses that the locals lived in. I suspect that the food that was probably wasted from the buffets laid out for us every day might have fed an entire town! We'd learned too, that many of the staff at the hotel ran several miles every day to and from work – and were expected to work for nothing for several months (and were then often 'let go'). It was a dilemma. Yet if we didn't go there on holiday the locals would be even worse off.

Our accommodation at Tsavo was in tents surrounded by timber frames – in an arc around a waterhole. The tents were large enough to stand up in and had flushing toilets and shower and sinks at the rear. The furniture was full size beds, drawers and wardrobes etc. We were warned to keep both ends of the tents secure to stop monkeys from getting in.

The snows on top of Kilimanjaro can be seen

When we asked what stopped the animals wandering through the camp at night were told that they didn't like the lights. We accepted this explanation until we remembered that we'd been told that the lights went out at nine o'clock!

Across the waterhole and in the distance we could, on a clear day, make out the snows on the summit of Mount Kilimanjaro. I had always wanted to see this as Baden Powell, founder of the Scout movement, was, I had always believed, buried on its slopes (though this is, apparently, not the case).

Each day we had a couple of game drives in the early morning and late afternoon. One day we had a walk around the waterhole. At one point we saw a crocodile and a bird close together. The bird seemed to be taunting the crocodile and I, for one, fully expected to see it swallowed whole if the crocodile lunged at it! As there was only about twenty feet of mud between us and the crocodile, it was a nerve wracking few moments as we made our way past them. We did remember, though, that we wouldn't have to out run the crocodile – just the slowest person in our group!

Tsavo is probably not the best reserve to see the 'Big Five' (lion, buffalo, black rhino, elephant and leopard) but you do see a lot of Guinea Fowl. Lots and lots of Guinea Fowl. To be fair, we did see buffalo, elephants, zebra, giraffes etc and some of the group did see lions

Part 13. New Adventures

and one of the three buses did encounter a leopard. Sadly, I was unwell the day they saw the lions and not in the bus that came across the leopard.

The second trip I did with SPICE to Kenya was three years later. We reversed the itinerary and visited a number of reserves before ending up in Mombasa. Jo came with me on this trip. As before, we flew into Nairobi where we stayed overnight. We had a trip to a giraffe sanctuary and to Karen Blixen's house (of 'Out of Africa' fame – the house itself being used for the external shots in the film).

Karen Blixen's House

The next day, we drove to Treetops – where the then Princess Elizabeth had been staying when she heard that her father had died and she was Queen. En route we stopped at Outspan hotel where there is a small scouting museum in the cottage that Baden Powell commissioned and lived in. Nearby is his grave marked with the tracking sign for 'gone home' of a dot within a circle. We had to leave most of our luggage at Outspan – taking just an airline hand-luggage size bag to Treetops.

Treetops Hotel

The journey to Treetops was 'interesting' to say the least with crazy traffic, several accidents including overturned lorries and a road surface that was more pot holes than tarmac.

Treetops hotel is built into the branches of trees and the rooms are tiny – just enough for a couple of bunk beds. The rooms are fitted with buzzers and you can choose to be warned of different levels of animals visiting the adjacent waterhole at night. We selected to be buzzed only for the top level such as lions and elephants.

Inside Treetops — the branches are well padded and Jo has her head in her reference book!

Part 13. New Adventures

While on a game drive at Treetops, we stopped at one of the highest points from which, we were assured, you could see Mount Kenya on a clear day. Sadly, this wasn't a clear day and all we could see were clouds in the distance. While wandering around this picnic spot, my right foot went down a hole and I tore my calf muscle. That caused me a lot of trouble over the following months.

From Treetops we drove to Lake Navaisha, crossing the equator en route and giving us an opportunity to stand with one foot in the northern hemisphere and the other in the southern. We took a boat trip out onto the lake getting a close up of the flamingos and pelicans. Watching the pelicans trying to take of was incredible; their huge wings beating down as they crashed across the water – scattering everything in their path – eventually lifting off from the surface but remaining low while they built up speed before finally managing to climb into the sky. Around the lake were what looked at first glance to be grey islands with birds sitting on them – but, on closer examination, turned out to be hippos. Other animals, too, came down to the water to drink – zebra and antelope particularly.

Gangway Please!

Astride the Equator

The lake had, at one time, like Habbaniya, been a staging post for flying boats majestically making their way down to Southern Africa. I could visualise them landing one the lake spraying huge spumes either side of the hull as it kissed the surface.

We left Navaisha and bumped our way along red dusty roads for the fabled Masai Mara. At times the roads just seemed to indicate a general direction of travel – with vehicles choosing their own path up to fifty yards either side of the original track.

Part 13. New Adventures

Our hotel was on the banks of a tributary of the Mara River. My calf muscle was troubling me so we decided to skip the afternoon's visit to a Masai village but told the coordinator that we would join them for the game drive. We relaxed for an hour or two then returned to reception to wait to be picked up for the game drive. When our vehicle didn't arrive, we asked reception to contact them by radio and were told that it had gone directly from the village to the game drive. We insisted on being picked up and we not at all happy with the mess up – and have no doubt that some of the others were equally unhappy at losing part of the game drive to collect us.

Cheetah cubs — there were six of them

The game at the Masai Mara was much more extensive than at Tsavo – we saw lions on every drive and several cheetahs. At one point a cheetah was walking parallel to the track we were on so we kept moving a few hundred yards so it would come past us each time. We kept that one in sight for around 40 minutes. Later we saw six cheetah cubs, just a few days old, well camouflaged in the dry brown grass.

The vistas in the Masai Mara are magnificent – with open views for miles to the distant horizon. At times we could see wildebeest intermingled with zebra from one horizon to the other. We watched as a lion stared at the herd of wildebeest –the closest ones staring back ready to react if the lion made a move as the rest of the herd moved along.

Part 13. New Adventures

From the Mara, we flew back to Nairobi where we changed planes for Mombasa. The airport in the reserve was a rough strip – with ramshackle buildings including a 'duty free shop', 'departure lounge' and 'security hut'. There was also a hut which housed the latrines – two holes in the ground that stank! Oh how they stank! If you needed to use the facility you really needed to be able to hold your breath for a long time.

The arrival and departure of the flights was a major event locally – with the schools bringing their pupils in smart uniforms to watch. Before the aircraft could land it was essential to clear the runway of animals that wandered on to it.

In Mombasa, Jo and I were mainly interested in diving – including a trip to watch and, if possible, dive with dolphins in the wild. We also visited a snake sanctuary.

As a result, we missed the group trip to Mombasa. On the last day, however, we were not due to leave the hotel for the airport until mid-afternoon so we arranged a trip accompanied by a guide and for us to be picked up by the coach in Mombasa. Having done the tour, we had drinks at the hotel where we'd be collected by the coach. Our guide really could not get around the fact that Jo was unmarried but in a relationship or that her partner wasn't with her; then he asked if her father was still around. I immediately thought "a lot closer than you can possibly imagine!" but we said nothing!

I'm sure Jo would have slipped one of the snakes into her luggage if she thought she could get away with it.

Flying

Simulators

As I may have mentioned, my original ambition was to be a pilot. I had the opportunity to take the controls of a Varsity during one 'air experience' flight from Stradishall and nearly got my gliding qualification. So, when SPICE offered a chance to try out a simulator or get into the cockpit of an aircraft, I booked on the events.

The first simulator was near Northampton and was based on a Boeing 737 cockpit. We each had a chance to 'take off' from Heathrow, fly a circuit then 'land' again.

Part 13. New Adventures

The next time was near Manchester airport. The company had converted an old twin-engine aircraft fuselage into a flight simulator. The simulator can be set up as a variety of aircraft from the original twin to large airliners and from WW2 fighters to modern equivalents.

For my first attempt, I stuck with the original twin design which was quite sedate and not too difficult to 'fly' including landing back onto the runway. The next time, I decided to be more adventurous. In the absence of an English Electric/ BAC Lightning option, I went for the Phantom. We 'took off' from RAF Valley in Anglesey – then it was through the valleys weaving between mountains. Eventually the inevitable happened and I 'hit' the hillside. Scrap one Phantom at about £24million. Try again – the instructor tells me that fast jets roll almost upside down to take the turns. I try and plough into the ground. Another rather used aircraft for the scrap yard.

OK, the Phantom was used by the navy as well as the RAF so let's try a carrier take-off and landing. The take-off was easy enough – then climb into the low cloud do a circuit and line up for the landing. Gear down, flaps down, arrestor hook down. Aim for the stern of the carrier. Oops made a mess of the approach – scratch another Phantom. Total bill so far £72 million. Try the landing again. Follow the lights – getting closer. Concentrate! My hands are getting sweaty – difficult to believe this is just a simulation it feels real. Touchdown! My goodness – I managed it. Ok final test – set up on approach back into RAF Valley. With a long runway stretching out in front of me, the landing is relatively straightforward after the aircraft carrier!

On my third visit I chose the famous Spitfire. The massive Merlin engine stretching ahead of me while the aircraft sits on its tail wheel all but eliminates any forward view so we weave from side to side to look out of the cockpit as we head for the runway. Must be careful not to lift the tail too much or the propeller will bite into the ground; careful too not to suddenly apply full power or the torque will twist the aircraft into a bank. 'In the air' it is very responsive and I practised a few loops & rolls. "OK let's beat up the airfield" says the instructor. Diving back down towards the ground we do a low-level pass at full speed. "How about a Victory roll" the instructor suggests. "Just what I'd been thinking", I pulled back on the controls and rolled to the left. Sadly, the landing wasn't as good as it might have been. Once again, the long nose restricted visibility and I misjudged the approach landing a few yards short of the airfield.

Part 13. New Adventures

Cockpit Visits

Next best to 'flying' a simulator is sitting in the cockpit of an aircraft. The English Electric/ BAC Lightning could have been my 'office' if I hadn't admitted having had hay fever when I applied to the RAF for pilot training! I'd sat in one at Coltishall in 1965 – but my dream is to actually fly in one of these beauties. There is one still operational

BAC Lightning at Bruntingthorpe

in South Africa but it's an expensive indulgence! For far less, I had the chance to climb back into the cockpit at Bruntingsthorpe!

Of course, it just as likely that I'd have ended up in bigger aircraft – perhaps a V bomber like the Vulcan or Victor. Again, I'd visited the cockpits of both at RAF St Athens as an Officer Cadet but when SPICE organised a trip to Wellesbourne to look at their Vulcan I just had to go. Space is incredibly tight in the Vulcan and it's difficult to imagine spending hours at a time in such compact areas.

Actual aircraft

As well as flight simulators, SPICE has also given me the opportunity to fly a couple of real aircraft.

Pilot's seat in a Vulcan

One of these trips was for two SPICE members (with an instructor) in a four-seat trainer flying from Coventry airport to Wellesbourne – then back again. One SPICE member would fly the aircraft one way and the other would fly it back.

During the briefing, Guy, our instructor, asked if either of us had flown before in a light aircraft. I said that I'd flown in a Chipmunk the previous year and in a Cessna back in the 60s.

Part 13. New Adventures

He asked if I'd taken the controls of either of them. "No, not those" I told him truthfully. Well it was the truth – I hadn't taken the controls of either the Cessna or the Chipmunk. He hadn't asked if I'd flown anything else.

Guy led us out to the aircraft; a PA28 Warrior. "looks a bit different to the Cessna" he remarked. "Yes, the wings are lower" I replied. He showed us how to do a Daily Inspection (DI) – checking the controls all worked and were properly attached to the aircraft; the navigation and landing lights all worked; the oil level was OK and there was fuel and it wasn't contaminated with water. Then it was time to get on board.

At the controls!

Choosing to do the return flight, I clambered into the back seat for the outward leg. It was a dull drizzly day with gusting cross winds that were forecast to increase later. The clouds were down to about two thousand feet. We taxied to the end of the runway, carried out pre-take off checks, radioed for clearance then took off. The first few hundred feet were a bit choppy but gradually settled down. My fellow Spicer handled the aircraft well – giving me something to aim for when it came to my turn. Before long it was time to descend into Wellesbourne. We joined the circuit then lined up with the runway at which point the instructor took over and put us back on the ground.

We taxied to the swop over point, and did another, pre-flight check. A second Spice aircraft with two other members on board were unable to stop their engine as the battery was low so they turned round and headed off after their crew had swopped places. We followed a few minutes later.

It was now my turn to sit in the left-hand seat. Having adjusted the seat, I checked the instruments – recognising most of them quite easily. We taxied along the perimeter track and pulled up in front of the Avro Vulcan V bomber on display. I'd been there the weekend before for a good look round the Vulcan including its cockpit – again with SPICE. I had first sat in the cockpit of one of these monsters when I had been an RAF officer cadet in 1965 – nearly fifty years ago. Then the Vulcan and Victor were part of the nuclear deterrent (the third of the V bombers, the Valiant, having been withdrawn due to fatigue problems).

Pre-flight checks complete we continued to the end of the runway where we sought permission to take off – permission grated, I responded with our call sign "Aeros eight-three".

Then we were off. As we climbed, we again hit some turbulence for a while – then the instructor handed over the controls to me. "Heading zero-eight-zero". I turned onto course. "Imagine a half pint of beer on the top of the instrument panel – or, in your case, a gin and tonic. Try to keep the horizon in line with the top of the drink". Horizon? What horizon? It

Part 13. New Adventures

was covered in cloud – so I glanced at the artificial horizon instrument. That was OK. Speed OK. Height stable – this was actually easier than the flight simulator on my PC at home. We were advised to watch out for another aircraft in our vicinity – Guy took control to take evasive action then handed back to me. "Head for that reservoir over there" he instructed. I applied right hand bank then as we came onto course eased off the pressure so that we ended up flying towards the lake. "That was perfect" he complimented sounding quite impressed with a rookie being able to perform such a turn. "I think I forgot to mention my gliding" I admitted.

As we approached Coventry, Guy asked if I had landed gliders. "Yes" I said. "Ok well you can land this then". "OK – but bear in mind that when I landed gliders, we aimed for the grass so if I put it down on the wrong place.....". We joined the circuit then started to line up with the runway. "Keep the landing point at the same position in your view all the time then you'll get there".

I did as instructed. I knew that there were now quite strong cross winds and that they were gusting and that we needed to compensate for these gusts – but I am sure that Guy handled that for me. As we crossed the threshold at the start of the runway, he instructed me to flare – holding the aircraft off the runway until we settled onto it. I don't remember any bounces so I think it was a fair landing.

Back in the office, I admitted that this was the third powered aircraft I had taken the controls of. When he asked what they'd been, I told him Varsity and Jet Provost. "Varsity?" he said – "That's a real aircraft!"

But it was the Jet Provost that has to be the best of the SPICE Events I have ever done. The 'JP' was the basic RAF jet trainer from the mid-fifties until the early nineties. Had I joined the RAF as a trainee pilot I would certainly have trained on one of the.

Powered by a single jet engine and with straight low set wings the instructor and trainee pilot sit side by side. The controls and instrumentation are pretty basic. The aircraft seemed to me to be very manoeuvrable – ideal to learn on.

Following a briefing, we took turns to climb in with the pilot. For my trip, we taxied to the end of the runway – lined up then increased power. As we accelerated down the runway, the pilot was winding the cockpit cover closed. Then it was into a steep climb before dropping the starboard wing and diving back towards the airfield; then, after telling me to brace my leg muscles, the pilot pulled back on the stick and we climbed again. Glancing out of the cockpit I could see the horizon at ninety degrees as we passed through the vertical; "Look above you" I could now see the horizon coming into view from behind my head; then we are upside down but it doesn't feel that way. G forces are holding us into our seats and it just seems as though the ground is in the wrong place not that we are inverted.

Coming out of the loop, we do a hesitation roll. In this manoeuvre, the pilot rolls ninety degrees so the wings are pointing straight up and down – then holds this position for a second or two, then another ninety degrees and we hang upside down. This time we know we are upside down and just retained by our seat straps. Another ninety and the wings are again vertical – then back to level flight; but only for an instant before we once again dive towards the earth and pull up in a loop – this time rolling off the top rather than completing a full circle.

The pilot turned to me – fully expecting, I suspect, to see me with a very green face or, perhaps even being sick into the bag he had provided at the start. "Are you enjoying it?" he asks. "I'm loving it, I tell him; but I'd like a go on the controls if I can." "Have you done any flying before?" he queries. "I've done some gliding" I assure him. "OK – take the controls then. Aim for that motorway junction down there; now pull up and hold the stick back; that's fine" as we perform another loop; "now put the stick over to the right" I do as instructed, knowing that it makes us roll. As we come back to the horizontal once more, I take of the pressure on the stick just as I would with the rudder of a yacht when turning onto another course. We then flew the rest of the circuit and line up for the landing at which point the pilot takes over and we touch down.

At the last count, I had done some two hundred different events with SPICE – this was just a few of them.

Chapter 60. Losing Mum Dec 2009

Mum hadn't been well for a number of years, some issues dating back to when she had surgery in 1961. She had also had knee operations and had moved in with my sister Linda and her husband Ian.

After a period in hospital in the autumn, she had gone back to Linda's. I think she'd had enough by then and she died just before Christmas 2009. She could look out of her window at the snow-covered ground – a scene that she particularly loved. Linda had called me to let me know that she was close to the end and I had driven over. By the time I arrived mum was asleep but I was able to say my goodbyes.

Following her funeral, we scattered her ashes, as she'd asked, on Whetley Common where she'd been born 87 years earlier. We had had to delay the scattering because of the bad weather and the day before we met up, it snowed again – perhaps mum was having one last laugh with us.

We received a letter of condolence from cousins that we hadn't seen for years after the funeral and have been able to re-establish contact with them. Sadly, the only time we've seen them have been at other funerals – but I suppose that's to be expected as everyone gets older!

Whetley Common — where mum wanted her ashes scattering

Chapter 61. South Africa

Not all of my adventurous holidays have been with SPICE. In 2010, Jo rang me to say that she had won a 'walking safari' in the Kruger National Park in South Africa – did I want to go with her?

The prize covered the three nights/ two days in one of the 'wilderness trails' – each roughly the size of a city. Access to these areas is restricted to eight visitors at a time – together with the local rangers. We would have to pay our travel costs and, obviously, it wouldn't be worth going there for just two days so there would be other costs to allow for.

I then asked when she was going to suggest cage diving with Great White Sharks. "That was going to be my next suggestions" she said.

We considered lots of possibilities – both of us being divers, we did consider a three-centre trip: Cape Town, Durban and Kruger; but we were advised not to try to fit in too much so we eventually settled on Cape Town and a tour of the Kruger – including the wilderness trail.

Southern point of Africa — where two oceans meet.

Part 13. New Adventures

Mum had left us both some money in her will and we knew that she would approve of us using a portion of it for this trip.

We flew out to Cape Town and picked up a hire car then drove to Gansbaai. As we had time in hand, we detoured along some back trails to Cape Agulhas — the southern tip of Africa. Our itinerary in this area included the cage dive with the Great Whites and visiting a penguin colony.

We had deliberately chosen an ethical dive boat that claimed not to use dummies to attract the sharks to the cage – but their boat was out of action and we were transferred to another boat that didn't have the same scruples. As we climbed on board Jo turned to me and asked if I thought we would need a bigger boat (a reference to a line from the film Jaws)

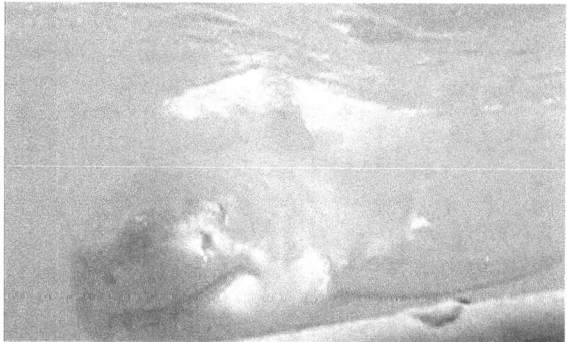

The shark experience involved climbing into cage attached to the side of the boat. As the sharks approached, we would duck our heads under the water to be able to see them. We were not equipped with full scuba gear and the cage wasn't lowered below the surface. It was certainly an experience seeing 'Jaws' that close. I was conscious of videos on the internet showing Great Whites breaking into the cages – but I didn't feel threatened. We were told to ensure that we kept our hands and feet inside the cage itself.

After our session was over, we clambered back out of the cage. The crew then said there were

Great White Sharks from the Cage

spaces in the cage for anyone wanting another go. I looked around for Jo – but she was

179

Part 13. New Adventures

already climbing back into the cage. As Gansbaai is on the Atlantic Ocean side of South Africa, the water was fed from the Antarctic and was cold – in spite of wearing wetsuits. Before heading over to our next stop in Simonstown, we visited the penguin colony at Boulder Bay. It seemed incongruous for penguins, whose natural environment as the Antarctic, to be on African soil – a continent better known for high temperatures; but, of course, as we had found out, the Atlantic waters were cold. We spend a couple of hours watching the Jackass penguins leaping from the rocks into the foaming waves – or struggling back onto the rocks, not always succeeding as the surf dragged them back into the water. Some low scrub on the shore provided them with cover for their nests.

In Simonstown, we had planned to go whale watching, charter a boat to go out to see Albatrosses, visit Kirstenbosch Gardens and go up Table Mountain.

left: Cable car up Table Mountain

right: Rock Hydrax aka Dassie – can you believe that their closest living relation is the elephant?

You can actually see the whales from the shore around False Bay – but it is certainly worth going on one of the boats. They are supposed to stay a safe distance from the whales but our boat virtually ran over the tail of one of the Southern Right Whales – which are the most commonly seen and recognisable by the V shaped spume from its blowhole.

The trip up Table Mountain was another experience not to be missed. I wasn't sure that I wanted to look down from the cable car so faced the mountain but, as it started to go up, the cable car rotated giving everyone a 360-degree view. On top of the mountain, we encountered Rock Hyraxes – or Dassies. It is incredible to think that the closest living relatives of these animals, which are about the size of wild rabbits, are elephants.

On the final evening of our time in Cape Town, we took a sunset cruise on a catamaran – with Jo doing a Titanic impression on the bow.

Jo doing a Titanic impression on the catamaran

Part 13. New Adventures

The next day we took the Premier Class train from Cape Town to Johannesburg. We could have flown and I suspect Jo would do so in future but I thought it would be great to see the country from ground level. The trip should have taken 24 hours – but we were an hour or so late getting into Jo'burg. We had booked sleeping compartments – but the air conditioning wasn't working. The meals were disappointing – they seemed to be trying to present the food as cordon bleu – with small portions but it fell short. When I asked for more potato at one meal, I was given one more potato.

Premier Class train from Cape Town to Johannesburg

We took a taxi from the station to the airport where we were due to pick up our vehicle for the Kruger. Although we were late arriving, the vehicle wasn't ready and we were at least a couple of hours late getting away. Our first stop was a supermarket where we need to pick up supplies and equipment. We were going to skirt the western edge of the Kruger, through the Blyde River Canyon before entering the park proper. We'd chosen a scenic route but by the time we got close to our overnight camp, the sun had set and we had to drive in the dark along hairpins. Not an enjoyable experience.

Next day we called in to view 'God's Window' and some waterfalls – then onto an area where there had been reports of Taita Falcons. Sadly, we didn't see any. Jo later realised that she had left her birding book where we'd stopped for the Falcons and we had a trek back to pick it up.

The website for our stop here had said that it was accessible in normal saloon cars. We'd booked a 4x4 looking vehicle (it was actually only two-wheel drive but had the clearance of an off-roader). We

God's window

were glad we had – I certainly wouldn't have liked to take a saloon car up that track.

There was an incredible thunderstorm that night – one flash had barely faded before the sky was lit up by another.

Part 13. New Adventures

The next day we finally entered the Kruger National Park and headed for Olifants Rest Camp where we were to be picked up for the Wilderness Trail. As we drove along, I became a bit concerned how little wildlife we were actually seeing. Was this the world-famous Kruger National Park?

We need not have worried. While we were sitting, eating a sandwich and looking out over the scrub towards the river, we became aware that the antelope seemed skittish.

Then a leopard ran out from cover and tried to catch the Impala. It disappeared behind some tall grass so we didn't see the end of the chase but I had managed to take two photographs of it running.

I'd previously seen all the 'big five' except the leopard and we had booked a single night in a private game reserve to increase our chances of being able to see one. Now we'd seen one on our first day in the Kruger.

one of the Waterfalls on the route

It was dark by the time we arrived at the wilderness camp. The fence around the compound looked as though it would struggle to keep chickens in their place – let alone anything remotely dangerous – and we had seen a leopard a few hours earlier! Our accommodation was in log cabins with thatched roofs – but the toilet, which was close to

Left to right: Wilderness Trail accommodation; dining area & toilet!

Part 13. New Adventures

the fence, was 'basic' to say the least and we were warned to have a good look round before sitting down!

The camp overlooked the Olifants River – which was near the border with Mozambique.

Next morning we had a very early start and were driven to our drop off point. The two rangers had briefed us that we should keep in single file and if we encountered any threats, they would fire a warning shot and, if that failed to deter, they would, very reluctantly, shoot to kill. Obviously none of us wanted that to happen.

At one point one of the rangers pointed out a footprint in the sand. "That's a lion's track" he told us. "There are three of them" he added. "We are going to track them!"

"Now hang on a moment", I thought, "they've told us that if we are threatened, they'll fire a warning shot then, if necessary, shoot to kill. That takes care of one lion – what about the other two? Those are single shot rifles and by the time they reload, it could be too late!"

Fortunately, we didn't catch up with the three lions – which had been spooked by hyenas trailing them to take advantage of any kills. On our way back to the vehicle, the rangers told us to take cover behind a clump of bushes and to keep quiet. They had spotted some men with rifles and thought they could be poachers. If so, we could be in far more danger from them than from lions. We were very relieved to find out that the other men were also rangers who had thought that we might be poachers.

A while later, we came across a herd of elephants and had to make a detour to keep out of their way.

It had been an incredible hike and it was still only mid-morning and time to return to camp for brunch. Then we

On the Wilderness Trail — tracking lions (on foot!)

Part 13. New Adventures

relaxed while the sun climbed in the sky and started to sink again towards the west. Jo, of course was off looking for birds.

Our second trek of the day was along the river bank – keeping up on some rocks that the hippos couldn't get up. There were scores of them in the river – occasionally fights would break out then peace would settle once more. We also saw a herd of elephants crossing the river and, again, had to ensure that we stayed out of their scent.

Back at camp we wandered down to the rocks above the river for 'sundowners' – what a day it had been.

The next morning, I had an upset stomach and decided the bush wasn't the place to get caught short. I decided to stay at the camp where I would be on my own until the cooks arrived to prepare brunch. As the vehicle disappeared over the hill and its engine noise faded to nothing, I returned to our cabin and sat on the veranda.

It felt quite strange knowing that there were no other human beings in the immediate vicinity. After living in a city where you can hardly escape crowds – especially on days when supporters are streaming down the road to Manchester United's Old Trafford ground – the silence was broken only by the river below the camp tumbling over the rocks, the wind in the trees and the occasional bird calling. It was idyllic. I'm not sure how I would have reacted, however, if I'd heard an elephant trumpet close by – or a lion roar! I could easily get inside the cabin if necessary (which is why I had chosen to sit on the veranda) – though whether that would have stood up against an elephant is another matter.

Well before they were expected, I heard the vehicle returning. They had reached the drop off point but the wind and threat of rain had made it dangerous to start the walk as it might have concealed the sound of threatening animals. They had, therefore abandoned the morning's walk.

The wind dropped later that morning and we were able to go out on a shortened walk along the river and up one of the tracks used by hippos. As my stomach had settled down by then I was able to join the group.

After the Wilderness trail, we picked up our own vehicle again and continued on our way to Satara.

While planning our trip, Jo and I had joined a forum where we'd received a lot of advice. Forumites visiting the Kruger tie yellow ribbons to their cars. We were driving along when an oncoming car flagged us down pointing the yellow ribbon on their car and at ours. We chatted at the side of the road – then agreed to meet up for drinks at our cabin that evening.

As we chatted over drinks, Wendy asked where Jo worked. When Jo told her she worked for the civil service, Wendy said she'd also been a Civil Servant – she'd been PA to Sir Ron de Vitt, Head of the Department of Constitutional Affairs. I said I'd met Sir Ron and she asked how. I explained that I was involved in staff associations and when probation had been merged into the new Ministry of Justice, we'd had a meeting with him. "You must know Chris Park then – he'd been lead on the DCA's Rainbow Network". I did indeed and sent Chris a text to say that we'd met Wendy and she said hi!

The other side of the world and we bump into mutual acquaintances! Incredible.

Part 13. New Adventures

A few days later we were booked into 'Elephant Plains' private game reserve. This had seemed our best prospect for seeing a leopard and worth the price. The fact that we had seen one on our very first day in the Kruger had removed the imperative of spotting one here but we ought to be lucky.

The accommodation was fantastic – individual cabins with four poster beds surrounded by mosquito nets. The tiles around the bath and sink in the en suite bathroom were animal pictures. The cabins were in immaculately manicured grounds and each had its own veranda overlooking the water hole.

There were more staff on duty than guests and the meals were incredible. Being on private grounds and with few vehicle movements, our drivers were able to take us off the main tracks – something that would be a no no in the main park.

Luxury accommodation at Elephant Plains

On our first drive that evening, we caught a glimpse a leopard disappearing down a track in the dark. Well, we had at least seen one!

The next morning, we had a second game drive. We came across a group of lions around a shrub. They lifted their heads as we drove up to within a few feet of them – then went back to sleep. That, it seems, is what lions do best! We were in an open topped 4x4 – no protection at all above waist height. Having lions – even asleep within feet of us was

"He's not showing signs of aggression!"

'interesting'. Eventually we decided to move on. As the driver carried out a three-point turn, one of the back wheels dropped into a dip by one of the lions' nose. He stood up and looked at us.

The driver assured us that it wasn't displaying any aggressiveness – but I wasn't that convinced. In any case, it seemed to me that a change from passive to aggressive might only take an instant – certainly faster than the vehicle could get out of danger!

Part 13. New Adventures

This is what we came to Elephant Plains to see

On the same drive, we came across another leopard – this time sitting in full view on top of a termite mound. Now THAT is why we had come here.

As we drove to our next camp, we came across a Black Rhino feeding in some shrub land that seemed to have been burnt. We also saw buffalo and elephants — which meant we had seen all of the 'Big Five' in just one day! It almost seemed too easy.

When it comes to safaris, I preferred the openness of the Masai Mara – with vistas over grassland stretching for mile upon mile. The Kruger, in contrast, is often restricted by thorn bushes and sometimes starts to feel a bit like a huge safari park in the UK. There is, however, no doubt that if you want to see the Big Five, the Kruger is a better bet than the Masai Mara. Whether it's a more satisfying experience is another question.

The other "Big 5" animals — Buffalo, Elephant and Black Rhino

If you want to read more about this incredible trip, Jo has written it up in far more detail that I have space for – http://safaritalk.net/topic/6038-jos-cape-to-kruger-safari/

Between us, Jo and I took more than 5,000 photographs and videos – even after discarding many each day. Rather than risk losing any of them, we decided to copy them onto DVDs – each of us keeping a set as well as the originals that had been transferred to my laptop.

Part 13. New Adventures

Chapter 62. Heart Attack 2011

On 30th March 2011, I was getting ready for work. I had a presentation on trans issues to give to some colleagues from Cheshire Probation that afternoon that was on my laptop. As I put my laptop into the bag, I dropped it. It had the only copy of the presentation – so I was concerned that I might have damaged it. Not surprisingly, I felt some tension in my chest.

Fortunately, the laptop wasn't damaged and the presentation was OK – so I continued getting ready for work. The tightness in my chest stayed, however. I thought about it – but was sure it was nothing serious – it certainly couldn't be anything like a heart attack as I had no actual pain.

As I started to do my make-up, sweat started to flow down my face. It may not be a heart attack but I didn't like what was happening so I went downstairs, unlocked the front door and left it on the latch then called 999.

"It sounds like a heart attack" I was told "take an aspirin and sit down – I'm sending an ambulance and a paramedic". I took the aspirin and put my phone charger into my handbag, then sent or left messages for Joanna, Chris and Elaine, my boss. Her's was that I might be a bit late into work as I was having a suspected heart attack.

Ironically, I had had my appraisal/ supervision session with her the previous afternoon. Over the past few months, I'd been managing two projects that were stressful – in one case because an individual involved kept promising to do things then not doing them. For some weeks, I'd been telling Elaine that once the projects were over, I would be taking time off for stress. "Don't forget, once we've completed the IAPS project, I'm taking time off" I'd remind her. During the supervision session, she'd said "I know we've been joking about stress – but how are you?" By then the cause of the stress had been taken off the project so I assured her that without him, things would be fine!

When the paramedic arrived, he hooked me up to a portable ECG machine and confirmed that I was, indeed, having a heart attack. I still didn't believe it. Once the ambulance arrived, I was offered the option of being taken to Salford Royal or Manchester Royal Infirmary. I was told that Salford Royal was closer but I'd probably be sent over to MRI for any treatment in any case. It seemed more sensible to go straight to MRI.

At MRI, I was taken straight into the treatment room and was just drowsy while they did a scan to find where the blockage was and then insert three stents through my wrist and into the heart. A couple of hours later I was in the recovery room sending texts to friends. Those friends were used to joke texts from me but didn't understand the joke of being told I'd had a heart attack. They eventually realised that it was no joke.

I was taken to Intensive Care – by then feeling the same as I had before the attack. A guy was brought into the ward and put in the bed next to mine. I heard him say to his visitors that he'd been in a meeting at work when he had felt unwell – and he was taken into Marsh room. "That's a coincidence", I thought. "There's a Marsh room at HQ". In fact, it wasn't a coincidence; he was also a member of probation staff and been taken ill where I worked!

Part 13. New Adventures

After cardiac rehabilitation, I made a gradual return to work to find that the two projects that had caused the stress in the first place were no further forward. I wasn't sure whether to be pleased that I was obviously 'indispensable' or peeved that no one had done the work while I'd been off!

There was some damage following the attack – around 30% loss of function – but I've tried not to let it get in the way even taking part in the Round the Island Yacht race less than three months later.

It has impacted on my diving – but I have been allowed to do shallow dives so that's not too bad. My first post attack dive was in Greece. After a checkout in the swimming pool, I did a shallow dive in the Ionian. The water was so warm, I decided not to bother with a wet suit and just wore a swimming costume. While the other divers did a second dive, I stayed on the boat and chatted to the instructor. He asked where I'd trained and when I said I'd done my advanced in Turkey he asked who with as his brother was a dive instructor near Bodrum. When I showed him my certification card, he said it was his brother who had trained me. It really is a small world.

In August 2013, I had arranged to do my Coastal Yachtmaster training with the Civil Service Sailing Association. A couple of weeks before the trip was due to start, I realised I would need a First Aid certificate so signed up for a course with the Red Cross. I knew that I'd be down on the floor dealing with 'casualties' and as I'd had a few twinges in mu right knee, wore a support. It was a hot day and I the support was uncomfortable so I eventually removed it. My knee then felt very painful. The next day I went to the GPs – he said that as it hadn't swollen up and wasn't hot, it was probably nothing to worry about but said he would refer me for an X-ray in any case which was done the same day.

At work the next day I was in a meeting and clearly in considerable discomfort – the Deputy Chief Officer asked if I should be in work – I told her that I was there to provide a briefing for the meeting but would then be going home. That night my knee started to swell up. I remembered that the GP had said the fact that it hadn't been swollen suggested it wasn't serious – so presumably the reverse might also apply. I returned to the GP on the Friday morning – the day I should have been leaving for my sailing course. The GP said that he didn't think it was a DVT but he would send me to Salford Royal for tests.

The tests were inconclusive so A&E said they would give me blood thinning injections, arrange for the practice nurse to give me them each day over the weekend and book me in for a scan.

By now I could hardly put my foot on the floor – it felt like I was walking on hot sharp glass. It was agony to even get from the sofa to the fridge or stand at the cooker to prepare food. I lost ten pounds in seven days!

The scan proved negative for DVD – but could be wrong and need another scan a week later. That also proved negative but in the meantime the X-ray showed that I have osteoarthritis in the knee.

I still haven't managed to do my Coastal Yachtmaster!

Part 14. Retirement

Chapter 63. Into Retirement

As I approached normal retirement age of 65, the government changed the rules and eliminating mandatory retirement giving me the option to continue working later if I wished. I'd already deferred my state pension after qualifying when I reached 60 so that it would be higher when I did start to draw it. My occupational pension combined with the state pension would still leave me close to the edge especially with an outstanding mortgage – so I did want to carry on working.

I'm not a city girl by nature and my plan was to retire somewhere in a more rural setting, closer to Jo (but not on her doorstep), somewhere with less grey skies than Manchester (not that difficult), ideally near the coast for some sailing, with lower levels of crime (again – not too difficult) but with a SPICE group. It also needed to be somewhere that I could get a house similar to my current one within my budget. The final two requirements might prove to be much more difficult to meet and satisfying all of them would probably be impossible.

The changes to the probation service looked likely to result in a gap in my work as IT Project Manager for anything up to a year or even eighteen months. I had hopes of persuading the powers that be to include me in the staff qualifying for a generous voluntary redundancy scheme – but this was refused. "There would be plenty of work for me" I was told. Perhaps so – but was it IT Project Management? I wasn't prepared to be just the 'odd job' person.

My estimate of the situation proved to be correct. IT Projects virtually dried up as our side of probation was sold off and the new owners decide their strategy for the future. There was one possibility on the horizon that appealed to me — a full time role as Lead of a combined Prison and Probation LGBT staff association; combining LAGIP and GALIPS. After several months waiting for the role to be finalised and advertised, I was told that I would probably not be eligible as it was a civil service role and I was not in the privatised section of probation.

At that stage, I handed in my notice and retired on 15th May 2015.

I had, by then, drafted my autobiography — which I published as a PDF file on CDs — not being aware at that time of the availability of Print on Demand from outlets such as Amazon of the option of e-books for Kindle and similar applications. I sold a few copies of the CDs at my retirement presentation.

I enjoyed my time with Probation until it was split into Community Rehabilitation Companies (the privatised sector) dealing with low-risk offenders and the National Probation Service which was absorbed into the Civil Service to deal with higher risk offenders. Many of

Part 14. Retirement

the staff at the time forecast that the changes would fail — and that assessment proved to be correct. The CRCs have now been recombined with the NPS — itself now part of Her Majesty's Prison and Probation Service.

The privatised part of Manchester Probation was combined with the equivalent part of Cheshire Probation and was one of five CRCs owned by Interserve. One of their 'innovative' plans was to develop a new IT offender case management system. I'd been Project Manager for the previous systems and had a fair idea what was going to be involved — and how long it would take to implement. But Interserve planned to do it in months and I thought that was totally impossible. It was obvious to me, however, that the Project Manager would be under a lot of stress and, having had one heart attack, I wasn't prepared to expose myself to the inevitable pressures.

In the end, I heard that the new system had still not been implemented well past what I'd considered the minimum time it would take.

It's not unusual for pensioners to declare that they do 't know how they found time to work — and that's certainly been my experience. I was asked several times after retiring if I missed working for probation. I could honestly say that I missed a lot of the friends I'd made — but not the work as it had become at the end.

Chapter 64. What next?

Diversity Role Models

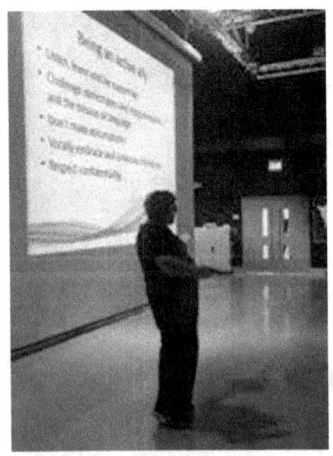

Giving a talk for Diversity Role Models

After retiring, I volunteered with Diversity Role Models, a charity that goes into schools to talk about homophobic, biphobic and transphobic bullying. The teams would typically comprise a facilitator and two or three role models. The facilitator would lead the session while the role models contributed with their personal experiences.

Most of the sessions were usually of one class of around 30 year 9 or 10 students. In the photograph on the left, the school decided to have whole year groups so each session was for around 180 students and we did five sessions that day.

I started with DRM as a Role Model but then became one of the facilitators. One of the features of the workshops was a 'Who's who' game. Each of the team would have three facts on the screen and the students had to try and decide which set of three facts related to which of us. My facts usually included: 'I've been in and out of every prison in Manchester', 'I've looped the loop in a jet' and 'I've come face to face with a Great White Shark'.

Training

In 2016, the National Offender Management Service introduced a new policy for working with transgender offenders. Having served on the NOMS diversity board and with extensive

Part 14. Retirement

experience of probation and prison systems, I developed a workshop to present to prison staff. I had a number of bookings from prisons around the country for these workshops — which covered the cost of a couple of long-haul holidays.

Chapter 65. Long Haul Holidays

Thailand 2016

In 2016, SPICE organised a holiday to Thailand — including several nights on a floating hotel on the River Kwai.

The trip involved changing flights in Dubai — which was a bit worrying as there had been reports of a transwoman being arrested there and eventually being expelled. To complicate matters, I'd had an ICD (combine pacemaker and defibrillator) fitted which meant I was likely to set off the metal detectors while going through security; not ideal for keeping a low profile. In fact, I didn't have any problems.

Bridge over the River Kwai.

One of our trips in Thailand was on the railway that ran alongside the River Kwai — we were amused to find a sign reading

'WARNING

BEWARE: DO NOT SIT ON THE STAIRWAY OR THE ROOF'

Not something you come across on UK trains!

Don't sit on the roof!

One particularly poignant visit on the trip was to Kanchanaburi Cemetery containing the graves of some of those who had died on the infamous Burma Railway.

Both my father and father-in-law had served in Burma during the war — and my mother-in-law had been held in a Japanese internment camp.

Kanchanaburi Cemetery

We took advantage of a trip to an elephant sanctuary while in Thailand — though we opted not to ride on one and chose one that was committed to eliminated such practices.

Part 14. Retirement

Australia and New Zealand 2017

I'd wanted to visit Australia and New Zealand for a long time — but I felt it needed to be for at least three weeks to justify the distance so it had had to wait until I'd retired.

Top of my bucket list in Oz were Uluru, diving the Great Barrier Reef, sailing the Whitsunday Islands, Blue Mountains and Sydney for the Bridge and Opera House — and seeing kangaroos and koala. After two weeks in Australia, I'd fly to Christchurch in New Zealand, pick up a hire car and drive up to Auckland, stopping for one night in Wellington with Diane, a friend from SPICE, who was working over there.

Uluru — aka Ayers Rock

Planning the trip was half the fun — working out flights and possible hotels. Eventually, the itinerary came together starting with a flight into Sydney having changed flights in Dubai — as I'd done for the trip to Thailand the previous year.

Sailing in the Whitsunday Islands

One hiccup in the planning was around the diving. The cardiac consultant was uncertain whether having had an ICD (Implantable cardioverter defibrillator — a combined pacemaker and defibrillator) fitted would allow me to dive. As I'd been told I couldn't dive unless I had it done, this was a pain! Checking the specification, I found it was OK at far greater depths than the rest of my body would stand! In the end, I had a specialist dive medical shortly before I flew out — which I passed. Unfortunately, I was out of practice and struggled to use the scuba kit on the actual dives and had to abort them. I did, however, managed to snorkel so probably saw most of the fish I'd have seen at normal dive depths.

In Sydney, I met up with Craig O'Brien and Anne, his wife. Craig is a fellow member of a Facebook group for students who had been at the English School of Paris in the 1950s/60s.

I also met up with a group of trans people attending an event at the Opera House. I also did a trip up into the Blue Mountains, where I rode the steepest (they claimed) railway in the world, and to a zoo which was the only place I managed to see kangaroos and koalas. I had

a mishap at the zoo when I sat down to eat a picnic — the bench was unstable and I fell backwards and hurt my hip.

Part 14. Retirement

New Zealand

My hip injury wasn't serious but it did make walking uncomfortable which impacted on the rest of my trip.

I picked up my hire car, a Toyota Yaris, in Christchurch, then found my hotel. The next morning, my route took me over the spine of South Island. As I went over the pass, I was caught up in heavy snow — which I hadn't expected. The only footwear I had with me were sandals.

Snowfall on my trip from Christchurch to Owen River

Diane - a SPICE friend and my hostess in Wellington

In Wellington, I made my way to the house of a friend from SPICE who had kindly offered to put me up for the night.

Over the next few days, I made my way up the North Island to Auckland for my flights to Sydney then back to the UK. I had looked at alternative routes — but returning via Sydney was far less expensive.

The timings meant that I spent several hours between flights at Sydney before my departure via to Dubai. The flight went via Bangkok where we had the option of staying on board or stretching our legs in the terminal. I was still having trouble walking far so elected to stay on board. From leaving my hotel in Auckland to arriving home, I was travelling for more than 40 hours. Not something I'd want to repeat.

Canada 2019

A trip through the Rockies — possibly on the Rocky Mountaineer — had been on my bucket list for a long time. And, if I was that side of the pond, I had to go and see my Aunt Hilda and her twin daughters Laura and Lynda who lived near Toronto. In 2019, the trip finally happened and I got to meet the girls and their families and spend time with Hilda and her husband George. They were superb hosts and took me around Toronto, including up the CN Tower, to Niagara Falls and to the

Cousins Laura and Lynda either side of me and Aunty Hilda far right.

Part 14. Retirement

Canadian Warplane Heritage Museum — home to one of only two airworthy Avro Lancaster bombers the other being part of the RAF Battle of Britain Memorial Flight.

V-RA (aka Vera) one of two airworthy Lancasters left in the world

The second part of my Canada trip was through the Rockies. I had decided against the train — opting instead to rent an SUV and drive myself.

This, I felt, gave me more flexibility to stop and look at anything that caught my eye — or make side trips such as up on to a glacier. I was disappointed not to see more wildlife on my journey through the Rockies— all I saw was a brown bear crossing the road ahead of me. By the time I got close enough to take a photograph, it had disappeared into the forest.

My trip ended in Vancouver where I took a boat trip to go whale / Orca (Killer Whales) watching.

Part 14. Retirement

Chapter 66. Writing

When I was 'between jobs' in about 1998, I started writing a novel. This was shelved when I was offered the job with the Probation Service. Once I retired, I tried to find the original file (written using Lotus Word Pro). During my search, I came across an on-line diary I'd kept when I first moved to Salford — we'd probably call it a blog these days. I decided to use that as the core of an anthology with other stories etc that I'd rediscovered.

One of the items reminded me on an incident when I was about 19 and living in London.

In 1966, while living in a tiny bed-sit in SW London, I caught a train to Bournemouth. It was an old styled corridor train and I changed in the toilets; putting on an orange bikini under my skirt and top. I took the Sandbanks ferry across to the beaches and dunes at Studland where I swam then sunbathed. As I lay there, I noticed a guy watching me so I quickly dressed and left.

It occurred to me that this could be used as the basis for a novel and I started to make notes — once again relegating my original story to the back burner. The new story, Summer Dreams' took on a life of its own.

SPICE had started creative writing sessions run by Lynn Trotter and I also joined Manchester Women Writers' Group which met in Manchester Central Library. Both groups provided very useful feedback on my efforts and saw my original works self-published on a major website. I've subsequently made them available through other outlets as not everyone likes to buy from that multinational company.

To date, my novels have featured trans and other gender diverse characters in authentic settings. I've tried to show that being trans is just a part of who they are and that they have much wider lives and dreams. Not all of them will be sympathetic — because trans people come in all types. I hope, however, to have avoided simplistic stereotypes.

The settings, such as Manchester's Gay Village, are as accurate as I can make them. The historical backgrounds, like the introduction of the Gender Recognition Act 2004 and the genuine personalities involved at that time may also be recognisable.

As well as works of fiction, I've produced two factual books:

A Tale of Two Lives

The original version of my autobiography, taking me up to the point of retirement, has now been updated to 2021.

Part 14. Retirement

A Practical Guide to Understanding Gender Variance

I've been involved in the trans community for more than twenty years; initially providing support on the internet then training as a counsellor and counselling supervisor; chairing trans and LGB&T support groups and providing workshops on trans issues to a range of audiences — and I've won several awards for this work.

This guide has been developed from those workshops and her personal experiences supporting other trans individuals. It is intended to be easy to read keeping jargon to a minimum and explaining terms in simple language. The information is laid out in logical sections — with a comprehensive contents section to find relevant details easily.

The book is aimed at anyone dealing with trans people

- Counsellors / Help-line Operators/ Befrienders
- Support/ Social Workers
- Union Staff
- Teachers and Lecturers
- Citizens Advice Bureaux
- Samaritans
- Criminal Justice System staff including
- Equality and Diversity Practitioners
- HR staff
- Other Managers
- LGBT+ organisations
- Family & Friends
- And Trans Individuals themselves

Contents include:

- Definitions
- Causality
- Social Transition
- Transsexual Journey to Surgery
- Travelling on: Post Transition / Surgery
- Trans Issues in Counselling
- Partners and Families
- Case Studies
- Legal History
- Discrimination & Hate Crime/ Incidents
- Employment
- Trans People in the Criminal Justice System
- Bibliography

Part 14. Retirement

Summer Dreams

"Summer Dreams" is an authentic story of the transgender community and illustrates the wide range of trans people's experiences, the problems, prejudices and fears that they face (and some of their own prejudices) — and the fact that being trans is just one facet of their lives. It was inspired by a true incident when the author was about 19.

But let Vicky tell you about Summer Dreams:

I was David, but now I'm Vicky.

I was sunbathing in sand dunes near Bournemouth in 2003, when Roger found me and changed my life. After spending a heavenly holiday with him as Vicky, I just couldn't face reverting to David. I knew, though, that becoming Vicky permanently was impossible.

There was only one option, I tried to kill myself.

Roger saved me then showed how life as Vicky was possible.

But is it too good to last?

Changes

Changes is a tale of corruption, blackmail, revenge, drug smuggling, murder, and self-discovery told from five points of view:

Nigel Hall has a comfortable life running his advertising agency and using girls and other activities including sailing and trips to casinos to entertain his clients.

George Collins enjoys perks that Nigel gives him and doesn't worry too much about the invoices he approves.

John Ives hadn't expected to take his cousin **Carol Ives's** part as Cinderella in a panto when she injured her ankle horse-riding nor that photos from the event would later give his fiancée an idea for getting him in and out of her parents' house without their knowledge. Nor did he expect to discover how much he enjoyed cross-dressing or that his fiancée would support him.

Then **Mary Sanchez**, the widow of OJ, a former business partner of Nigel, returns from the USA. She takes over the company George works for and extracts revenge on Nigel, who she blames for OJ's death.

The consequences impact on all of them.

Part 14. Retirement

Operation Busted Flush
a matter of survival

The White House administration's treatment of transgender people - especially those in the military – in 2016-20, made me wonder what would happen if a group of trans veterans decided to take action.

As one reader said:

I want to see the movie of this book

Reviewed in the United Kingdom on 29 November 2020

Transgender avengers form a crack team to take down a corrupt and authoritarian US president before he causes more harm to their community. Good action-adventure romp with wish fulfilment for all those who have watched in despair over the past years as our hard won trans rights are attacked by governments worldwide. Thoroughly enjoyed it.

Transgender Tales
Adventures and Misadventures on the Journey from Transvestite to Transsexual

An online diary I kept between 1997 and 1999 when I first moved to Salford. I chatted to lots of other trans people on line, many of who had never been anywhere "dressed" so I invited them to visit and go down Manchester's Gay Village. This tells the story of those trips and others that I made with Vanity Club UK — a TV/TS club.

It also tells of my thoughts over that period when I started by identifying as transvestite but began to wonder if I was actually transsexual and if I would eventually need to transition permanently

There are descriptions of how I came out as trans to two of my oldest friends, at work and to my family — and the consequences of those steps

Three stories that I wrote at the time for Northern Concord's magazine "Crosstalk" under the name Helen Williamson. A poem "Can You Tell Me What I Am?" which was written when I was questioning if I was TV or TS. And a number of other humorous anecdotes from the period.

I hope you enjoy it!

What readers say:

"Some great short stories about the dilemmas of being a TV in the early 80s 90s. The diaries reveal a hidden community proudly remembered for its peer support, mentoring and deep friendship. full of spirit and life."

Part 14. Retirement

Chapter 67. Covid

The less said about that the better. Virtually all my contact with other people, including my continuing counselling work, moved onto Zoom — how I wished I'd bought a few of their shares at the start of lockdown!

Chapter 68. Conclusion

I think most people want to feel that they've made a difference in the world, that they've left 'footprints in the sand', that others may have been helped by what they've done. I would certainly like to think this is the case.

Maybe these ramblings will entertain and even give a greater understanding of trans individuals. I hope that they might help other trans individuals by showing that, in spite of ups and downs (and I've had my share) we can survive transition and even have a fulfilling life afterwards. That, surely, is the whole point of transition – becoming who we really are and making the best of that life.

Helen Dale

March 2015 – updated 2021

www.ingramcontent.com/pod-product-compliance
Lightning Source LLC
Chambersburg PA
CBHW071414070526
44578CB00003B/572